Food Code
2009 Recommendations of the
United States Public Health Service
Food and Drug Administration

The Food Code is a model for safeguarding public health and ensuring food is unadulterated and honestly presented when offered to the consumer. It represents FDA's best advice for a uniform system of provisions that address the safety and protection of food offered at retail and in food service.

This model is offered for adoption by local, state, and federal governmental jurisdictions for administration by the various departments, agencies, bureaus, divisions, and other units within each jurisdiction that have been delegated compliance responsibilities for food service, retail food stores, or food vending operations. Alternatives that offer an equivalent level of public health protection to ensure that food at retail and foodservice is safe are recognized in this model.

This guidance represents FDA's current thinking on safeguarding public health and ensuring food is unadulterated and honestly presented when offered to the consumer. It does not create or confer any rights for or on any person and does not operate to bind FDA or the public. This guidance is being issued in accordance with FDA's Good Guidance Practices regulation (21 CFR 10.115; 65 FR 56468; September 19, 2000; revised as of April 1, 2008).

1997 - *Food Code, 1997 Recommendations of the United States Public Health Service, Food and Drug Administration,* National Technical Information Service Publication PB97-133656

1999 - *Food Code, 1999 Recommendations of the United States Public Health Service, Food and Drug Administration,* National Technical Information Service Publication PB99-115925

2001 - *Food Code, 2001Recommendations of the United States Public Health Service, Food and Drug Administration,* National Technical Information Service Publication PB2002-100819

2003 - *Supplement to the 2001 Food Code,* National Technical Information Service Publication PB2003-106843

2005 - *Food Code, 2005 Recommendations of the United States Public Health Service, Food and Drug Administration,* National Technical Information Service Publication PB2005-102200

2007 - *Supplement to the 2005 Food Code,* National Technical Information Service Publication PB2007-112622

JOINT INTRODUCTION to the 2009 FOOD CODE

The Food and Drug Administration (FDA) and the Centers for Disease Control and Prevention (CDC) of the U.S. Department of Health and Human Services (HHS) and the Food Safety and Inspection Service of the U.S. Department of Agriculture (USDA) are pleased to release the 2009 edition of the Food Code. The Food Code is a model code and reference document for state, city, county and tribal agencies that regulate restaurants, retail food stores, vending operations and foodservice operations in institutions such as schools, hospitals, nursing homes and child care centers.

The Food Code establishes practical, science-based guidance and enforceable provisions for mitigating risk factors known to cause foodborne illness. Food safety is a priority for HHS and USDA, and we strongly encourage the adoption and implementation of the 2009 Food Code at all levels of government.

Among the key findings of the Food Safety Working Group created by President Obama was the need to modernize statutes that require effective sanitation and preventive controls in food establishments. An increasingly globalized food supply chain, the aging of our population, increases in the number of immunocompromised and immunosuppressed individuals, and the trend toward greater consumption of foods prepared outside the home demand sustained vigilance by industry and the regulatory community to promote food safety in retail and foodservice establishments.

Implementation of the Food Code also supports many of the food safety objectives of Healthy People 2010, the comprehensive, nationwide set of health promotion and disease prevention objectives designed to serve as a 10-year strategy for improving health in the United States. Healthy People 2010 objectives include reducing infections caused by foodborne pathogens, reducing outbreaks of foodborne illness, and improving food employee behaviors and food preparation practices that directly relate to foodborne illness in retail food establishments. Similar objectives are planned for the next generation of the initiative, Healthy People 2020.

Food Code adoption and implementation is important for achieving uniform national food safety standards and for enhancing the efficiency and effectiveness of our nation's food safety system. As of January 2009, 49 of 50 states and 3 of 6 territories of the United States report having retail codes patterned after prior editions of the Food Code. Many federal agencies and tribal governments have adopted the Code as well. We commend these jurisdictions and agencies and urge all to update their existing codes and initiate rule-making that is consistent with the 2009 Food Code.

The federal government is committed to enhanced coordination of food safety efforts with state, local, and tribal agencies, and the food industry to protect our food supply. Establishing uniform and enforceable standards of food safety in retail and foodservice establishments is an important part of strengthening our nation's food protection system. HHS and USDA will continue to take progressive steps to partner with all who have a stake in food safety and are committed to reducing the incidence of foodborne illness in the United States.

Margaret A. Hamburg, M.D.
Commissioner
Food and Drug Administration
U.S. Department of Health and Human Services

Alfred V. Almanza
Administrator
Food Safety and Inspection Service
U.S Department of Agriculture

Thomas R. Frieden, M.D. M.P.H.
Director
Centers for Disease Control and Prevention
U.S. Department of Health and Human Services

Preface

1. FOODBORNE ILLNESS ESTIMATES, RISK FACTORS, AND INTERVENTIONS
2. PHS MODEL CODES HISTORY, PURPOSE, AND AUTHORITY
3. PUBLIC HEALTH AND CONSUMER EXPECTATIONS
4. ADVANTAGE OF UNIFORM STANDARDS
5. MODIFICATIONS AND IMPROVEMENTS IN THIS EDITION
6. DISCUSSION OF THE FOOD CODE AS A HACCP MODEL AND THE
   INTENTION TO INCORPORATE OTHER MODELS
7. CODE ADOPTION/CERTIFIED COPIES
8. INFORMATION TO ASSIST THE USER
9. THE CODE REVISION PROCESS
10. ACKNOWLEDGMENTS

1. FOODBORNE ILLNESS ESTIMATES, RISK FACTORS, AND INTERVENTIONS

Foodborne illness in the United States is a major cause of personal distress, preventable death, and avoidable economic burden. Meade et. al. (1999) estimated that foodborne diseases cause approximately 76 million illnesses, 325,000 hospitalizations, and 5,000 deaths in the United States each year.

For many victims, foodborne illness results only in discomfort or lost time from the job. For some, especially preschool age children, older adults in health care facilities, and those with impaired immune systems, foodborne illness is more serious and may be life threatening.

The annual cost of foodborne illness in terms of pain and suffering, reduced productivity, and medical costs are estimated to be $10 - $83 billion. As stated by Meade et. al., the nature of food and foodborne illness has changed dramatically in the United States over the last century. While technological advances such as pasteurization and proper canning have all but eliminated some disease, new causes of foodborne illness have been identified. Surveillance of foodborne illness is complicated by several factors. The first is underreporting. Although foodborne illnesses can be severe or even fatal, milder cases are often not detected through routine surveillance. Second, many pathogens transmitted through food are also spread through water or from person to person, thus obscuring the role of foodborne transmission. Finally, pathogens or agents that have not yet been identified and thus cannot be diagnosed cause some proportion of foodborne illness.

Epidemiological outbreak data repeatedly identify five major risk factors related to employee behaviors and preparation practices in retail and food service establishments as contributing to foodborne illness:

- Improper holding temperatures,
- Inadequate cooking, such as undercooking raw shell eggs,
- Contaminated equipment,
- Food from unsafe sources, and
- Poor personal hygiene

The Food Code addresses controls for risk factors and further establishes 5 key public health interventions to protect consumer health. Specifically, these interventions are: demonstration of knowledge, employee health controls, controlling hands as a vehicle of contamination, time and temperature parameters for controlling pathogens, and the consumer advisory. The first two interventions are found in Chapter 2 and the last three in Chapter 3.

Healthy People 2010 and Healthy People 2020 are national initiatives that work through the cooperative federal-state-private sector and which establish 10-year objectives to improve the health of all Americans through prevention. Food Safety Objective 10-6 in Healthy People 2010 is: *Improve food employee behaviors and food preparation practices that directly relate to foodborne illness in retail food establishments.* This includes food operations such as retail food stores, food service establishments, health care facilities, schools and other "food establishments" as defined in the Food Code. In 2010, the Healthy People 2020 objectives will be released along with guidance for achieving the new 10-year targets.

The Food and Drug Administration (FDA) endeavors to assist the approximately 75 state and territorial agencies and more than 3,000 local departments that assume primary responsibility for preventing foodborne illness and for licensing and inspecting establishments within the retail segment of the food industry. This industry segment consists of more than one million establishments and employs a work force of over 16 million.

2. PHS MODEL CODES HISTORY, PURPOSE, AND AUTHORITY

(A) History and Purpose

U.S. Public Health Service (PHS) activities in the area of food protection began at the turn of the 20th century with studies on the role of milk in the spread of disease. These studies led to the conclusion that effective disease prevention requires the application of comprehensive food sanitation measures from production to consumption. Additional studies identified and evaluated measures which would most effectively control disease, including work which led to improved processes for pasteurization.

Next, model codes were developed to assist state and local governments in initiating and maintaining effective programs for prevention of foodborne illness. The first of these, which is now titled *Grade A Pasteurized Milk Ordinance – Recommendations of the PHS/FDA,* was initially published in 1924. Subsequently, the PHS published recommended model food codes that address the various components of the retail segment of the food industry. These code editions are listed chronologically on pp. iii and iv. Through the years all states, hundreds of local jurisdictions, and many federal agencies have adopted some edition of model food codes recommended by the PHS.

Today, FDA's purpose in maintaining an updated model food code is to assist food control jurisdictions at all levels of government by providing them with a scientifically sound technical and legal basis for regulating the retail segment of the food industry. The retail segment includes those establishments or locations in the food distribution chain where the consumer takes possession of the food.

The model Food Code is neither federal law nor federal regulation and is not preemptive. Rather, it represents FDA's best advice for a uniform system of regulation to ensure that food at retail is safe and properly protected and presented. Although not federal requirements (until adopted by federal bodies for use within federal jurisdictions), the model Food Code provisions are designed to be consistent with federal food laws and regulations, and are written for ease of legal adoption at all levels of government. A list of jurisdictions that have reported to FDA their status in adopting the Food Code is available on the FDA CFSAN Web Page at http://www.fda.gov/Food/FoodSafety/RetailFoodProtection/FederalStateCooperative Programs/ucm108156.htm . The list is self-reported and FDA has not yet evaluated whether all the adopted codes are equivalent to the model Food Code.

Providing model food codes and model code interpretations and opinions is the mechanism through which FDA, as a lead federal food control agency, promotes uniform implementation of national food regulatory policy among the several thousand federal, state, and local agencies and tribes that have primary responsibility for the regulation or oversight of retail level food operations.

(B) Authority

PHS authority for providing assistance to state and local governments is derived from the Public Health Service Act [42 USC 243]. Section 311(a) states in part: "... The Secretary shall ... assist states and their political subdivisions in the prevention and suppression of communicable diseases, and with respect to other public health matters, shall cooperate with and aid state and local authorities in the enforcement of their ... health regulations and shall advise the several states on matters relating to the preservation and improvement of the public health." Responsibility for carrying out the provisions of the Act relative to food protection was delegated within the PHS to the Commissioner of Food and Drugs in 1968 [21 CFR 5.10(a)(2) and (3)].

Under authority of the Economy Act, June 30, 1932 as amended [31 USC 1535], FDA provides assistance to federal agencies.

Assistance provided to local, state, and federal governmental bodies is also based on FDA's authorities and responsibilities under the Federal Food, Drug, and Cosmetic Act [21 USC 301].

3. PUBLIC HEALTH AND CONSUMER EXPECTATIONS

It is a shared responsibility of the food industry and the government to ensure that food provided to the consumer is safe and does not become a vehicle in a disease outbreak or in the transmission of communicable disease. This shared responsibility extends to ensuring that consumer expectations are met and that food is unadulterated, prepared in a clean environment, and honestly presented.

Under FDA's 2009 Mission Statement the agency is responsible for:

Protecting the public health by assuring the safety and security of our nation's food supply… and for advancing the public health by helping to make foods safer and more affordable; and helping the public get the accurate, science-based information they need about foods to improve their health.

Accordingly, the provisions of the Food Code provide a system of prevention and overlapping safeguards designed to minimize foodborne illness; ensure employee health, industry manager knowledge, safe food, nontoxic and cleanable equipment, and acceptable levels of sanitation on food establishment premises; and promote fair dealings with the consumer.

4. ADVANTAGE OF UNIFORM STANDARDS

The advantages of well-written, scientifically sound, and up-to-date model codes have long been recognized by industry and government officials.

Industry conformance with acceptable procedures and practices is far more likely where regulatory officials "speak with one voice" about what is required to protect the public health, why it is important, and which alternatives for compliance may be accepted.

Model codes provide a guide for use in establishing what is required. They are useful to business in that they provide accepted standards that can be applied in training and quality assurance programs. They are helpful to local, state, and federal governmental bodies that are developing or updating their own codes.

The model Food Code provides guidance on food safety, sanitation, and fair dealing that can be uniformly adopted for the retail segment of the food industry. The document is the cumulative result of the efforts and recommendations of many contributing individuals, agencies, and organizations with years of experience using earlier model code editions. It embraces the concept that our quality of life, state of health, and the public welfare are directly affected by how we collectively provide and protect our food.

The model Food Code provisions are consistent with, and where appropriate incorporate, federal performance standards for the same products and processes. Federal performance standards in effect define public food safety expectations for the product, usually in terms of lethality to a pathogenic microorganism of particular concern. Use of performance standards as the measure of regulatory compliance means establishments are free to use innovative approaches in producing safe products, in lieu of adherence to traditional processing approaches, such as specified cooking times and temperatures, that achieve the same end. Federally inspected establishments demonstrate compliance with performance standards by showing that their process adheres to an appropriately designed, validated HACCP plan.

Retail processors may be given the same opportunity as federally-regulated establishments to use innovative techniques in the production of safe foods. Retail establishments may apply to the regulatory authority for a variance to use a specific federal food safety performance standard for a product or a process in lieu of compliance with otherwise applicable specifications in the Food Code. However, to show compliance with the federal performance standard, the retail processor must, like a federally inspected establishment, show that processing controls are in place to ensure that the standard is being met. Thus, a request for a variance based on a federal performance standard must be supported by a validated HACCP plan with record keeping and documented verification being made available to the regulatory authority.

5. MODIFICATIONS AND IMPROVEMENTS IN THIS EDITION

The revisions contained in this edition reflect changes, additions, deletions, and format modifications listed in the Supplement to the 2005 FDA Food Code and recommendations developed during the 2008 Biennial meeting of the Conference for Food Protection. The revisions also reflect input provided by those who have been intimately involved with studying, teaching, and using the earlier editions. Most of these enhancements involve added clarification or new information. Some reflect evolving regulatory policy contained in new or revised federal regulations.

The needed clarifications and missing Code provisions were identified by FDA and others during standardization and certification activities, State Training Team courses, regional food protection seminars, the deliberations of food equipment standards organizations, and the verbal and written requests for clarification received by FDA field and headquarters components.

Changes in provisions related to federal laws and regulations administered by other federal agencies such as the United States Department of Agriculture were jointly developed with those agencies.

New to the 2009 Food Code is a revised designation system for Code provisions. The former use of "critical" or "non-critical" has been changed in recognition that there is a need for better identifying risk-based controls contained within the Code's provisions.

A Summary of Changes is provided at the end of the Food Code. General enhancements include:

(1) Added and improved definitions that are more precise and more consistent with terminology and definitions found in related laws and regulations;

(2) Modified provisions to make them more consistent with national requirements and standards administered by other federal agencies and international bodies; more flexible without compromising public health; and more internally consistent with other Food Code provisions;

(3) Clarified other provisions regarding their intent, thereby reducing confusion and the potential for inconsistent application;

(4) Improved user aids contained in the Annexes such as added references and updated public health reasons, model forms, guides, and lists; and

(5) Expanded the Index with additional terms to assist a broader base of users in finding topics of interest.

6. DISCUSSION OF THE CODE AS A HACCP MODEL AND THE INTENTION TO INCORPORATE OTHER MODELS

It is important to note that preapproval of HACCP plans for food establishments operating pursuant to a variance is provided for under the Food Code, but such plan preapproval is not a part of another HACCP regulatory model, the Fish and Fishery Products regulation 21 CFR 123, effective December 18, 1997 (a Third Edition issued June 2001). Additionally, there are differences between the two models in the required content of the HACCP plan. For example, the HACCP plans mandated by the Food Code must include flow diagrams, product formulations, training plans, and a corrective action plan. Flow diagrams and product formulations are suggested but not mandated components of the Fish and Fishery Products regulation.

These differences are necessitated by differences in the nature of the regulations and the regulatory structure set up to enforce them. HACCP plans developed under the Food Code variance process are provided to the regulatory authority to enable the regulatory authority to assess whether the establishment has designed a system of controls sufficient to ensure the safety of the product. The plans will be reviewed outside the food establishment and, in most cases, in the absence of any historical performance information for the product at that establishment. Therefore, the plan must contain sufficient detail to allow the regulator to fully understand the operations and the intended controls. Products requiring a variance are those which are deemed to be potentially hazardous (time/temperature control for safety) and for which retail production would otherwise be prohibited.

To assist food establishments in applying HACCP principles at retail, FDA has issued a document entitled: *Managing Food Safety: A HACCP Principles Guide for Operators of Food Service, Retail Food Stores, and Other Food Establishments at the Retail Level.* This document is available from FDA and can be found on the FDA Web Page at http://www.fda.gov/Food/FoodSafety/RetailFoodProtectionManagingFoodSafetyHACCP Principles/Operators/default.htm

Under the Fish and Fishery Products regulation, every seafood processor is required to perform a hazard analysis, and must have and implement a written HACCP Plan whenever a hazard analysis reveals a food safety hazard that is reasonably likely to occur. HACCP plans developed pursuant to the Fish and Fishery Products regulation are for all products in the class and are not for products for which production is presently prohibited. Plans will be reviewed on site, with records available to judge, among other things, the adequacy of past corrective actions.

It is intended that the Food Code will be amended to incorporate federal HACCP regulations and guidelines by inclusion in the text of the Food Code, by reference, or through the issuance of interpretations. This will provide alternatives to the preapproval of HACCP plans, such as simplified HACCP plans in line with the Fish and Fishery Products model, if the product is produced under a HACCP plan developed in conformance with such regulation or guideline. In so doing, the need for preapproved plans under the more intensive regimen of the Food Code will be significantly reduced.

HACCP plans are key to the use of performance standards as measures of regulatory compliance. Performance standards issued by the Food Safety and Inspection Service are applicable to a broad range of meat, poultry, and egg products. Federal performance standards are acceptable, equivalent alternatives to the command-and-control provisions that now provide specific times and temperatures for processing various products. Federal performance standards may be used to determine the safety of a product or process under the Food Code if authorized under a variance granted in accord with the Code's variance provisions, and demonstrated by adherence to a validated HACCP plan, consistent with the Code's HACCP provisions.

7. CODE ADOPTION/CERTIFIED COPIES

The model Food Code is provided for use by food regulatory jurisdictions at all levels of government. At the state and local levels the model may be:

(A) Enacted into <u>statute</u> as an act of the state legislative body;

(B) Promulgated as a <u>regulation</u>, if the state legislative body has delegated rule-making authority to a governmental administrative agency; or

(C) Adopted as an <u>ordinance</u>, if the local legislative body has been delegated rule-making authority or regulatory powers.

Typically, code adoption bodies publish a notice of their intent to adopt a code, make copies available for public inspection, and provide an opportunity for public input prior to adoption. This is usually done in one of two ways.

The recommended method is the "short form" or "adoption by reference" approach where a simple statement is published stating that certified copies of the proposed code are on file for public review. This approach may be used by governmental bodies located in states that have enabling laws authorizing the adoption of codes by reference. An advantage to this approach is a substantial reduction in the cost of publishing and printing.

Certified copies of the Food Code for use in adopting the model by reference are available through the FDA Retail Food Protection Team, HFS-320, 5100 Paint Branch Parkway, College Park, MD 20740-3835. Refer to item 2. *(A)* of this Preface to access a listing of jurisdictions' adoptions.

The alternative method is the "long form" or "section-by-section" approach where the proposed code is published in its entirety.

Both methods of adoption allow for the modification of specific provisions to accommodate existing law, administrative procedure, or regulatory policy. Annex 7 contains model adoption forms for use by governmental bodies who wish to use either of these methods.

8. INFORMATION TO ASSIST THE USER

Many of the improvements contained in the model Food Code, as listed under item 5 of this Preface, are provided to make the document easier to use. Other characteristics of the new edition, if they are understood by the user, make it easier to follow and apply. These include structure, nomenclature, and methodology.

Food Code provisions address essentially four areas: personnel (Chapter 2), food (Chapter 3), equipment/facilities/supplies (Chapters 4, 5, 6, 7), and compliance and enforcement (Chapter 8). A new user will find it helpful to review the Table of Contents together with the Code Reference Sheet (Annex 7, Guide 3-B) in order to quickly gain an understanding of the scope and sequence of subjects included within these four areas. The structural nomenclature of the document is as follows:

Chapter	9
Part	9-1
Subpart	9-101
Section (§)	9-101.11
Paragraph (¶)	9-101.11(A)
Subparagraph	9-101.11(A)(1)

Code provisions are either appropriate for citing and debiting on an inspection report or they are not. Those not intended for citing/debiting are identified by the digits following the decimal point in the numbering system. These "nondebitable" provisions fall into two categories, those that end with two digits after the decimal point and the last digit is a zero, e.g., § 1-201.10; and those that end with three digits after the decimal point and the last 2 digits are zeros, e.g., § 8-805.100.

Two types of internal cross referencing are widely used throughout the Code to eliminate the need for restating provisions.

A. The first type of cross reference uses phrases that contain the word "under", e.g., "as specified **under** ... (followed by the relevant portion of the Code)."

The purpose of this type of cross reference is to:

1) Alert the reader to relevant information, and

2) Provide a system by which each violation is recorded under the <u>one</u> most appropriate provision. This type of cross reference signals to the reader the provision of the Code <u>under</u> which a certain violation is properly cited/debited.

B. The second type of cross reference uses phrases that contain the word "in," e.g., "as specified **in**... (followed by the relevant portion of the Code)."

The purpose of this type of cross reference is to:

1) Indicate the specific provisions of a separate document such as a federal regulation that are being incorporated by reference <u>in</u> the requirement of the Code, e.g., ¶ 3-201.11(C); or

2) Refer the reader to a nondebitable provision of the Code which provides further information for consideration, such as provision for an exception or for an allowance to comply via an alternative method.

For example, ¶ 3-201.16 (A) begins with "Except as specified in ¶ (B)…" and ¶ (B) states the relevant exceptions to ¶ (A). Paragraph 3-201.11(E) states in part, "… as specified in ¶ 3-401.11(C)" and ¶ 3-401.11(C) provides for an allowance to serve or sell raw or undercooked, whole-meat, intact beef steaks in a ready-to-eat form.

If you review the exception in ¶ 3-201.16(B) and the allowance in ¶ 3-401.11(C), you will see that exceptions and allowances often contain conditions of compliance, i.e., conditions that must be met in order for the exception or allowance to convey.

Based on the violation being cited, the substance of the text being referred to, and the context in which the reference is made, users of the Code must infer the intent of the cross reference. That is, the user must determine if the cross reference simply alerts the user to additional information about the requirement or if the cross reference:

- sends (via the word "under") the citing/debiting to another Code provision; or
- incorporates (via the word "in") the referenced requirements into the Code provision.

The Food Code presents requirements by principle rather than by subject. For example, equipment requirements are presented under headings such as Materials, Design and Construction, Numbers and Capacities, Location and Installation, and Maintenance and Operation rather than by refrigerators, sinks, and thermometers. In this way provisions need be stated only once rather than repeated for each piece or category of equipment. Where there are special requirements for certain equipment, the requirement is delineated under the appropriate principle (e.g., Design and Construction) and listed separately in the index.

Portions of some sections are written in *italics*. These provisions are not requirements, but are provided to convey relevant information about specific exceptions and alternative means for compliance. Italics are pursuant to a preceding provision that states a requirement, to which the italics offer an exception or another possibility. Italicized sections usually involve the words "except for," "may", "need not" or "does not apply." See ¶ 3-202.18(D).

Requirements contained in the Food Code are presented as being in one of three categories of importance: PRIORITY ITEM (i.e. a provision in this Code whose application contributes directly to the elimination, prevention or reduction to an acceptable level, hazards associated with foodborne illness or injury and there is no other provision that more directly controls the hazard); **PRIORITY FOUNDATION ITEM** (i.e., a provision in this Code whose application supports, facilitates or enables one or more PRIORITY ITEMS); and, **CORE ITEM** (i.e., a provision in this Code that is not designated as a PRIORITY ITEM or a PRIORITY FOUNDATION ITEM and that usually relates to general sanitation, operational controls, sanitation standard operating procedures (SSOPs), facilities or structures, equipment design, or general maintenance.

A "P" or "Pf" designation after a paragraph or subparagraph indicates that the provision within that section is a PRIORITY ITEM or PRIORITY FOUNDATION ITEM. Any unmarked provisions within a section are CORE ITEMS.

The following conventions are used in the Food Code. "Shall" means the act is imperative, i.e., "shall" constitutes a command. "May not" means absolute prohibition. "May" is permissive and means the act is allowed. The term "means" is followed by a declared fact.

Defined words and terms are in "small caps" in the text of the Food Code chapters to alert the reader to the fact that there is a specific meaning assigned to those words and terms and that the meaning of a provision is to be interpreted in the defined context. A concerted effort was also made to place in "small caps" all forms and combinations of those defined words and terms that were intended to carry the weight of the definition.

The annexes located at the back of the document can provide tremendous assistance to those charged with applying Food Code provisions. No reference is made in the text of a provision to the annexes which support its requirements. This is necessary in order to keep future laws or other requirements based on the model Food Code "clean." However, the annexes are provided specifically to assist the regulatory authority apply the provisions uniformly and effectively.

It is, therefore, important for users to preview the subject and essence of each of the annexes before using the document. Some of the annexes (e.g., References, Public Health Reasons) are structured to present the information by the specific Food Code item number to which they apply. Other annexes provide information and materials intended to be helpful to the user such as model forms that can be used, a delineation of the principles of HACCP, guidelines for establishment inspection, and criteria for certain food processes for use in evaluating proposed HACCP plans.

9. THE CODE REVISION PROCESS

(A) Food Code Revision and Publication Cycles

FDA is issuing a new edition of the Food Code every 4 years. During the 4-year span of time between editions, FDA may issue supplements to an existing edition. Each new edition will incorporate the changes made in the supplement as well as any new revisions.

(B) Submission of Food Code Change Suggestions

FDA will continue to receive concerns and recommendations for modification of the Food Code from any individual or organization.

Given the purpose of the document as discussed in item 2. of this Preface, the Agency will be especially interested in addressing problems identified by those in government and industry who are responsible for implementing the Food Code. FDA will also be especially responsive to those needed policy and technical changes raised by an organization that uses a democratic process for addressing problems and concerns.

Included are organizations that provide a process that encourages representative participation in deliberations by government, industry, and academic and consumer interests, followed by public health ratification such as a state-by-state vote by officially designated delegates. The Conference for Food Protection (retail food issues), the National Conference on Interstate Milk Shipments (milk and dairy products issues), and the Interstate Shellfish Sanitation Conference (molluscan shellfish issues) are examples of such organizations. These organizations receive problems submitted by any interested individual, but specify the forms on which the issues must be detailed and provide specific time frames during which they may be submitted.

FDA encourages interested individuals to consider raising issues and suggesting solutions involving the federal-state cooperative programs based on FDA's model codes through these organizations.

10. ACKNOWLEDGMENTS

Many individuals devoted considerable time and effort in addressing concerns and developing recommendations that are now reflected in the Food Code. These individuals represent a wide diversity of regulators, educators, industry leaders, and consumer representatives acting through their agencies, companies, professional groups, or trade organizations. It is only through the dedicated efforts and contributions of experienced professionals that a scientifically sound, well focused, and up-to-date model code is possible. FDA acknowledges with gratitude the substantial assistance of those who contributed to public health and food safety in the development of the Food Code.

Contents

Chapter 1

Purpose and Definitions

Chapter 2	
	Management and Personnel

Chapter 3	
	Food

Chapter 5	
	Water, Plumbing, and Waste

Chapter 6

Physical Facilities

Annex 1

Compliance and Enforcement

Annex 2

References

Annex 3

Public Health Reasons/Administrative Guidelines

Annex 4

Management of Food Safety Practices – Achieving Active Managerial
Control of Foodborne Illness Risk Factors

1) Employee health information

- a) Form 1-A Conditional Employee or Food Employee Interview
- b) Form 1-B Conditional or Food Employee Reporting Agreement
- c) Form 1-C Conditional Employee or Food Employee Medical Referral
- d) Form 1-D Application for Bare Hand Contact Procedure

2) Adoption information

    a)   Form 2-A   Adoption by Reference
    b)   Form 2-B   Adoption by Section-by-Section Reference

3) Inspection information

    a)   Form 3-A   Food Establishment Inspection Report
    b)   Guide 3-B   Instructions for Marking the Food Establishment Inspection Report, Including Food Code References for Risk Factors/Interventions and Good Retail Practices

4) Summary information

    a)   Chart 4-A   Summary Chart for Minimum Cooking Food Temperatures and Holding Times Required by Chapter 3
    b)   Chart 4-B   Summary Chart for Minimum Food Temperatures and Holding Times Required by Chapter 3 for Reheating Foods for Hot Holding
    c)   Chart 4-C   Summary Chart – Ready-to-eat, Potentially Hazardous Food (Time/Temperature, Control for Safety Food) Date Marking § 3-501.17(A) – (E) and Disposition § 3-501.18
    d)   Chart 4-D   FDA Food Code Mobile Food Establishment Matrix
    e)   Summary   Summary of Changes in the FDA Food Code

1 Purpose and Definitions

Parts

1-1   TITLE, INTENT, SCOPE

Subparts

Title

1-101.10   Food Code.

These provisions shall be known as the Food Code, hereinafter referred to as "this Code."

Intent

1-102.10   Food Safety, Illness Prevention, and Honest Presentation.

The purpose of this Code is to safeguard public health and provide to CONSUMERS FOOD that is safe, unADULTERATED, and honestly presented.

Scope

1-103.10   Statement.

This Code establishes definitions; sets standards for management and personnel, FOOD operations, and EQUIPMENT and facilities; and provides for FOOD ESTABLISHMENT plan review, PERMIT issuance, inspection, EMPLOYEE RESTRICTION, and PERMIT suspension.

Applicability and *Terms Defined*	**1-201.10**	**Statement of Application and Listing of** **Terms.**

(A) The following definitions shall apply in the interpretation and application of this Code.

(B) Terms Defined. As used in this Code, each of the terms listed in ¶ 1-201.10(B) shall have the meaning stated below.

Accredited Program.

(1) **"Accredited program"** means a food protection manager certification program that has been evaluated and listed by an accrediting agency as conforming to national standards for organizations that certify individuals.

(2) **"Accredited program"** refers to the certification process and is a designation based upon an independent evaluation of factors such as the sponsor's mission; organizational structure; staff resources; revenue sources; policies; public information regarding program scope, eligibility requirements, re-certification, discipline and grievance procedures; and test development and administration.

(3) *"Accredited program" does not refer to training functions or educational programs.*

Additive.

(1) **"Food additive"** has the meaning stated in the Federal Food, Drug, and Cosmetic Act, § 201(s) and 21 CFR 170.3(e)(1).

(2) **"Color additive"** has the meaning stated in the Federal Food, Drug, and Cosmetic Act, § 201(t) and 21 CFR 70.3(f).

"Adulterated" has the meaning stated in the Federal Food, Drug, and Cosmetic Act, § 402.

"Approved" means acceptable to the REGULATORY AUTHORITY based on a determination of conformity with principles, practices, and generally recognized standards that protect public health.

Asymptomatic.

(1) **"Asymptomatic"** means without obvious symptoms; not showing or producing indications of a disease or other medical condition, such as an individual infected with a pathogen but not exhibiting or producing any signs or symptoms of vomiting, diarrhea, or jaundice.

(2) **"Asymptomatic"** includes not showing symptoms because symptoms have resolved or subsided, or because symptoms never manifested.

"a_w" means water activity which is a measure of the free moisture in a FOOD, is the quotient of the water vapor pressure of the substance divided by the vapor pressure of pure water at the same temperature, and is indicated by the symbol A_w.

"Balut" means an embryo inside a fertile EGG that has been incubated for a period sufficient for the embryo to reach a specific stage of development after which it is removed from incubation before hatching.

"Beverage" means a liquid for drinking, including water.

"Bottled drinking water" means water that is SEALED in bottles, packages, or other containers and offered for sale for human consumption, including bottled mineral water.

"Casing" means a tubular container for sausage products made of either natural or artificial (synthetic) material.

"Certification number" means a unique combination of letters and numbers assigned by a SHELLFISH CONTROL AUTHORITY to a MOLLUSCAN SHELLFISH DEALER according to the provisions of the National Shellfish Sanitation Program.

"CFR" means CODE OF FEDERAL REGULATIONS. Citations in this Code to the CFR refer sequentially to the Title, Part, and Section numbers, such as 40 CFR 180.194 refers to Title 40, Part 180, Section 194.

CIP.

(1) **"CIP"** means cleaned in place by the circulation or flowing by mechanical means through a piping system of a detergent solution, water rinse, and SANITIZING solution onto or over EQUIPMENT surfaces that require cleaning, such as the method used, in part, to clean and SANITIZE a frozen dessert machine.

(2) **"CIP"** *does not include the cleaning of* EQUIPMENT *such as band saws, slicers, or mixers that are subjected to in-place manual cleaning without the use of a CIP system.*

"Commingle" means:

(1) To combine SHELLSTOCK harvested on different days or from different growing areas as identified on the tag or label, or

(2) To combine SHUCKED SHELLFISH from containers with different container codes or different shucking dates.

Comminuted.

(1) **"Comminuted"** means reduced in size by methods including chopping, flaking, grinding, or mincing.

(2) **"Comminuted"** includes FISH or MEAT products that are reduced in size and restructured or reformulated such as gefilte FISH, gyros, ground beef, and sausage; and a mixture of 2 or more types of MEAT that have been reduced in size and combined, such as sausages made from 2 or more MEATS.

"Conditional employee" means a potential FOOD EMPLOYEE to whom a job offer is made, conditional on responses to subsequent medical questions or examinations designed to identify potential FOOD EMPLOYEES who may be suffering from a disease that can be transmitted through FOOD and done in compliance with Title 1 of the Americans with Disabilities Act of 1990.

"Confirmed disease outbreak" means a FOODBORNE DISEASE OUTBREAK in which laboratory analysis of appropriate specimens identifies a causative agent and epidemiological analysis implicates the FOOD as the source of the illness.

"Consumer" means a PERSON who is a member of the public, takes possession of FOOD, is not functioning in the capacity of an operator of a FOOD ESTABLISHMENT or FOOD PROCESSING PLANT, and does not offer the FOOD for resale.

Core Item.

(1) **"Core item"** means a provision in this Code that is not designated as a PRIORITY ITEM or a PRIORITY FOUNDATION ITEM.

(2) **"Core item"** includes an item that usually relates to general sanitation, operational controls, sanitation standard operating procedures (SSOPs), facilities or structures, equipment design, or general maintenance.

"Corrosion-resistant material" means a material that maintains acceptable surface cleanability characteristics under prolonged influence of the FOOD to be contacted, the normal use of cleaning compounds and SANITIZING solutions, and other conditions of the use environment.

"Counter-mounted equipment" means EQUIPMENT that is not portable and is designed to be mounted off the floor on a table, counter, or shelf.

"Critical control point" means a point or procedure in a specific FOOD system where loss of control may result in an unacceptable health RISK.

"Critical limit" means the maximum or minimum value to which a physical, biological, or chemical parameter must be controlled at a CRITICAL CONTROL POINT to minimize the RISK that the identified FOOD safety HAZARD may occur.

"Cut leafy greens" means fresh leafy greens whose leaves have been cut, shredded, sliced, chopped, or torn. The term "leafy greens" includes iceberg lettuce, romaine lettuce, leaf lettuce, butter lettuce, baby leaf lettuce (i.e., immature lettuce or leafy greens), escarole, endive, spring mix, spinach, cabbage, kale, arugula and chard. The term "leafy greens" does not include herbs such as cilantro or parsley.

"Dealer" means a PERSON who is authorized by a SHELLFISH CONTROL AUTHORITY for the activities of SHELLSTOCK shipper, shucker-packer, repacker, reshipper, or depuration processor of MOLLUSCAN SHELLFISH according to the provisions of the National Shellfish Sanitation Program.

"Disclosure" means a written statement that clearly identifies the animal-derived FOODS which are, or can be ordered, raw, undercooked, or without otherwise being processed to eliminate pathogens, or items that contain an ingredient that is raw, undercooked, or without otherwise being processed to eliminate pathogens.

Drinking Water.

(1) **"Drinking water"** means water that meets criteria as specified in 40 CFR 141 National Primary Drinking Water Regulations.

(2) **"Drinking water"** is traditionally known as "potable water."

(3) **"Drinking water"** includes the term "water" *except where the term used connotes that the water is not potable, such as "boiler water," "mop water," "rainwater," "wastewater," and "nondrinking" water.*

"Dry storage area" means a room or area designated for the storage of PACKAGED or containerized bulk FOOD that is not POTENTIALLY HAZARDOUS (TIME/TEMPERATURE CONTROL FOR SAFETY FOOD) and dry goods such as SINGLE-SERVICE items.

Easily Cleanable.

(1) **"Easily cleanable"** means a characteristic of a surface that:

(a) Allows effective removal of soil by normal cleaning methods;

(b) Is dependent on the material, design, construction, and installation of the surface; and

(c) Varies with the likelihood of the surface's role in introducing pathogenic or toxigenic agents or other contaminants into FOOD based on the surface's APPROVED placement, purpose, and use.

(2) **"Easily cleanable"** includes a tiered application of the criteria that qualify the surface as EASILY CLEANABLE as specified in Subparagraph (1) of this definition to different situations in which varying degrees of cleanability are required such as:

(a) The appropriateness of stainless steel for a FOOD preparation surface as opposed to the lack of need for stainless steel to be used for floors or for tables used for CONSUMER dining; or

(b) The need for a different degree of cleanability for a utilitarian attachment or accessory in the kitchen as opposed to a decorative attachment or accessory in the CONSUMER dining area.

"Easily movable" means:

(1) Portable; mounted on casters, gliders, or rollers; or provided with a mechanical means to safely tilt a unit of EQUIPMENT for cleaning; and

(2) Having no utility connection, a utility connection that disconnects quickly, or a flexible utility connection line of sufficient length to allow the EQUIPMENT to be moved for cleaning of the EQUIPMENT and adjacent area.

Egg.

(1) **"Egg"** means the shell EGG of avian species such as chicken, duck, goose, guinea, quail, RATITES or turkey.

(2) *"Egg" does not include*:

(a) *A BALUT;*

(b) *The egg of reptile species such as alligator; or*

(c) *An EGG PRODUCT.*

Egg Product.

    (1) **"Egg Product"** means all, or a portion of, the contents found inside EGGS separated from the shell and pasteurized in a FOOD PROCESSING PLANT, with or without added ingredients, intended for human consumption, such as dried, frozen or liquid eggs.

    (2) *"Egg Product" does not include FOOD which contains EGGS only in a relatively small proportion such as cake mixes.*

"Employee" means the PERMIT HOLDER, PERSON IN CHARGE, FOOD EMPLOYEE, PERSON having supervisory or management duties, PERSON on the payroll, family member, volunteer, PERSON performing work under contractual agreement, or other PERSON working in a FOOD ESTABLISHMENT.

"Enterohemorrhagic *Escherichia coli"* (EHEC) means *E. coli* which cause hemorrhagic colitis, meaning bleeding enterically or bleeding from the intestine. The term is typically used in association with *E. coli* that have the capacity to produce Shiga toxins and to cause attaching and effacing lesions in the intestine. EHEC is a subset of STEC, whose members produce additional virulence factors. Infections with EHEC may be asymptomatic but are classically associated with bloody diarrhea (hemorrhagic colitis) and hemolytic uremic syndrome (HUS) or thrombotic thrombocytopenic purpura (TTP). Examples of serotypes of EHEC include: *E. coli* O157:H7; *E. coli* O157:NM; *E. coli* O26:H11; *E. coli* O145:NM; *E. coli* O103:H2; or *E. coli* O111:NM. *Also see* SHIGA TOXIN-PRODUCING *E. COLI.*

"EPA" means the U.S. Environmental Protection Agency.

Equipment.

    (1) **"Equipment"** means an article that is used in the operation of a FOOD ESTABLISHMENT such as a freezer, grinder, hood, ice maker, MEAT block, mixer, oven, reach-in refrigerator, scale, sink, slicer, stove, table, TEMPERATURE MEASURING DEVICE for ambient air, VENDING MACHINE, or WAREWASHING machine.

    (2) *"Equipment" does not include apparatuses used for handling or storing large quantities of PACKAGED FOODS that are received from a supplier in a cased or overwrapped lot, such as hand trucks, forklifts, dollies, pallets, racks, and skids.*

"Exclude" means to prevent a PERSON from working as an EMPLOYEE in a FOOD ESTABLISHMENT or entering a FOOD ESTABLISHMENT as an EMPLOYEE.

"FDA" means the U.S. Food and Drug Administration.

7

Fish.

(1) **"Fish"** means fresh or saltwater finfish, crustaceans and other forms of aquatic life (including alligator, frog, aquatic turtle, jellyfish, sea cucumber, and sea urchin and the roe of such animals) other than birds or mammals, and all mollusks, if such animal life is intended for human consumption.

(2) **"Fish"** includes an edible human FOOD product derived in whole or in part from FISH, including FISH that have been processed in any manner.

"Food" means a raw, cooked, or processed edible substance, ice, BEVERAGE, or ingredient used or intended for use or for sale in whole or in part for human consumption, or chewing gum.

"Foodborne disease outbreak" means the occurrence of two or more cases of a similar illness resulting from the ingestion of a common FOOD.

"Food-contact surface" means:

(1) A surface of EQUIPMENT or a UTENSIL with which FOOD normally comes into contact; or

(2) A surface of EQUIPMENT or a UTENSIL from which FOOD may drain, drip, or splash:

(a) Into a FOOD, or

(b) Onto a surface normally in contact with FOOD.

"Food employee" means an individual working with unPACKAGED FOOD, FOOD EQUIPMENT or UTENSILS, or FOOD-CONTACT SURFACES.

Food Establishment.

(1) **"Food establishment"** means an operation that:

(a) stores, prepares, packages, serves, vends food directly to the consumer, or otherwise provides FOOD for human consumption such as a restaurant; satellite or catered feeding location; catering operation if the operation provides FOOD directly to a CONSUMER or to a conveyance used to transport people; market; vending location; conveyance used to transport people; institution; or FOOD bank; and

(b) relinquishes possession of FOOD to a CONSUMER directly, or indirectly through a delivery service such as home delivery of grocery orders or restaurant takeout orders, or delivery service that is provided by common carriers.

(2) **"Food establishment"** includes:

(a) An element of the operation such as a transportation vehicle or a central preparation facility that supplies a vending location or satellite feeding location *unless the vending or feeding location is permitted by the* REGULATORY AUTHORITY; and

(b) An operation that is conducted in a mobile, stationary, temporary, or permanent facility or location; where consumption is on or off the PREMISES; and regardless of whether there is a charge for the FOOD.

(3) ***"Food establishment"*** *does not include:*

(a) *An establishment that offers only pre*PACKAGED FOODS *that are not* POTENTIALLY HAZARDOUS (TIME/TEMPERATURE CONTROL FOR SAFETY) FOODS;

(b) *A produce stand that only offers whole, uncut fresh fruits and vegetables;*

(c) *A* FOOD PROCESSING PLANT*; including those that are located on the* PREMISES *of a* FOOD ESTABLISHMENT

(d) *A kitchen in a private home if only* FOOD *that is not* POTENTIALLY HAZARDOUS (TIME/TEMPERATURE CONTROL FOR SAFETY) FOOD, *is prepared for sale or service at a function such as a religious or charitable organization's bake sale if allowed by* LAW *and if the* CONSUMER *is informed by a clearly visible placard at the sales or service location that the* FOOD *is prepared in a kitchen that is not subject to regulation and inspection by the* REGULATORY AUTHORITY*;*

(e) *An area where* FOOD *that is prepared as specified in Subparagraph (3)(d) of this definition is sold or offered for human consumption;*

(f) *A kitchen in a private home, such as a small family day-care provider; or a bed-and-breakfast operation that prepares and offers* FOOD *to guests if the home is owner occupied, the number of available guest bedrooms does not exceed 6, breakfast is the only meal offered, the number of guests served does not exceed 18, and the* CONSUMER *is informed by statements contained in published advertisements, mailed brochures, and placards posted at the registration area that the* FOOD *is prepared in a kitchen that is not regulated and inspected by the* REGULATORY AUTHORITY*; or*

(g) *A private home that receives catered or home-delivered* FOOD.

Food Processing Plant.

(1) **"Food processing plant"** means a commercial operation that manufactures, packages, labels, or stores FOOD for human consumption, and provides FOOD for sale or distribution to other business entities such as FOOD PROCESSING PLANTS or FOOD ESTABLISHMENTS.

(2) *"Food processing plant"* does not include a FOOD ESTABLISHMENT.

Game Animal.

(1) **"Game animal"** means an animal, the products of which are FOOD, that is not classified as livestock, sheep, swine, goat, horse, mule, or other equine in 9 CFR 301.2 Definitions, or as Poultry, or FISH.

(2) **"Game animal"** includes mammals such as reindeer, elk, deer, antelope, water buffalo, bison, rabbit, squirrel, opossum, raccoon, nutria, or muskrat, and nonaquatic reptiles such as land snakes.

(3) *"Game animal"* does not include RATITES.

"General use pesticide" means a pesticide that is not classified by EPA for restricted use as specified in 40 CFR 152.175 Pesticides classified for restricted use.

"Grade A standards" means the requirements of the United States Public Health Service/FDA "Grade A Pasteurized Milk Ordinance" with which certain fluid and dry milk and milk products comply.

"HACCP plan" means a written document that delineates the formal procedures for following the HAZARD Analysis and CRITICAL CONTROL POINT principles developed by The National Advisory Committee on Microbiological Criteria for Foods.

Handwashing Sink.

(1) **"Handwashing sink"** means a lavatory, a basin or vessel for washing, a wash basin, or a PLUMBING FIXTURE especially placed for use in personal hygiene and designed for the washing of the hands.

(2) **"Handwashing sink"** includes an automatic handwashing facility.

"Hazard" means a biological, chemical, or physical property that may cause an unacceptable CONSUMER health RISK.

"Health practitioner" means a physician licensed to practice medicine, or if allowed by LAW, a nurse practitioner, physician assistant, or similar medical professional.

"Hermetically sealed container" means a container that is designed and intended to be secure against the entry of microorganisms and, in the case of low acid canned FOODS, to maintain the commercial sterility of its contents after processing.

"Highly susceptible population" means PERSONS who are more likely than other people in the general population to experience foodborne disease because they are:

(1) Immunocompromised; preschool age children, or older adults; and

(2) Obtaining FOOD at a facility that provides services such as custodial care, health care, or assisted living, such as a child or adult day care center, kidney dialysis center, hospital or nursing home, or nutritional or socialization services such as a senior center.

"Imminent health hazard" means a significant threat or danger to health that is considered to exist when there is evidence sufficient to show that a product, practice, circumstance, or event creates a situation that requires immediate correction or cessation of operation to prevent injury based on:

(1) The number of potential injuries, and

(2) The nature, severity, and duration of the anticipated injury.

"Injected" means manipulating MEAT to which a solution has been introduced into its interior by processes that are referred to as "injecting," "pump marinating," or "stitch pumping".

Juice.

(1) **"Juice"** means the aqueous liquid expressed or extracted from one or more fruits or vegetables, purées of the edible portions of one or more fruits or vegetables, or any concentrates of such liquid or purée.

(2) ***"Juice"*** *does not include, for purposes of HACCP, liquids, purées, or concentrates that are not used as BEVERAGES or ingredients of BEVERAGES.*

"Kitchenware" means FOOD preparation and storage UTENSILS.

"Law" means applicable local, state, and federal statutes, regulations, and ordinances.

"Linens" means fabric items such as cloth hampers, cloth napkins, table cloths, wiping cloths, and work garments including cloth gloves.

Major Food Allergen.

(1) **"Major food allergen"** means:

(a) Milk, EGG, FISH (such as bass, flounder, cod, and including crustacean shellfish such as crab, lobster, or shrimp), tree nuts (such as almonds, pecans, or walnuts), wheat, peanuts, and soybeans; or

(b) A FOOD ingredient that contains protein derived from a FOOD, as specified in Subparagraph (1)(a) of this definition.

(2) *"Major food allergen" does not include:*

(a) *Any highly refined oil derived from a FOOD specified in Subparagraph (1)(a) of this definition and any ingredient derived from such highly refined oil; or*

(b) *Any ingredient that is exempt under the petition or notification process specified in the Food Allergen Labeling and Consumer Protection Act of 2004 (Public Law 108-282).*

"Meat" means the flesh of animals used as FOOD including the dressed flesh of cattle, swine, sheep, or goats and other edible animals, *except FISH, POULTRY, and wild GAME ANIMALS as specified under Subparagraphs 3-201.17(A)(3) and (4).*

Mechanically Tenderized.

(1) **"Mechanically tenderized"** means manipulating meat with deep penetration by processes which may be referred to as "blade tenderizing," "jaccarding," "pinning," "needling," or using blades, pins, needles or any mechanical device.

(2) **"Mechanically tenderized"** does not include processes by which solutions are INJECTED into meat.

"mg/L" means milligrams per liter, which is the metric equivalent of parts per million (ppm).

"Molluscan shellfish" means any edible species of fresh or frozen oysters, clams, mussels, and scallops or edible portions thereof, *except when the scallop product consists only of the shucked adductor muscle.*

Non-Continuous Cooking.

(1) **"Non-continuous cooking"** means the cooking of FOOD in a FOOD ESTABLISHMENT using a process in which the initial heating of the FOOD is

intentionally halted so that it may be cooled and held for complete cooking at a later time prior to sale or service.

(2) **"Non-continuous cooking"** does not include cooking procedures that only involve temporarily interrupting or slowing an otherwise continuous cooking process.

Packaged.

(1) **"Packaged"** means bottled, canned, cartoned, securely bagged, or securely wrapped, whether PACKAGED in a FOOD ESTABLISHMENT or a FOOD PROCESSING PLANT.

(2) *"Packaged" does not include a wrapper, carry-out box, or other nondurable container used to containerize FOOD with the purpose of facilitating FOOD protection during service and receipt of the FOOD by the CONSUMER.*

"Permit" means the document issued by the REGULATORY AUTHORITY that authorizes a PERSON to operate a FOOD ESTABLISHMENT.

"Permit holder" means the entity that:

(1) Is legally responsible for the operation of the FOOD ESTABLISHMENT such as the owner, the owner's agent, or other PERSON; and

(2) Possesses a valid PERMIT to operate a FOOD ESTABLISHMENT.

"Person" means an association, a corporation, individual, partnership, other legal entity, government, or governmental subdivision or agency.

"Person in charge" means the individual present at a FOOD ESTABLISHMENT who is responsible for the operation at the time of inspection.

Personal Care Items.

(1) **"Personal care items"** means items or substances that may be poisonous, toxic, or a source of contamination and are used to maintain or enhance a PERSON'S health, hygiene, or appearance.

(2) **"Personal care items"** include items such as medicines; first aid supplies; and other items such as cosmetics, and toiletries such as toothpaste and mouthwash.

"pH" means the symbol for the negative logarithm of the hydrogen ion concentration, which is a measure of the degree of acidity or alkalinity of a solution.

Values between 0 and 7 indicate acidity and values between 7 and 14 indicate alkalinity. The value for pure distilled water is 7, which is considered neutral.

"Physical facilities" means the structure and interior surfaces of a FOOD ESTABLISHMENT including accessories such as soap and towel dispensers and attachments such as light fixtures and heating or air conditioning system vents.

"Plumbing fixture" means a receptacle or device that:

(1) Is permanently or temporarily connected to the water distribution system of the PREMISES and demands a supply of water from the system; or

(2) Discharges used water, waste materials, or SEWAGE directly or indirectly to the drainage system of the PREMISES.

"Plumbing system" means the water supply and distribution pipes; PLUMBING FIXTURES and traps; soil, waste, and vent pipes; sanitary and storm sewers and building drains, including their respective connections, devices, and appurtenances within the PREMISES; and water-treating EQUIPMENT.

"Poisonous or toxic materials" means substances that are not intended for ingestion and are included in 4 categories:

(1) Cleaners and SANITIZERS, which include cleaning and SANITIZING agents and agents such as caustics, acids, drying agents, polishes, and other chemicals;

(2) Pesticides, *except SANITIZERS*, which include substances such as insecticides and rodenticides;

(3) Substances necessary for the operation and maintenance of the establishment such as nonfood grade lubricants and PERSONAL CARE ITEMS that may be deleterious to health; and

(4) Substances that are not necessary for the operation and maintenance of the establishment and are on the PREMISES for retail sale, such as petroleum products and paints.

Potentially Hazardous Food (Time/Temperature Control for Safety Food).

(1) **"Potentially hazardous food (time/temperature control for safety food)"** means a FOOD that requires time/temperature control for safety (TCS) to limit pathogenic microorganism growth or toxin formation.

(2) **"Potentially hazardous food (time/temperature control for safety food)"** includes:

(a) An animal FOOD that is raw or heat-treated; a plant FOOD that is heat-treated or consists of raw seed sprouts, cut melons, cut leafy greens, cut tomatoes or mixtures of cut tomatoes that are not modified in a way so that they are unable to support pathogenic microorganism growth or toxin formation, or garlic-in-oil mixtures that are not modified in a way so that they are unable to support pathogenic microorganism growth or toxin formation; and

(b) Except as specified in Subparagraph (3)(d) of this definition, a FOOD that because of the interaction of its A_W and PH values is designated as Product Assessment Required (PA) in Table A or B of this definition:

Table A. Interaction of PH and A_W for control of spores in FOOD heat-treated to destroy vegetative cells and subsequently PACKAGED

A_W values	PH values		
	4.6 or less	> 4.6 - 5.6	> 5.6
≤0.92	non-PHF*/non-TCS FOOD**	non-PHF/non-TCS FOOD	non-PHF/non-TCS FOOD
> 0.92 - .95	non-PHF/non-TCS FOOD	non-PHF/non-TCS FOOD	PA***
> 0.95	non-PHF/non-TCS FOOD	PA	PA

* PHF means POTENTIALLY HAZARDOUS FOOD
** TCS FOOD means TIME/TEMPERATURE CONTROL FOR SAFETY FOOD
*** PA means Product Assessment required

Table B. Interaction of pH and A$_w$ for control of vegetative cells and spores in FOOD not heat-treated or heat-treated but not PACKAGED

A$_w$ values	pH values			
	< 4.2	4.2 - 4.6	> 4.6 - 5.0	> 5.0
< 0.88	non-PHF*/ non-TCS food**	non-PHF/ non-TCS food	non-PHF/ non-TCS food	non-PHF/ non-TCS food
0.88 – 0.90	non-PHF/ non-TCS food	non-PHF/ non-TCS food	non-PHF/ non-TCS food	PA***
> 0.90 – 0.92	non-PHF/ non-TCS food	non-PHF/ non-TCS food	PA	PA
> 0.92	non-PHF/ non-TCS food	PA	PA	PA

*   PHF means POTENTIALLY HAZARDOUS FOOD
**   TCS FOOD means TIME/TEMPERATURE CONTROL FOR SAFETY FOOD
*** PA means Product Assessment required

(3) **"Potentially hazardous food (time/temperature control for safety food)"** does not include:

(a) An air-cooled hard-boiled EGG with shell intact, or an EGG with shell intact that is not hard-boiled, but has been pasteurized to destroy all viable **salmonellae;**

(b) A FOOD in an unopened HERMETICALLY SEALED CONTAINER that is commercially processed to achieve and maintain commercial sterility under conditions of non-refrigerated storage and distribution;

(c) A FOOD that because of its pH or A$_w$ value, or interaction of A$_w$ and pH values, is designated as a non-PHF/non-TCS FOOD in Table A or B of this definition;

(d) A FOOD that is designated as Product Assessment Required (PA) in Table A or B of this definition and has undergone a Product Assessment showing that the growth or toxin formation of pathogenic microorganisms that are reasonably likely to occur in that FOOD is precluded due to:

16

(i) Intrinsic factors including added or natural characteristics of the FOOD such as preservatives, antimicrobials, humectants, acidulants, or nutrients,

(ii) Extrinsic factors including environmental or operational factors that affect the FOOD such as packaging, modified atmosphere such as REDUCED OXYGEN PACKAGING, shelf life and use, or temperature range of storage and use, or

(iii) A combination of intrinsic and extrinsic factors; or

(e) A FOOD that does not support the growth or toxin formation of pathogenic microorganisms in accordance with one of the Subparagraphs (3)(a) - (3)(d) of this definition even though the FOOD may contain a pathogenic microorganism or chemical or physical contaminant at a level sufficient to cause illness or injury.

"Poultry" means:

(1) Any domesticated bird (chickens, turkeys, ducks, geese, guineas, RATITES, or squabs), whether live or dead, as defined in 9 CFR 381.1 Poultry Products Inspection Regulations Definitions, Poultry; and

(2) Any migratory waterfowl or game bird, pheasant, partridge, quail, grouse, or pigeon, whether live or dead, as defined in 9 CFR 362.1 Voluntary Poultry Inspection Regulations, Definitions.

"Premises" means:

(1) The PHYSICAL FACILITY, its contents, and the contiguous land or property under the control of the PERMIT HOLDER; or

(2) The PHYSICAL FACILITY, its contents, and the land or property not described in Subparagraph (1) of this definition if its facilities and contents are under the control of the PERMIT HOLDER and may impact FOOD ESTABLISHMENT personnel, facilities, or operations, and a FOOD ESTABLISHMENT is only one component of a larger operation such as a health care facility, hotel, motel, school, recreational camp, or prison.

"Primal cut" means a basic major cut into which carcasses and sides of MEAT are separated, such as a beef round, pork loin, lamb flank, or veal breast.

Priority Item.

(1) **"Priority item"** means a provision in this Code whose application contributes directly to the elimination, prevention or reduction to an acceptable level, hazards

17

associated with foodborne illness or injury and there is no other provision that more directly controls the hazard.

(2) **"Priority item"** includes items with a quantifiable measure to show control of hazards such as cooking, reheating, cooling, handwashing; and

(3) **"Priority item"** is an item that is denoted in this Code with a superscript P- [P].

Priority Foundation Item.

(1) **"Priority foundation item"** means a provision in this Code whose application supports, facilitates or enables one or more PRIORITY ITEMS.

(2) **"Priority foundation item"** includes an item that requires the purposeful incorporation of specific actions, equipment or procedures by industry management to attain control of risk factors that contribute to foodborne illness or injury such as personnel training, infrastructure or necessary equipment, HACCP plans, documentation or record keeping, and labeling; and

(3) **"Priority foundation item"** is an item that is denoted in this Code with a superscript Pf - [Pf].

"Public water system" has the meaning stated in 40 CFR 141 National Primary Drinking Water Regulations.

"Ratite" means a flightless bird such as an emu, ostrich, or rhea.

Ready-to-Eat Food.

(1) **"Ready-to-eat food"** means FOOD that:

    (a) Is in a form that is edible without additional preparation to achieve FOOD safety, as specified under one of the following: ¶ 3-401.11(A) or (B), § 3-401.12, or § 3-402.11, or as specified in ¶ 3-401.11(C), or

    (b) Is a raw or partially cooked animal FOOD and the consumer is advised as specified in Subparagraphs 3-401.11(D)(1) and (3); or

    (c) Is prepared in accordance with a variance that is granted as specified in Subparagraph 3-401.11(D) (4); and

    (d) May receive additional preparation for palatability or aesthetic, epicurean, gastronomic, or culinary purposes.

(2) **"Ready-to-eat food"** includes:

(a) Raw animal FOOD that is cooked as specified under § 3-401.11 or 3-401.12, or frozen as specified under § 3-402.11;

(b) Raw fruits and vegetables that are washed as specified under § 3-302.15;

(c) Fruits and vegetables that are cooked for hot holding, as specified under § 3-401.13;

(d) All POTENTIALLY HAZARDOUS FOOD (TIME/TEMPERATURE CONTROL FOR SAFETY FOOD) that is cooked to the temperature and time required for the specific FOOD under Subpart 3-401 and cooled as specified under § 3-501.14;

(e) Plant FOOD for which further washing, cooking, or other processing is not required for FOOD safety, and from which rinds, peels, husks, or shells, if naturally present are removed;

(f) Substances derived from plants such as spices, seasonings, and sugar;

(g) A bakery item such as bread, cakes, pies, fillings, or icing for which further cooking is not required for FOOD safety;

(h) The following products that are produced in accordance with USDA guidelines and that have received a lethality treatment for pathogens: dry, fermented sausages, such as dry salami or pepperoni; salt-cured MEAT and POULTRY products, such as prosciutto ham, country cured ham, and Parma ham; and dried MEAT and POULTRY products, such as jerky or beef sticks; and

(i) FOODS manufactured as specified in 21 CFR Part 113, Thermally Processed Low-Acid Foods Packaged in Hermetically Sealed Containers.

Reduced Oxygen Packaging.

(1) **"Reduced oxygen packaging"** means:

(a) The reduction of the amount of oxygen in a PACKAGE by removing oxygen; displacing oxygen and replacing it with another gas or combination of gases; or otherwise controlling the oxygen content to a level below that normally found in the atmosphere (approximately 21% at sea level); and

(b) A process as specified in Subparagraph (1)(a) of this definition that involves a FOOD for which the HAZARDS *Clostridium botulinum* or *Listeria monocytogenes* require control in the final PACKAGED form.

(2) **"Reduced oxygen packaging"** includes:

(a) Vacuum PACKAGING, in which air is removed from a PACKAGE of FOOD and the PACKAGE is HERMETICALLY SEALED so that a vacuum remains inside the PACKAGE;

(b) Modified atmosphere PACKAGING, in which the atmosphere of a PACKAGE of FOOD is modified so that its composition is different from air but the atmosphere may change over time due to the permeability of the PACKAGING material or the respiration of the FOOD. Modified atmosphere PACKAGING includes reduction in the proportion of oxygen, total replacement of oxygen, or an increase in the proportion of other gases such as carbon dioxide or nitrogen;

(c) Controlled atmosphere PACKAGING, in which the atmosphere of a PACKAGE of FOOD is modified so that until the PACKAGE is opened, its composition is different from air, and continuous control of that atmosphere is maintained, such as by using oxygen scavengers or a combination of total replacement of oxygen, nonrespiring FOOD, and impermeable PACKAGING material;

(d) Cook chill PACKAGING, in which cooked FOOD is hot filled into impermeable bags which have the air expelled and are then sealed or crimped closed. The bagged FOOD is rapidly chilled and refrigerated at temperatures that inhibit the growth of psychrotrophic pathogens; or

(e) Sous vide PACKAGING, in which raw or partially cooked FOOD is placed in a hermetically sealed, impermeable bag, cooked in the bag, rapidly chilled, and refrigerated at temperatures that inhibit the growth of psychrotrophic pathogens.

"Refuse" means solid waste not carried by water through the SEWAGE system.

"Regulatory authority" means the local, state, or federal enforcement body or authorized representative having jurisdiction over the FOOD ESTABLISHMENT.

"Reminder" means a written statement concerning the health RISK of consuming animal FOODS raw, undercooked, or without otherwise being processed to eliminate pathogens.

"Re-service" means the transfer of FOOD that is unused and returned by a CONSUMER after being served or sold and in the possession of the CONSUMER, to another PERSON.

"Restrict" means to limit the activities of a FOOD EMPLOYEE so that there is no RISK of transmitting a disease that is transmissible through FOOD and the FOOD EMPLOYEE does not work with exposed FOOD, clean EQUIPMENT, UTENSILS, LINENS, or unwrapped SINGLE-SERVICE or SINGLE-USE ARTICLES.

"Restricted egg" means any check, dirty EGG, incubator reject, inedible, leaker, or loss as defined in 9 CFR 590.

"Restricted use pesticide" means a pesticide product that contains the active ingredients specified in 40 CFR 152.175 Pesticides classified for restricted use, and that is limited to use by or under the direct supervision of a certified applicator.

"Risk" means the likelihood that an adverse health effect will occur within a population as a result of a HAZARD in a FOOD.

"Safe material" means:

(1) An article manufactured from or composed of materials that may not reasonably be expected to result, directly or indirectly, in their becoming a component or otherwise affecting the characteristics of any FOOD;

(2) An additive that is used as specified in § 409 of the Federal Food, Drug, and Cosmetic Act; or

(3) Other materials that are not ADDITIVES and that are used in conformity with applicable regulations of the Food and Drug Administration.

"Sanitization" means the application of cumulative heat or chemicals on cleaned FOOD-CONTACT SURFACES that, when evaluated for efficacy, is sufficient to yield a reduction of 5 logs, which is equal to a 99.999% reduction, of representative disease microorganisms of public health importance.

"Sealed" means free of cracks or other openings that allow the entry or passage of moisture.

"Service animal" means an animal such as a guide dog, signal dog, or other animal individually trained to provide assistance to an individual with a disability.

"Servicing area" means an operating base location to which a mobile FOOD ESTABLISHMENT or transportation vehicle returns regularly for such things as vehicle and equipment cleaning, discharging liquid or solid wastes, refilling water tanks and ice bins, and boarding FOOD.

21

"Sewage" means liquid waste containing animal or vegetable matter in suspension or solution and may include liquids containing chemicals in solution.

"Shellfish control authority" means a state, federal, foreign, tribal, or other government entity legally responsible for administering a program that includes certification of MOLLUSCAN SHELLFISH harvesters and DEALERs for interstate commerce.

"Shellstock" means raw, in-shell MOLLUSCAN SHELLFISH.

"Shiga toxin-producing *Escherichia coli*" (STEC) means any *E. coli* capable of producing Shiga toxins (also called verocytotoxins or "Shiga-like" toxins). Examples of serotypes of STEC include both O157 and non-O157 *E. coli*. *Also see* ENTEROHEMORRHAGIC *ESCHERICHIA COLI.*

"Shucked shellfish" means MOLLUSCAN SHELLFISH that have one or both shells removed.

"Single-service articles" means TABLEWARE, carry-out UTENSILS, and other items such as bags, containers, placemats, stirrers, straws, toothpicks, and wrappers that are designed and constructed for one time, one PERSON use after which they are intended for discard.

Single-Use Articles.

(1) **"Single-use articles"** means UTENSILS and bulk FOOD containers designed and constructed to be used once and discarded.

(2) **"Single-use articles"** includes items such as wax paper, butcher paper, plastic wrap, formed aluminum FOOD containers, jars, plastic tubs or buckets, bread wrappers, pickle barrels, ketchup bottles, and number 10 cans which do not meet the materials, durability, strength, and cleanability specifications under §§ 4-101.11, 4-201.11, and 4-202.11 for multiuse UTENSILS.

"Slacking" means the process of moderating the temperature of a FOOD such as allowing a FOOD to gradually increase from a temperature of -23°C (-10°F) to -4°C (25°F) in preparation for deep-fat frying or to facilitate even heat penetration during the cooking of previously block-frozen FOOD such as shrimp.

"Smooth" means:

(1) A FOOD-CONTACT SURFACE having a surface free of pits and inclusions with a cleanability equal to or exceeding that of (100 grit) number 3 stainless steel;

(2) A nonFOOD-CONTACT SURFACE of EQUIPMENT having a surface equal to that of commercial grade hot-rolled steel free of visible scale; and

(3) A floor, wall, or ceiling having an even or level surface with no roughness or projections that render it difficult to clean.

"Tableware" means eating, drinking, and serving UTENSILS for table use such as flatware including forks, knives, and spoons; hollowware including bowls, cups, serving dishes, and tumblers; and plates.

"Temperature measuring device" means a thermometer, thermocouple, thermistor, or other device that indicates the temperature of FOOD, air, or water.

"Temporary food establishment" means a FOOD ESTABLISHMENT that operates for a period of no more than 14 consecutive days in conjunction with a single event or celebration.

"USDA" means the U.S. Department of Agriculture.

"Utensil" means a FOOD-CONTACT implement or container used in the storage, preparation, transportation, dispensing, sale, or service of FOOD, such as KITCHENWARE or TABLEWARE that is multiuse, SINGLE-SERVICE, or SINGLE-USE; gloves used in contact with FOOD; temperature sensing probes of FOOD TEMPERATURE MEASURING DEVICES; and probe-type price or identification tags used in contact with FOOD.

"Variance" means a written document issued by the REGULATORY AUTHORITY that authorizes a modification or waiver of one or more requirements of this Code if, in the opinion of the REGULATORY AUTHORITY, a health HAZARD or nuisance will not result from the modification or waiver.

"Vending machine" means a self-service device that, upon insertion of a coin, paper currency, token, card, or key, or by optional manual operation, dispenses unit servings of FOOD in bulk or in packages without the necessity of replenishing the device between each vending operation.

"Vending machine location" means the room, enclosure, space, or area where one or more VENDING MACHINES are installed and operated and includes the storage areas and areas on the PREMISES that are used to service and maintain the VENDING MACHINES.

"Warewashing" means the cleaning and SANITIZING of UTENSILS and FOOD-CONTACT SURFACES of EQUIPMENT.

"Whole-muscle, intact beef" means whole muscle beef that is not injected, mechanically tenderized, reconstructed, or scored and marinated, from which beef steaks may be cut.

Chapter 2 — Management and Personnel

Chapter

2 Management and Personnel

Parts

- 2-1 SUPERVISION
- 2-2 EMPLOYEE HEALTH
- 2-3 PERSONAL CLEANLINESS
- 2-4 HYGIENIC PRACTICES

2-1 SUPERVISION

Subparts

2-101 Responsibility
2-102 Knowledge
2-103 Duties

Responsibility

2-101.11 Assignment.

(A) Except as specified in ¶ (B) of this section, the PERMIT HOLDER shall be the PERSON IN CHARGE or shall designate a PERSON IN CHARGE and shall ensure that a PERSON IN CHARGE is present at the FOOD ESTABLISHMENT during all hours of operation.^Pf

(B) In a FOOD ESTABLISHMENT with two or more separately PERMITTED departments that are the legal responsibility of the same PERMIT HOLDER and that are located on the same PREMISES, the PERMIT HOLDER may, during specific time periods when food is not being prepared, packaged, or served, designate a single PERSON IN CHARGE who is present on the PREMISES during all hours of operation, and who is responsible for each separately PERMITTED FOOD ESTABLISHMENT on the PREMISES.^Pf

25

Knowledge **2-102.11**   **Demonstration.**

Based on the RISKS inherent to the FOOD operation, during inspections and upon request the PERSON IN CHARGE shall demonstrate to the REGULATORY AUTHORITY knowledge of foodborne disease prevention, application of the HAZARD Analysis and CRITICAL CONTROL POINT principles, and the requirements of this Code. The PERSON IN CHARGE shall demonstrate this knowledge by:

(A) Complying with this Code by having no violations of PRIORITY ITEMS during the current inspection; [Pf]

(B) Being a certified FOOD protection manager who has shown proficiency of required information through passing a test that is part of an ACCREDITED PROGRAM;[Pf] or

(C) Responding correctly to the inspector's questions as they relate to the specific FOOD operation. The areas of knowledge include:

(1) Describing the relationship between the prevention of foodborne disease and the personal hygiene of a FOOD EMPLOYEE; [Pf]

(2) Explaining the responsibility of the PERSON IN CHARGE for preventing the transmission of foodborne disease by a FOOD EMPLOYEE who has a disease or medical condition that may cause foodborne disease; [Pf]

(3) Describing the symptoms associated with the diseases that are transmissible through FOOD; [Pf]

(4) Explaining the significance of the relationship between maintaining the time and temperature of POTENTIALLY HAZARDOUS FOOD (TIME/TEMPERATURE CONTROL FOR SAFETY FOOD) and the prevention of foodborne illness; [Pf]

(5) Explaining the HAZARDS involved in the consumption of raw or undercooked MEAT, POULTRY, EGGS, and FISH; [Pf]

(6) Stating the required FOOD temperatures and times for safe cooking of POTENTIALLY HAZARDOUS FOOD (TIME/TEMPERATURE CONTROL FOR SAFETY FOOD) including MEAT, POULTRY, EGGS, and FISH; [Pf]

(7) Stating the required temperatures and times for the safe refrigerated storage, hot holding, cooling, and reheating of POTENTIALLY HAZARDOUS FOOD (TIME/TEMPERATURE CONTROL FOR SAFETY FOOD); [Pf]

(8) Describing the relationship between the prevention of foodborne illness and the management and control of the following:

(a) Cross contamination, [Pf]

(b) Hand contact with READY-TO-EAT FOODS, [Pf]

(c) Handwashing, [Pf] and

(d) Maintaining the FOOD ESTABLISHMENT in a clean condition and in good repair; [Pf]

(9) Describing FOODS identified as MAJOR FOOD ALLERGENS and the symptoms that a MAJOR FOOD ALLERGEN could cause in a sensitive individual who has an allergic reaction. [Pf]

(10) Explaining the relationship between FOOD safety and providing EQUIPMENT that is:

(a) Sufficient in number and capacity, [Pf] and

(b) Properly designed, constructed, located, installed, operated, maintained, and cleaned; [Pf]

(11) Explaining correct procedures for cleaning and SANITIZING UTENSILS and FOOD-CONTACT SURFACES of EQUIPMENT; [Pf]

(12) Identifying the source of water used and measures taken to ensure that it remains protected from contamination such as providing protection from backflow and precluding the creation of cross connections; [Pf]

(13) Identifying POISONOUS OR TOXIC MATERIALS in the FOOD ESTABLISHMENT and the procedures necessary to ensure that they are safely stored, dispensed, used, and disposed of according to LAW; [Pf]

27

(14) Identifying CRITICAL CONTROL POINTS in the operation from purchasing through sale or service that when not controlled may contribute to the transmission of foodborne illness and explaining steps taken to ensure that the points are controlled in accordance with the requirements of this Code; [Pf]

(15) Explaining the details of how the PERSON IN CHARGE and FOOD EMPLOYEES comply with the HACCP PLAN if a plan is required by the LAW, this Code, or an agreement between the REGULATORY AUTHORITY and the FOOD ESTABLISHMENT; [Pf]

(16) Explaining the responsibilities, rights, and authorities assigned by this Code to the:

    (a) FOOD EMPLOYEE, [Pf]

    (b) CONDITIONAL EMPLOYEE, [Pf]

    (c) PERSON IN CHARGE, [Pf]

    (d) REGULATORY AUTHORITY; [Pf] and

(17) Explaining how the PERSON IN CHARGE, FOOD EMPLOYEES, and CONDITIONAL EMPLOYEES comply with reporting responsibilities and EXCLUSION or RESTRICTION of FOOD EMPLOYEES. [Pf]

2-102.20   Food Protection Manager Certification.

A PERSON IN CHARGE who demonstrates knowledge by being a FOOD protection manager that is certified by a FOOD protection manager certification program that is evaluated and listed by a Conference for Food Protection-recognized accrediting agency as conforming to the Conference for Food Protection Standards for Accreditation of Food Protection Manager Certification Programs is deemed to comply with ¶ 2-102.11(B).

Duties   **2-103.11   Person in Charge.**

The PERSON IN CHARGE shall ensure that:

(A) FOOD ESTABLISHMENT operations are not conducted in a private home or in a room used as living or sleeping quarters as specified under § 6-202.111; [Pf]

(B) PERSONS unnecessary to the FOOD ESTABLISHMENT operation are not allowed in the FOOD preparation, FOOD storage, or WAREWASHING areas, except that brief visits and tours may be authorized by the PERSON IN CHARGE if steps are taken to ensure that exposed FOOD; clean EQUIPMENT, UTENSILS, and LINENS; and unwrapped SINGLE-SERVICE and SINGLE-USE ARTICLES are protected from contamination; [Pf]

(C) EMPLOYEES and other PERSONS such as delivery and maintenance PERSONS and pesticide applicators entering the FOOD preparation, FOOD storage, and WAREWASHING areas comply with this Code; [Pf]

(D) EMPLOYEES are effectively cleaning their hands, by routinely monitoring the EMPLOYEES' handwashing; [Pf]

(E) EMPLOYEES are visibly observing FOODS as they are received to determine that they are from APPROVED sources, delivered at the required temperatures, protected from contamination, unADULTERED, and accurately presented, by routinely monitoring the EMPLOYEES' observations and periodically evaluating FOODS upon their receipt; [Pf]

(F) EMPLOYEES are properly cooking POTENTIALLY HAZARDOUS FOOD (TIME/TEMPERATURE CONTROL FOR SAFETY FOOD), being particularly careful in cooking those FOODS known to cause severe foodborne illness and death, such as EGGS and COMMINUTED MEATS, through daily oversight of the EMPLOYEES' routine monitoring of the cooking temperatures using appropriate temperature measuring devices properly scaled and calibrated as specified under § 4-203.11 and ¶ 4-502.11(B); [Pf]

(G) EMPLOYEES are using proper methods to rapidly cool POTENTIALLY HAZARDOUS FOODS (TIME/TEMPERATURE CONTROL FOR SAFETY FOODS) that are not held hot or are not for consumption within 4 hours, through daily oversight of the EMPLOYEES' routine monitoring of FOOD temperatures during cooling; [Pf]

(H) CONSUMERS who order raw; or partially cooked READY-TO-EAT FOODS of animal origin are informed as specified under § 3-603.11 that the FOOD is not cooked sufficiently to ensure its safety; [Pf]

(I) EMPLOYEES are properly SANITIZING cleaned multiuse EQUIPMENT and UTENSILS before they are reused, through routine monitoring of solution temperature and exposure time for hot water SANITIZING, and chemical concentration, pH, temperature, and exposure time for chemical SANITIZING; [Pf]

(J) CONSUMERS are notified that clean TABLEWARE is to be used when they return to self-service areas such as salad bars and buffets as specified under § 3-304.16; [Pf]

(K) Except when APPROVAL is obtained from the REGULATORY AUTHORITY as specified in ¶ 3-301.11(D), EMPLOYEES are preventing cross-contamination of READY-TO-EAT FOOD with bare hands by properly using suitable UTENSILS such as deli tissue, spatulas, tongs, single-use gloves, or dispensing EQUIPMENT; [Pf]

(L) EMPLOYEES are properly trained in FOOD safety, including food allergy awareness, as it relates to their assigned duties; [Pf] and

(M) FOOD EMPLOYEES and CONDITIONAL EMPLOYEES are informed of their responsibility to report in accordance with LAW, to the PERSON IN CHARGE, information about their health and activities as they relate to diseases that are transmissible through FOOD, as specified under ¶ 2-201.11(A). [Pf]

2-2	**EMPLOYEE HEALTH**
	Subpart
	2-201 **Responsibilities of Permit Holder, Person in Charge, Food Employees, and Conditional Employees**

Responsibilities and Reporting Symptoms and Diagnosis	**2-201.11** **Responsibility of Permit Holder, Person in Charge, and Conditional Employees.**

(A) The PERMIT HOLDER shall require FOOD EMPLOYEES and CONDITIONAL EMPLOYEES to report to the PERSON IN CHARGE information about their health and activities as they relate to diseases that are transmissible through FOOD. A FOOD EMPLOYEE or CONDITIONAL EMPLOYEE shall report the information in a manner that allows the PERSON IN CHARGE to reduce the RISK of foodborne disease transmission, including providing necessary additional information, such as the date of onset of symptoms and an illness, or of a diagnosis without symptoms, if the FOOD EMPLOYEE or CONDITIONAL EMPLOYEE:

reportable symptoms

(1) Has any of the following symptoms:

　(a) Vomiting,[P]

　(b) Diarrhea,[P]

　(c) Jaundice,[P]

　(d) Sore throat with fever,[P] or

　(e) A lesion containing pus such as a boil or infected wound that is open or draining and is:

　　(i) On the hands or wrists, *unless an impermeable cover such as a finger cot or stall protects the lesion and a SINGLE-USE glove is worn over the impermeable cover,*[P]

　　(ii) On exposed portions of the arms, *unless the lesion is protected by an impermeable cover,*[P] or

31

(iii) On other parts of the body, *unless the lesion is covered by a dry, durable, tight-fitting bandage;*[P]

reportable diagnosis

(2) Has an illness diagnosed by a HEALTH PRACTITIONER due to:

(a) Norovirus,[P]

(b) Hepatitis A virus,[P]

(c) *Shigella* spp.,[P]

(d) ENTEROHEMORRHAGIC or SHIGA TOXIN-PRODUCING *ESCHERICHIA COLI,*[P] or

(e) *Salmonella* Typhi;[P]

reportable past illness

(3) Had a previous illness, diagnosed by a HEALTH PRACTITIONER, within the past 3 months due to *Salmonella* Typhi, without having received antibiotic therapy, as determined by a HEALTH PRACTITIONER;[P]

reportable history of exposure

(4) Has been exposed to, or is the suspected source of, a CONFIRMED DISEASE OUTBREAK, because the FOOD EMPLOYEE or CONDITIONAL EMPLOYEE consumed or prepared FOOD implicated in the outbreak, or consumed FOOD at an event prepared by a PERSON who is infected or ill with:

(a) Norovirus within the past 48 hours of the last exposure,[P]

(b) ENTEROHEMORRHAGIC or SHIGA TOXIN-PRODUCING *ESCHERICHIA COLI, or Shigella* spp. within the past 3 days of the last exposure,[P]

(c) *Salmonella* Typhi within the past 14 days of the last exposure,[P] or

(d) Hepatitis A virus within the past 30 days of the last exposure;[P] or

reportable history of exposure

(5) Has been exposed by attending or working in a setting where there is a CONFIRMED DISEASE OUTBREAK, or living in the same household as, and has knowledge about, an individual who works or attends a setting where there is a CONFIRMED

32

DISEASE OUTBREAK, or living in the same household as, and has knowledge about, an individual diagnosed with an illness caused by:

(a) Norovirus within the past 48 hours of the last exposure,[P]

(b) ENTEROHEMORRHAGIC or SHIGA TOXIN-PRODUCING *ESCHERICHIA COLI, or Shigella* spp. within the past 3 days of the last exposure,[P]

(c) *Salmonella* Typhi within the past 14 days of the last exposure,[P] or

(d) Hepatitis A virus within the past 30 days of the last exposure.[P]

responsibility of person in charge to notify the regulatory authority

(B) The PERSON IN CHARGE shall notify the REGULATORY AUTHORITY when a FOOD EMPLOYEE is:

(1) Jaundiced,[Pf] or

(2) Diagnosed with an illness due to a pathogen as specified under Subparagraphs (A)(2)(a) - (e) of this section.[Pf]

responsibility of the person in charge to prohibit a conditional employee from becoming a food employee

(C) The PERSON IN CHARGE shall ensure that a CONDITIONAL EMPLOYEE:

(1) Who exhibits or reports a symptom, or who reports a diagnosed illness as specified under Subparagraphs (A)(1) - (3) of this section, is prohibited from becoming a FOOD EMPLOYEE until the CONDITIONAL EMPLOYEE meets the criteria for the specific symptoms or diagnosed illness as specified under § 2-201.13;[P] and

(2) Who will work as a FOOD EMPLOYEE in a FOOD ESTABLISHMENT that serves as a HIGHLY SUSCEPTIBLE POPULATION and reports a history of exposure as specified under Subparagraphs (A)(4) – (5), is prohibited from becoming a FOOD EMPLOYEE until the CONDITIONAL EMPLOYEE meets the criteria as specified under ¶ 2-201.13(I). [P]

responsibility of the person in charge to exclude or restrict

(D) The PERSON IN CHARGE shall ensure that a FOOD EMPLOYEE who exhibits or reports a symptom, or who reports a diagnosed illness or a history of exposure as specified under Subparagraphs (A)(1) - (5) of this section is:

33

(1) EXCLUDED as specified under ¶¶ 2-201.12 (A) - (C), and Subparagraphs (D)(1), (E)(1), (F)(1), or (G)(1) and in compliance with the provisions specified under ¶¶ 2-201.13(A) - (G); ^{P} or

(2) RESTRICTED as specified under Subparagraphs 2-201.12 (D)(2), (E)(2), (F)(2), (G)(2), or ¶¶ 2-201.12(H) or (I) and in compliance with the provisions specified under ¶¶ 2-201.13(D) - (I). ^{P}

responsibility of food employees and conditional employees to report

(E) A FOOD EMPLOYEE or CONDITIONAL EMPLOYEE shall report to the PERSON IN CHARGE the information as specified under ¶ (A) of this section.^{Pf}

responsibility of food employees to comply

(F) A FOOD EMPLOYEE shall:

(1) Comply with an EXCLUSION as specified under ¶¶ 2-201.12(A) - (C) and Subparagraphs 2-201.12(D)(1), (E)(1), (F)(1), or (G)(1) and with the provisions specified under ¶¶ 2-201.13(A) - (G); ^{P} or

(2) Comply with a RESTRICTION as specified under Subparagraphs 2-201.12(D)(2), (E)(2), (F)(2), (G)(2), or ¶¶ 2-201.12 (H) or (I) and comply with the provisions specified under ¶¶ 2-201.13(D) - (I). ^{P}

conditions of exclusion and restriction

2-201.12   Exclusions and Restrictions.

The PERSON IN CHARGE shall EXCLUDE or RESTRICT a FOOD EMPLOYEE from a FOOD ESTABLISHMENT in accordance with the following:

symptomatic with vomiting or diarrhea

(A) *Except when the symptom is from a noninfectious condition,* EXCLUDE a FOOD EMPLOYEE if the FOOD EMPLOYEE is:

(1) Symptomatic with vomiting or diarrhea;^{P} or

(2) Symptomatic with vomiting or diarrhea and diagnosed with an infection from Norovirus, *Shigella* spp., or ENTEROHEMORRHAGIC or SHIGA TOXIN-PRODUCING *E. COLI.*^{P}

jaundiced or diagnosed with **hepatitis A infection**

(B) EXCLUDE a FOOD EMPLOYEE who is:

(1) Jaundiced and the onset of jaundice occurred within the last 7 calendar days, *unless the FOOD EMPLOYEE provides to the PERSON IN CHARGE written medical documentation from a HEALTH PRACTITIONER specifying that the jaundice is not caused by hepatitis A virus or other fecal-orally transmitted infection;*[P]

(2) Diagnosed with an infection from hepatitis A virus within 14 calendar days from the onset of any illness symptoms, or within 7 calendar days of the onset of jaundice;[P] or

(3) Diagnosed with an infection from hepatitis A virus without developing symptoms.[P]

diagnosed or reported previous infection due to **S. Typhi**

(C) EXCLUDE a FOOD EMPLOYEE who is diagnosed with an infection from *Salmonella* Typhi, or reports a previous infection with *Salmonella* Typhi within the past 3 months as specified under Subparagraph 2-201.11(A)(3). [P]

diagnosed with an asymptomatic infection from **Norovirus**

(D) If a FOOD EMPLOYEE is diagnosed with an infection from Norovirus and is ASYMPTOMATIC:

(1) EXCLUDE the FOOD EMPLOYEE who works in a FOOD ESTABLISHMENT serving a HIGHLY SUSCEPTIBLE POPULATION;[P] or

(2) RESTRICT the FOOD EMPLOYEE who works in a FOOD ESTABLISHMENT not serving a HIGHLY SUSCEPTIBLE POPULATION.[P]

diagnosed with **Shigella spp.** *infection and asymptomatic*

(E) If a FOOD EMPLOYEE is diagnosed with an infection from *Shigella* spp. and is ASYMPTOMATIC:

(1) EXCLUDE the FOOD EMPLOYEE who works in a FOOD ESTABLISHMENT serving a HIGHLY SUSCEPTIBLE POPULATION;[P] or

(2) RESTRICT the FOOD EMPLOYEE who works in a FOOD ESTABLISHMENT not serving a HIGHLY SUSCEPTIBLE POPULATION.[P]

35

*diagnosed with **EHEC** or **STEC** and asymptomatic*	(F) If a FOOD EMPLOYEE is diagnosed with an infection from ENTEROHEMORRHAGIC or SHIGA TOXIN-PRODUCING *E. COLI*, and is ASYMPTOMATIC: (1) EXCLUDE the FOOD EMPLOYEE who works in a FOOD ESTABLISHMENT serving a HIGHLY SUSCEPTIBLE POPULATION;^P or (2) RESTRICT the FOOD EMPLOYEE who works in a FOOD ESTABLISHMENT not serving a HIGHLY SUSCEPTIBLE POPULATION.^P
*symptomatic with **sore throat with fever***	(G) If a FOOD EMPLOYEE is ill with symptoms of acute onset of sore throat with fever: (1) EXCLUDE the FOOD EMPLOYEE who works in a FOOD ESTABLISHMENT serving a HIGHLY SUSCEPTIBLE POPULATION;^P or (2) RESTRICT the FOOD EMPLOYEE who works in a FOOD ESTABLISHMENT not serving a HIGHLY SUSCEPTIBLE POPULATION.^P
*symptomatic with **uncovered infected wound or pustular boil***	(H) If a FOOD EMPLOYEE is infected with a skin lesion containing pus such as a boil or infected wound that is open or draining and not properly covered as specified under Subparagraph 2-201.11(A)(1)(e), RESTRICT the FOOD EMPLOYEE.^P
***exposed** to foodborne pathogen and works in food establishment serving HSP*	(I) If a FOOD EMPLOYEE is exposed to a foodborne pathogen as specified under Subparagraphs 2-201.11(A)(4) or (5), RESTRICT the FOOD EMPLOYEE who works in a FOOD ESTABLISHMENT serving a HIGHLY SUSCEPTIBLE POPULATION.^P

Managing Exclusions and Restrictions

2-201.13   Removal, Adjustment, or Retention of Exclusions and Restrictions.

The PERSON IN CHARGE shall adhere to the following conditions when removing, adjusting, or retaining the EXCLUSION or RESTRICTION of a FOOD EMPLOYEE:

(A) *Except when a FOOD EMPLOYEE is diagnosed with an infection from hepatitis A virus or Salmonella Typhi:*

removing exclusion for food employee who was symptomatic and not diagnosed	(1) Reinstate a FOOD EMPLOYEE who was EXCLUDED as specified under Subparagraph 2-201.12(A)(1) if the FOOD EMPLOYEE:

(a) Is ASYMPTOMATIC for at least 24 hours;[P] or

(b) Provides to the PERSON IN CHARGE written medical documentation from a HEALTH PRACTITIONER that states the symptom is from a noninfectious condition.[P]

Norovirus diagnosis

(2) If a FOOD EMPLOYEE was diagnosed with an infection from Norovirus and EXCLUDED as specified under Subparagraph 2-201.12(A)(2):

adjusting exclusion for food employee who was symptomatic and is now asymptomatic

(a) RESTRICT the FOOD EMPLOYEE, who is ASYMPTOMATIC for at least 24 hours and works in a FOOD ESTABLISHMENT not serving a HIGHLY SUSCEPTIBLE POPULATION, until the conditions for reinstatement as specified under Subparagraphs (D)(1) or (2) of this section are met;[P] or

retaining exclusion for food employee who was asymptomatic and is now asymptomatic and works in food establishment serving HSP

(b) Retain the EXCLUSION for the FOOD EMPLOYEE, who is ASYMPTOMATIC for at least 24 hours and works in a FOOD ESTABLISHMENT that serves a HIGHLY SUSCEPTIBLE POPULATION, until the conditions for reinstatement as specified under Subparagraphs (D)(1) or (2) of this section are met.[P]

Shigella spp. diagnosis

(3) If a FOOD EMPLOYEE was diagnosed with an infection from *Shigella* spp. and EXCLUDED as specified under Subparagraph 2-201.12(A)(2):

adjusting exclusion for food employee who was symptomatic and is now asymptomatic

(a) RESTRICT the FOOD EMPLOYEE, who is ASYMPTOMATIC for at least 24 hours and works in a FOOD ESTABLISHMENT not serving a HIGHLY SUSCEPTIBLE POPULATION, until the conditions for reinstatement as specified under Subparagraphs (E)(1) or (2) of this section are met;[P] or

retaining exclusion for food employee who was asymptomatic and is now asymptomatic

(b) Retain the EXCLUSION for the FOOD EMPLOYEE, who is ASYMPTOMATIC for at least 24 hours and works in a FOOD ESTABLISHMENT that serves a HIGHLY SUSCEPTIBLE POPULATION, until the conditions for reinstatement as specified under Subparagraphs (E)(1) or (2) , or (E)(1) and (3)(a) of this section are met.[P]

EHEC or STEC diagnosis

(4) If a FOOD EMPLOYEE was diagnosed with an infection from ENTEROHEMORRHAGIC or SHIGA TOXIN-PRODUCING *ESCHERICHIA COLI* and EXCLUDED as specified under Subparagraph 2-201.12(A)(2):

adjusting exclusion for food employee who was symptomatic and is now asymptomatic

(a) RESTRICT the FOOD EMPLOYEE, who is ASYMPTOMATIC for at least 24 hours and works in a FOOD ESTABLISHMENT not serving a HIGHLY SUSCEPTIBLE POPULATION, until the conditions for reinstatement as specified under Subparagraphs (F)(1) or (2) of this section are met;[P] or

retaining exclusion for food employee who was symptomatic and is now asymptomatic and works in food establishment serving HSP

(b) Retain the EXCLUSION for the FOOD EMPLOYEE, who is ASYMPTOMATIC for at least 24 hours and works in a FOOD ESTABLISHMENT that serves a HIGHLY SUSCEPTIBLE POPULATION, until the conditions for reinstatement as specified under Subparagraphs (F)(1) or (2) are met.[P]

hepatitis A virus or jaundice diagnosis - *removing exclusions*

(B) Reinstate a FOOD EMPLOYEE who was EXCLUDED as specified under ¶ 2-201.12(B) if the PERSON IN CHARGE obtains APPROVAL from the REGULATORY AUTHORITY and one of the following conditions is met;

(1) The FOOD EMPLOYEE has been jaundiced for more than 7 calendar days;[P]

(2) The anicteric FOOD EMPLOYEE has been symptomatic with symptoms other than jaundice for more than 14 calendar days;[P] or

(3) The FOOD EMPLOYEE provides to the PERSON IN CHARGE written medical documentation from a HEALTH PRACTITIONER stating that the FOOD EMPLOYEE is free of a hepatitis A virus infection.[P]

S. Typhi diagnosis - **removing exclusions**

(C) Reinstate a FOOD EMPLOYEE who was EXCLUDED as specified under ¶ 2-201.12(C) if:

(1) The PERSON IN CHARGE obtains APPROVAL from the REGULATORY AUTHORITY;[P] and

(2) The FOOD EMPLOYEE provides to the PERSON IN CHARGE written medical documentation from a HEALTH PRACTITIONER

that states the FOOD EMPLOYEE is free from *S.* Typhi infection.[P]

Norovirus diagnosis - removing exclusion or restriction

(D) Reinstate a FOOD EMPLOYEE who was EXCLUDED as specified under Subparagraphs 2-201.12(A)(2) or (D)(1) who was RESTRICTED under Subparagraph 2-201.12(D)(2) if the PERSON IN CHARGE obtains APPROVAL from the REGULATORY AUTHORITY and one of the following conditions is met:

(1) The EXCLUDED or RESTRICTED FOOD EMPLOYEE provides to the PERSON IN CHARGE written medical documentation from a HEALTH PRACTITIONER stating that the FOOD EMPLOYEE is free of a Norovirus infection;[P]

(2) The FOOD EMPLOYEE was EXCLUDED or RESTRICTED after symptoms of vomiting or diarrhea resolved, and more than 48 hours have passed since the FOOD EMPLOYEE became ASYMPTOMATIC;[P] or

(3) The FOOD EMPLOYEE was EXCLUDED or RESTRICTED and did not develop symptoms and more than 48 hours have passed since the FOOD EMPLOYEE was diagnosed.[P]

Shigella spp. diagnosis - removing exclusion or restriction

(E) Reinstate a FOOD EMPLOYEE who was EXCLUDED as specified under Subparagraphs 2-201.12(A)(2) or (E)(1) or who was RESTRICTED under Subparagraph 2-201.12(E)(2) if the PERSON IN CHARGE obtains APPROVAL from the REGULATORY AUTHORITY and one of the following conditions is met:

(1) The EXCLUDED or RESTRICTED FOOD EMPLOYEE provides to the PERSON IN CHARGE written medical documentation from a HEALTH PRACTITIONER stating that the FOOD EMPLOYEE is free of a *Shigella* spp. infection based on test results showing 2 consecutive negative stool specimen cultures that are taken:

(a) Not earlier than 48 hours after discontinuance of antibiotics,[P] and

(b) At least 24 hours apart;[P]

(2) The FOOD EMPLOYEE was EXCLUDED or RESTRICTED after symptoms of vomiting or diarrhea resolved, and more than 7 calendar days have passed since the FOOD EMPLOYEE became ASYMPTOMATIC;[P] or

(3) The FOOD EMPLOYEE was EXCLUDED or RESTRICTED and did not develop symptoms and more than 7 calendar days have passed since the FOOD EMPLOYEE was diagnosed.[P]

EHEC or STEC diagnosis - removing exclusion or restriction

(F) Reinstate a FOOD EMPLOYEE who was EXCLUDED or RESTRICTED as specified under Subparagraphs 2-201.12(A)(2) or (F)(1) or who was RESTRICTED under Subparagraph 2-201.12(F)(2) if the PERSON IN CHARGE obtains APPROVAL from the REGULATORY AUTHORITY and one of the following conditions is met:

(1) The EXCLUDED or RESTRICTED FOOD EMPLOYEE provides to the PERSON IN CHARGE written medical documentation from a HEALTH PRACTITIONER stating that the FOOD EMPLOYEE is free of an infection from ENTEROHEMORRHAGIC or SHIGA TOXIN-PRODUCING *ESCHERICHIA COLI* based on test results that show 2 consecutive negative stool specimen cultures that are taken:

(a) Not earlier than 48 hours after discontinuance of antibiotics;[P] and

(b) At least 24 hours apart;[P]

(2) The FOOD EMPLOYEE was EXCLUDED or RESTRICTED after symptoms of vomiting or diarrhea resolved and more than 7 calendar days have passed since the FOOD EMPLOYEE became ASYMPTOMATIC;[P] or

(3) The FOOD EMPLOYEE was EXCLUDED or RESTRICTED and did not develop symptoms and more than 7 days have passed since the FOOD EMPLOYEE was diagnosed.[P]

sore throat with fever - removing exclusion or restriction

(G) Reinstate a FOOD EMPLOYEE who was EXCLUDED or RESTRICTED as specified under Subparagraphs 2-201.12(G)(1) or (2) if the FOOD EMPLOYEE provides to the PERSON IN CHARGE written medical documentation from a HEALTH PRACTITIONER stating that the FOOD EMPLOYEE meets one of the following conditions:

(1) Has received antibiotic therapy for *Streptococcus pyogenes* infection for more than 24 hours;[P]

(2) Has at least one negative throat specimen culture for *Streptococcus pyogenes* infection;[P] or

40

(3) Is otherwise determined by a HEALTH PRACTITIONER to be free of a *Streptococcus pyogenes* infection.[P]

uncovered infected wound or pustular boil - removing restriction

(H) Reinstate a FOOD EMPLOYEE who was RESTRICTED as specified under ¶ 2-201.12(H) if the skin, infected wound, cut, or pustular boil is properly covered with one of the following:

(1) An impermeable cover such as a finger cot or stall and a single-use glove over the impermeable cover if the infected wound or pustular boil is on the hand, finger, or wrist;[P]

(2) An impermeable cover on the arm if the infected wound or pustular boil is on the arm;[P] or

(3) A dry, durable, tight-fitting bandage if the infected wound or pustular boil is on another part of the body.[P]

exposure to foodborne pathogen and works in food establishment serving HSP – removing restriction

(I) Reinstate a FOOD EMPLOYEE who was RESTRICTED as specified under ¶ 2-201.12(I) and was exposed to one of the following pathogens as specified under Subparagraph 2-201.11(A)(4) or (5):

Norovirus

(1) Norovirus and one of the following conditions is met:

(a) More than 48 hours have passed since the last day the FOOD EMPLOYEE was potentially exposed;[P] or

(b) More than 48 hours have passed since the FOOD EMPLOYEE'S household contact became ASYMPTOMATIC.[P]

Shigella spp., EHEC, or STEC

(2) *Shigella* spp. or ENTEROHEMORRHAGIC or SHIGA TOXIN-PRODUCING *ESCHERICHIA COLI* and one of the following conditions is met:

(a) More than 3 calendar days have passed since the last day the FOOD EMPLOYEE was potentially exposed;[P] or

(b) More than 3 calendar days have passed since the FOOD EMPLOYEE'S household contact became ASYMPTOMATIC.[P]

S. Typhi

(3) *S.* Typhi and one of the following conditions is met:

(a) More than 14 calendar days have passed since the last day the FOOD EMPLOYEE was potentially exposed;[P] or

(b) More than 14 calendar days have passed since the FOOD EMPLOYEE'S household contact became ASYMPTOMATIC.[P]

hepatitis A

(4) Hepatitis A virus and one of the following conditions is met:

(a) The FOOD EMPLOYEE is immune to hepatitis A virus infection because of a prior illness from hepatitis A;[P]

(b) The FOOD EMPLOYEE is immune to hepatitis A virus infection because of vaccination against hepatitis A;[P]

(c) The FOOD EMPLOYEE is immune to hepatitis A virus infection because of IgG administration;[P]

(d) More than 30 calendar days have passed since the last day the FOOD EMPLOYEE was potentially exposed;[P]

(e) More than 30 calendar days have passed since the FOOD EMPLOYEE'S household contact became jaundiced;[P] or

(f) The FOOD EMPLOYEE does not use an alternative procedure that allows bare hand contact with READY-TO-EAT FOOD until at least 30 days after the potential exposure, as specified in Subparagraphs (I)(4)(d) and (e) of this section, and the FOOD EMPLOYEE receives additional training about:

(i) Hepatitis A symptoms and preventing the transmission of infection,[P]

(ii) Proper handwashing procedures,[P] and

(iii) Protecting READY-TO-EAT FOOD from contamination introduced by bare hand contact.[P]

2-3 PERSONAL CLEANLINESS

Subparts

2-301	**Hands and Arms**
2-302	**Fingernails**
2-303	**Jewelry**
2-304	**Outer Clothing**

Hands and Arms **2-301.11   Clean Condition.**

FOOD EMPLOYEES shall keep their hands and exposed portions of their arms clean.[P]

2-301.12   Cleaning Procedure.

(A) Except as specified in ¶ (D) of this section, FOOD EMPLOYEES shall clean their hands and exposed portions of their arms, including surrogate prosthetic devices for hands or arms for at least 20 seconds, using a cleaning compound in a HANDWASHING SINK that is equipped as specified under § 5-202.12 and Subpart 6-301. [P]

(B) FOOD EMPLOYEES shall use the following cleaning procedure in the order stated to clean their hands and exposed portions of their arms, including surrogate prosthetic devices for hands and arms:

(1) Rinse under clean, running warm water; [P]

(2) Apply an amount of cleaning compound recommended by the cleaning compound manufacturer; [P]

(3) Rub together vigorously for at least 10 to 15 seconds while:

(a) Paying particular attention to removing soil from underneath the fingernails during the cleaning procedure, [P] and

(b) Creating friction on the surfaces of the hands and arms or surrogate prosthetic devices for hands and arms, finger tips, and areas between the fingers; [P]

43

(4) Thoroughly rinse under clean, running warm water; [P] and

(5) Immediately follow the cleaning procedure with thorough drying using a method as specified under § 6-301.12. [P]

(C) *To avoid recontaminating their hands or surrogate prosthetic devices, FOOD EMPLOYEES may use disposable paper towels or similar clean barriers when touching surfaces such as manually operated faucet handles on a HANDWASHING SINK or the handle of a restroom door.*

(D) *If APPROVED and capable of removing the types of soils encountered in the FOOD operations involved, an automatic handwashing facility may be used by FOOD EMPLOYEES to clean their hands or surrogate prosthetic devices.*

2-301.13 Special Handwash Procedures.

Reserved.

2-301.14 When to Wash.

FOOD EMPLOYEES shall clean their hands and exposed portions of their arms as specified under § 2-301.12 immediately before engaging in FOOD preparation including working with exposed FOOD, clean EQUIPMENT and UTENSILS, and unwrapped SINGLE-SERVICE and SINGLE-USE ARTICLES[P] and:

(A) After touching bare human body parts other than clean hands and clean, exposed portions of arms; [P]

(B) After using the toilet room; [P]

(C) After caring for or handling SERVICE ANIMALS or aquatic animals as specified in ¶ 2-403.11(B); [P]

(D) Except as specified in ¶ 2-401.11(B), after coughing, sneezing, using a handkerchief or disposable tissue, using tobacco, eating, or drinking; [P]

(E) After handling soiled EQUIPMENT or UTENSILS; [P]

(F) During FOOD preparation, as often as necessary to remove soil and contamination and to prevent cross contamination when changing tasks; [P]

(G) When switching between working with raw FOOD and working with READY-TO-EAT FOOD; [P]

(H) Before donning gloves for working with FOOD; [P] and

(I) After engaging in other activities that contaminate the hands. [P]

2-301.15   Where to Wash.

FOOD EMPLOYEES shall clean their hands in a HANDWASHING SINK or APPROVED automatic handwashing facility and may not clean their hands in a sink used for FOOD preparation or WAREWASHING, or in a service sink or a curbed cleaning facility used for the disposal of mop water and similar liquid waste. [Pf]

2-301.16   Hand Antiseptics.

(A) A hand antiseptic used as a topical application, a hand antiseptic solution used as a hand dip, or a hand antiseptic soap shall:

(1) Comply with one of the following:

(a) Be an APPROVED drug that is listed in the FDA publication **Approved Drug Products with Therapeutic Equivalence Evaluations** as an APPROVED drug based on safety and effectiveness; [Pf] or

(b) Have active antimicrobial ingredients that are listed in the FDA monograph for OTC Health-Care Antiseptic Drug Products as an antiseptic handwash, [Pf] and

(2) Comply with one of the following:

(a) Have components that are exempted from the requirement of being listed in federal FOOD ADDITIVE regulations as specified in 21 CFR 170.39 - Threshold of regulation for substances used in food-contact articles; [Pf] or

45

(b) Comply with and be listed in:

(i) 21 CFR 178 - Indirect Food Additives: Adjuvants, Production Aids, and Sanitizers as regulated for use as a FOOD ADDITIVE with conditions of safe use, [Pf] or

(ii) 21 CFR 182 - Substances Generally Recognized as Safe, 21 CFR 184 - Direct Food Substances Affirmed as Generally Recognized as Safe, or 21 CFR 186 - Indirect Food Substances Affirmed as Generally Recognized as Safe for use in contact with food, [Pf] and

(3) Be applied only to hands that are cleaned as specified under § 2-301.12. [Pf]

(B) If a hand antiseptic or a hand antiseptic solution used as a hand dip does not meet the criteria specified under Subparagraph (A)(2) of this section, use shall be:

(1) Followed by thorough hand rinsing in clean water before hand contact with FOOD or by the use of gloves; [Pf] or

(2) Limited to situations that involve no direct contact with FOOD by the bare hands. [Pf]

(C) A hand antiseptic solution used as a hand dip shall be maintained clean and at a strength equivalent to at least 100 MG/L chlorine. [Pf]

Fingernails   2-302.11   **Maintenance.**

(A) FOOD EMPLOYEES shall keep their fingernails trimmed, filed, and maintained so the edges and surfaces are cleanable and not rough. [Pf]

(B) *Unless wearing intact gloves in good repair*, a FOOD EMPLOYEE may not wear fingernail polish or artificial fingernails when working with exposed FOOD. [Pf]

Jewelry   2-303.11   **Prohibition.**

Except for *a plain ring such as a wedding band*, while preparing FOOD, FOOD EMPLOYEES may not wear jewelry including medical information jewelry on their arms and hands.

Outer Clothing   2-304.11   **Clean Condition.**

FOOD EMPLOYEES shall wear clean outer clothing to prevent contamination of FOOD, EQUIPMENT, UTENSILS, LINENS, and SINGLE-SERVICE and SINGLE-USE ARTICLES.

2-4	**HYGIENIC PRACTICES**
	Subparts
	2-401 **Food Contamination Prevention**
	2-402 **Hair Restraints**
	2-403 **Animals**

Food
Contamination
Prevention

2-401.11   **Eating, Drinking, or Using Tobacco.**

(A) Except as specified in ¶ (B) of this section, an EMPLOYEE shall eat, drink, or use any form of tobacco only in designated areas where the contamination of exposed FOOD; clean EQUIPMENT, UTENSILS, and LINENS; unwrapped SINGLE-SERVICE and SINGLE-USE ARTICLES; or other items needing protection can not result.

(B) *A FOOD EMPLOYEE may drink from a closed BEVERAGE container if the container is handled to prevent contamination of:*

(1) *The EMPLOYEE'S hands;*

(2) *The container; and*

(3) *Exposed FOOD; clean EQUIPMENT, UTENSILS, and LINENS; and unwrapped SINGLE-SERVICE and SINGLE-USE ARTICLES.*

2-401.12   **Discharges from the Eyes, Nose, and Mouth.**

FOOD EMPLOYEES experiencing persistent sneezing, coughing, or a runny nose that causes discharges from the eyes, nose, or mouth may not work with exposed FOOD; clean EQUIPMENT, UTENSILS, and LINENS; or unwrapped SINGLE-SERVICE or SINGLE-USE ARTICLES.

Hair Restraints

2-402.11   Effectiveness.

(A) Except as provided in ¶ (B) of this section, FOOD EMPLOYEES shall wear hair restraints such as hats, hair coverings or nets, beard restraints, and clothing that covers body hair, that are designed and worn to effectively keep their hair from contacting exposed FOOD; clean EQUIPMENT, UTENSILS, and LINENS; and unwrapped SINGLE-SERVICE and SINGLE-USE ARTICLES.

(B) *This section does not apply to FOOD EMPLOYEES such as counter staff who only serve BEVERAGES and wrapped or PACKAGED FOODS, hostesses, and wait staff if they present a minimal RISK of contaminating exposed FOOD; clean EQUIPMENT, UTENSILS, and LINENS; and unwrapped SINGLE-SERVICE and SINGLE-USE ARTICLES.*

Animals

2-403.11   Handling Prohibition.

(A) Except as specified in ¶ (B) of this section, FOOD EMPLOYEES may not care for or handle animals that may be present such as patrol dogs, SERVICE ANIMALS, or pets that are allowed as specified in Subparagraphs 6-501.115(B)(2)-(5). [Pf]

(B) *FOOD EMPLOYEES with SERVICE ANIMALS may handle or care for their SERVICE ANIMALS and FOOD EMPLOYEES may handle or care for FISH in aquariums or MOLLUSCAN SHELLFISH or crustacea in display tanks if they wash their hands as specified under § 2-301.12 and ¶ 2-301.14(C).*

<table>
<tr><td>Chapter</td><td></td></tr>
<tr><td>

3
</td><td>

Food
</td></tr>
</table>

Parts

3-1   CHARACTERISTICS

Subparts

3-101   Condition

Condition   **3-101.11   Safe, Unadulterated, and Honestly Presented.**

FOOD shall be safe, unADULTERATED, and, as specified under § 3-601.12, honestly presented.[P]

3-2	SOURCES, SPECIFICATIONS, AND ORIGINAL CONTAINERS AND RECORDS
	Subparts
	3-201 Sources
	3-202 Specifications for Receiving
	3-203 Original Containers and Records

Sources

3-201.11   Compliance with Food Law.

(A) FOOD shall be obtained from sources that comply with LAW. [P]

(B) FOOD prepared in a private home may not be used or offered for human consumption in a FOOD ESTABLISHMENT. [P]

(C) PACKAGED FOOD shall be labeled as specified in LAW, including 21 CFR 101 FOOD Labeling, 9 CFR 317 Labeling, Marking Devices, and Containers, and 9 CFR 381 Subpart N Labeling and Containers, and as specified under §§ 3-202.17 and 3-202.18. [Pf]

(D) FISH, *other than those specified in paragraph 3-402.11(B), that are intended for consumption in raw or undercooked form and allowed as specified in Subparagraph 3-401.11(D), may be offered for sale or service if they are obtained from a supplier that freezes the FISH as specified under § 3-402.11; or if they are frozen on the PREMISES as specified under § 3-402.11 and records are retained as specified under § 3-402.12.*

(E) WHOLE-MUSCLE, INTACT BEEF steaks that are intended for consumption in an undercooked form without a CONSUMER advisory as specified in ¶ 3-401.11(C) shall be:

    (1) Obtained from a FOOD PROCESSING PLANT that, upon request by the purchaser, packages the steaks and labels them, to indicate that the steaks meet the definition of WHOLE-MUSCLE, INTACT BEEF, [Pf] or

    (2) Deemed acceptable by the REGULATORY AUTHORITY based on other evidence, such as written buyer specifications or invoices, that indicates that the steaks meet the definition of WHOLE-MUSCLE, INTACT BEEF, [Pf] and

(3) If individually cut in a FOOD ESTABLISHMENT:

> (a) Cut from WHOLE-MUSCLE INTACT BEEF that is labeled by
> a FOOD PROCESSING PLANT as specified in Subparagraph
> (E)(1) of this section or identified as specified in
> Subparagraph (E)(2) of this section, [Pf]
>
> (b) Prepared so they remain intact, [Pf] and
>
> (c) If PACKAGED for undercooking in a FOOD
> ESTABLISHMENT, labeled as specified in Subparagraph
> (E)(1) of this section or identified as specified in (E)(2) of
> this section. [Pf]

(F) MEAT and POULTRY that is not a READY-TO-EAT FOOD and is in
a PACKAGED form when it is offered for sale or otherwise offered
for consumption, shall be labeled to include safe handling
instructions as specified in LAW, including 9 CFR 317.2(l) and 9
CFR 381.125(b).

(G) EGGS that have not been specifically treated to destroy all
viable *Salmonellae* shall be labeled to include safe handling
instructions as specified in LAW, including 21 CFR 101.17(h).

3-201.12   Food in a Hermetically Sealed Container.

FOOD in a HERMETICALLY SEALED CONTAINER shall be obtained
from a FOOD PROCESSING PLANT that is regulated by the FOOD
regulatory agency that has jurisdiction over the plant. [P]

3-201.13   Fluid Milk and Milk Products.

Fluid milk and milk products shall be obtained from sources that
comply with GRADE A STANDARDS as specified in LAW. [P]

3-201.14   Fish.

(A) FISH that are received for sale or service shall be:

> (1) Commercially and legally caught or harvested; [P] or
>
> (2) APPROVED for sale or service. [P]

51

(B) M<small>OLLUSCAN</small> <small>SHELLFISH</small> that are recreationally caught may not be received for sale or service. ^P

3-201.15　Molluscan Shellfish.

(A) M<small>OLLUSCAN</small> <small>SHELLFISH</small> shall be obtained from sources according to L<small>AW</small> and the requirements specified in the U.S. Department of Health and Human Services, Public Health Service, Food and Drug Administration, National Shellfish Sanitation Program Guide for the Control of Molluscan Shellfish. ^P

(B) M<small>OLLUSCAN</small> <small>SHELLFISH</small> received in interstate commerce shall be from sources that are listed in the Interstate Certified Shellfish Shippers List. ^P

3-201.16　Wild Mushrooms.

(A) Except as specified in ¶ (B) of this section, mushroom species picked in the wild shall be obtained from sources where each mushroom is individually inspected and found to be safe by an A<small>PPROVED</small> mushroom identification expert. ^P

(B) *This section does not apply to:*

　　(1) *Cultivated wild mushroom species that are grown, harvested, and processed in an operation that is regulated by the F<small>OOD</small> regulatory agency that has jurisdiction over the operation; or*

　　(2) *Wild mushroom species if they are in packaged form and are the product of a F<small>OOD</small> P<small>ROCESSING</small> P<small>LANT</small> that is regulated by the F<small>OOD</small> regulatory agency that has jurisdiction over the plant.*

3-201.17　Game Animals.

(A) If G<small>AME</small> A<small>NIMALS</small> are received for sale or service they shall be:

　　(1) Commercially raised for F<small>OOD</small> ^P and:

(a) Raised, slaughtered, and processed under a voluntary inspection program that is conducted by the agency that has animal health jurisdiction, [P] or

(b) Under a routine inspection program conducted by a regulatory agency other than the agency that has animal health jurisdiction, [P] and

(c) Raised, slaughtered, and processed according to:

(i) LAWS governing MEAT and POULTRY as determined by the agency that has animal health jurisdiction and the agency that conducts the inspection program, [P] and

(ii) Requirements which are developed by the agency that has animal health jurisdiction and the agency that conducts the inspection program with consideration of factors such as the need for antemortem and postmortem examination by an APPROVED veterinarian or veterinarian's designee; [P]

(2) Under a voluntary inspection program administered by the USDA for game animals such as exotic animals (reindeer, elk, deer, antelope, water buffalo, or bison) that are "inspected and APPROVED" in accordance with 9 CFR 352 Exotic animals; voluntary inspection or rabbits that are "inspected and certified" in accordance with 9 CFR 354 voluntary inspection of rabbits and edible products thereof; [P]

(3) As allowed by LAW, for wild GAME ANIMALS that are live-caught:

(a) Under a routine inspection program conducted by a regulatory agency such as the agency that has animal health jurisdiction, [P] and

(b) Slaughtered and processed according to:

(i) LAWS governing MEAT and POULTRY as determined by the agency that has animal health jurisdiction and the agency that conducts the inspection program, [P] and

(ii) Requirements which are developed by the agency that has animal health jurisdiction and the agency that conducts the inspection program with consideration of factors such as the need for antemortem and postmortem examination by an APPROVED veterinarian or veterinarian's designee; [P] or

(4) As allowed by LAW, for field-dressed wild GAME ANIMALS under a routine inspection program that ensures the animals:

(a) Receive a postmortem examination by an APPROVED veterinarian or veterinarian's designee, [P] or

(b) Are field-dressed and transported according to requirements specified by the agency that has animal health jurisdiction and the agency that conducts the inspection program, [P] and

(c) Are processed according to LAWS governing MEAT and POULTRY as determined by the agency that has animal health jurisdiction and the agency that conducts the inspection program. [P]

(B) A GAME ANIMAL may not be received for sale or service if it is a species of wildlife that is listed in 50 CFR 17 Endangered and threatened wildlife and plants.

Specifications for Receiving

3-202.11   Temperature.

(A) Except as specified in ¶ (B) of this section, refrigerated, POTENTIALLY HAZARDOUS FOOD (TIME/TEMPERATURE CONTROL FOR SAFETY FOOD) shall be at a temperature of 5°C (41°F) or below when received. [P]

(B) *If a temperature other than 5°C (41°F) for a POTENTIALLY HAZARDOUS FOOD (TIME/TEMPERATURE CONTROL FOR SAFETY FOOD) is specified in LAW governing its distribution, such as LAWS governing milk and MOLLUSCAN SHELLFISH, the FOOD may be received at the specified temperature.*

(C) Raw EGGS shall be received in refrigerated equipment that maintains an ambient air temperature of 7°C (45°F) or less. [P]

(D) POTENTIALLY HAZARDOUS FOOD (TIME/TEMPERATURE CONTROL FOR SAFETY FOOD) that is cooked to a temperature and for a time specified under §§ 3-401.11 - 3-401.13 and received hot shall be at a temperature of 57°C (135°F) or above. [P]

(E) A FOOD that is labeled frozen and shipped frozen by a FOOD PROCESSING PLANT shall be received frozen. [Pf]

(F) Upon receipt, POTENTIALLY HAZARDOUS FOOD (TIME/TEMPERATURE CONTROL FOR SAFETY FOOD) shall be free of evidence of previous temperature abuse. [Pf]

3-202.12   Additives.

FOOD may not contain unAPPROVED FOOD ADDITIVES or ADDITIVES that exceed amounts specified in 21 CFR 170-180 relating to FOOD ADDITIVES, generally recognized as safe or prior sanctioned substances that exceed amounts specified in 21 CFR 181-186, substances that exceed amounts specified in 9 CFR Subpart C Section 424.21(b) Food ingredients and sources of radiation, or pesticide residues that exceed provisions specified in 40 CFR 180 Tolerances for pesticides chemicals in food, and   exceptions. [P]

3-202.13   Eggs.

EGGS shall be received clean and sound and may not exceed the restricted EGG tolerances for U.S. Consumer Grade B as specified in United States Standards, Grades, and Weight Classes for Shell Eggs, AMS 56.200 *et seq.*, administered by the Agricultural Marketing Service of USDA. [P]

3-202.14   Eggs and Milk Products, Pasteurized.

(A) EGG PRODUCTS shall be obtained pasteurized. [P]

(B) Fluid and dry milk and milk products shall:

(1) Be obtained pasteurized; [P] and

(2) Comply with GRADE A STANDARDS as specified in LAW. [P]

(C) Frozen milk products, such as ice cream, shall be obtained pasteurized as specified in 21 CFR 135 - Frozen desserts. [P]

(D) Cheese shall be obtained pasteurized *unless alternative procedures to pasteurization are specified in the CFR, such as 21 CFR 133 - Cheeses and related cheese products, for curing certain cheese varieties.* [P]

3-202.15   Package Integrity.

FOOD packages shall be in good condition and protect the integrity of the contents so that the FOOD is not exposed to ADULTERATION or potential contaminants. [Pf]

3-202.16   Ice.

Ice for use as a FOOD or a cooling medium shall be made from DRINKING WATER. [P]

3-202.17   Shucked Shellfish, Packaging and Identification.

(A) Raw SHUCKED SHELLFISH shall be obtained in nonreturnable packages which bear a legible label that identifies the: [Pf]

   (1) Name, address, and CERTIFICATION NUMBER of the shucker, packer or repacker of the MOLLUSCAN SHELLFISH; [Pf] and

   (2) The "sell by" or "best if used by" date for packages with a capacity of less than 1.89 L (one-half gallon) or the date shucked for packages with a capacity of 1.89 L (one-half gallon) or more. [Pf]

(B) A package of raw SHUCKED SHELLFISH that does not bear a label or which bears a label which does not contain all the information as specified under ¶ (A) of this section shall be subject to a hold order, as allowed by LAW, or seizure and destruction in accordance with 21 CFR Subpart D - Specific Administrative Decisions Regarding Interstate Shipments, Section 1240.60(d) Molluscan shellfish.

3-202.18   Shellstock Identification.

(A) SHELLSTOCK shall be obtained in containers bearing legible source identification tags or labels that are affixed by the harvester or DEALER that depurates, ships, or reships the SHELLSTOCK, as specified in the National Shellfish Sanitation Program Guide for the Control of Molluscan Shellfish, and that list: [Pf]

(1) Except as specified under ¶ (C) of this section, on the harvester's tag or label, the following information in the following order: [Pf]

(a) The harvester's identification number that is assigned by the SHELLFISH CONTROL AUTHORITY, [Pf]

(b) The date of harvesting, [Pf]

(c) The most precise identification of the harvest location or aquaculture site that is practicable based on the system of harvest area designations that is in use by the SHELLFISH CONTROL AUTHORITY and including the abbreviation of the name of the state or country in which the shellfish are harvested, [Pf]

(d) The type and quantity of shellfish, [Pf] and

(e) The following statement in bold, capitalized type: "This tag is required to be attached until container is empty or retagged and thereafter kept on file for 90 days"; [Pf] and

(2) Except as specified in ¶ (D) of this section, on each DEALER's tag or label, the following information in the following order: [Pf]

(a) The DEALER'S name and address, and the CERTIFICATION NUMBER assigned by the SHELLFISH CONTROL AUTHORITY, [Pf]

(b) The original shipper's CERTIFICATION NUMBER including the abbreviation of the name of the state or country in which the shellfish are harvested, [Pf]

(c) The same information as specified for a harvester's tag under Subparagraphs (A)(1)(b)-(d) of this section, [Pf] and

57

(d) The following statement in bold, capitalized type: "This tag is required to be attached until container is empty and thereafter kept on file for 90 days." [Pf]

(B) A container of SHELLSTOCK that does not bear a tag or label or that bears a tag or label that does not contain all the information as specified under ¶ (A) of this section shall be subject to a hold order, as allowed by LAW, or seizure and destruction in accordance with 21 CFR Subpart D - Specific Administrative Decisions Regarding Interstate Shipments, Section 1240.60(d).

(C) If a place is provided on the harvester's tag or label for a DEALER's name, address, and CERTIFICATION NUMBER, the DEALER's information shall be listed first.

(D) *If the harvester's tag or label is designed to accommodate each DEALER's identification as specified under Subparagraphs (A)(2)(a) and (b) of this section, individual DEALER tags or labels need not be provided.*

3-202.19   Shellstock, Condition.

When received by a FOOD ESTABLISHMENT, SHELLSTOCK shall be reasonably free of mud, dead shellfish, and shellfish with broken shells. Dead shellfish or SHELLSTOCK with badly broken shells shall be discarded.

3-202.110   Juice Treated.

Commercially Processed

Pre-PACKAGED JUICE shall:

(A) Be obtained from a processor with a HACCP system as specified in 21 CFR Part 120 Hazard Analysis and Critical Control (HACCP) Systems; [Pf] and

(B) Be obtained pasteurized or otherwise treated to attain a 5-log reduction of the most resistant microorganism of public health significance as specified in 21 CFR Part 120.24 Process Controls. [P]

3-203.11 Molluscan Shellfish, Original Container.

(A) Except as specified in ¶¶ (B) - (D) of this section, MOLLUSCAN SHELLFISH may not be removed from the container in which they are received other than immediately before sale or preparation for service.

Original Containers and Records

(B) *For display purposes, SHELLSTOCK may be removed from the container in which they are received, displayed on drained ice, or held in a display container, and a quantity specified by a CONSUMER may be removed from the display or display container and provided to the CONSUMER if:*

    (1) The source of the SHELLSTOCK on display is identified as specified under § 3-202.18 and recorded as specified under § 3-203.12; and

    (2) The SHELLSTOCK are protected from contamination.

(C) *SHUCKED SHELLFISH may be removed from the container in which they were received and held in a display container from which individual servings are dispensed upon a CONSUMER'S request if:*

    (1) The labeling information for the shellfish on display as specified under § 3-202.17 is retained and correlated to the date when, or dates during which, the shellfish are sold or served; and

    (2) The shellfish are protected from contamination.

(D) *SHUCKED SHELLFISH may be removed from the container in which they were received and repacked in CONSUMER self service containers where allowed by LAW if:*

    (1) The labeling information for the shellfish is on each CONSUMER self service container as specified under § 3-202.17 and ¶¶ 3-602.11(A) and (B)(1) - (5);

    (2) The labeling information as specified under § 3-202.17 is retained and correlated with the date when, or dates during which, the shellfish are sold or served;

(3) *The labeling information and dates specified under Subparagraph (D)(2) of this section are maintained for 90 days; and*

(4) *The shellfish are protected from contamination.*

3-203.12 Shellstock, Maintaining Identification.

(A) Except as specified under Subparagraph (C) (2) of this section, SHELLSTOCK tags or labels shall remain attached to the container in which the SHELLSTOCK are received until the container is empty. [Pf]

(B) The date when the last SHELLSTOCK from the container is sold or served shall be recorded on the tag or label. [Pf]

(C) The identity of the source of SHELLSTOCK that are sold or served shall be maintained by retaining SHELLSTOCK tags or labels for 90 calendar days from the date that is recorded on the tag or label, as specified under ¶ B of this section, by: [Pf]

(1) Using an APPROVED record keeping system that keeps the tags or labels in chronological order correlated to the date that is recorded on the tag or label, as specified under ¶ B of this section; [Pf] and

(2) If SHELLSTOCK are removed from its tagged or labeled container:

(a) Preserving source identification by using a record keeping system as specified under Subparagraph (C)(1) of this section, [Pf] and

(b) Ensuring that SHELLSTOCK from one tagged or labeled container are not COMMINGLED with SHELLSTOCK from another container with different CERTIFICATION NUMBERS; different harvest dates; or different growing areas as identified on the tag or label before being ordered by the CONSUMER. [Pf]

3-3	PROTECTION FROM CONTAMINATION AFTER RECEIVING

Subparts

3-301	Preventing Contamination by Employees
3-302	Preventing Food and Ingredient Contamination
3-303	Preventing Contamination from Ice Used as a Coolant
3-304	Preventing Contamination from Equipment,
3-305	Preventing Contamination from the Premises
3-306	Preventing Contamination by Consumers
3-307	Preventing Contamination from Other Sources

Preventing Contamination by Employees

3-301.11   **Preventing Contamination from Hands.**

(A) FOOD EMPLOYEES shall wash their hands as specified under § 2-301.12.

(B) *Except when washing fruits and vegetables as specified under § 3-302.15 or as specified in ¶ (D) of this section,* FOOD EMPLOYEES may not contact exposed, READY-TO-EAT FOOD with their bare hands and shall use suitable UTENSILS such as deli tissue, spatulas, tongs, single-use gloves, or dispensing EQUIPMENT. [P]

(C) FOOD EMPLOYEES shall minimize bare hand and arm contact with exposed FOOD that is not in a READY-TO-EAT form. [Pf]

(D) *FOOD EMPLOYEES not serving a HIGHLY SUSCEPTIBLE POPULATION may contact exposed, READY-TO-EAT FOOD with their bare hands if:*

    (1) *The PERMIT HOLDER obtains prior APPROVAL from the REGULATORY AUTHORITY;*

    (2) *Written procedures are maintained in the FOOD ESTABLISHMENT and made available to the REGULATORY AUTHORITY upon request that include:*

        (a) *For each bare hand contact procedure, a listing of the specific READY-TO-EAT FOODS that are touched by bare hands,*

(b) *Diagrams and other information showing that handwashing facilities, installed, located, equipped, and maintained as specified under §§ 5-203.11, 5-204.11, 5-205.11, 6-301.11, 6-301.12, and 6-301.14, are in an easily accessible location and in close proximity to the work station where the bare hand contact procedure is conducted;*

(3) *A written EMPLOYEE health policy that details how the FOOD ESTABLISHMENT complies with §§ 2-201.11, 2-201.12, and 2-201.13 including:*

(a) *Documentation that FOOD EMPLOYEES and CONDITIONAL EMPLOYEES acknowledge that they are informed to report information about their health and activities as they relate to gastrointestinal symptoms and diseases that are transmittable through FOOD as specified under ¶ 2-201.11(A),*

(b) *Documentation that FOOD EMPLOYEES and CONDITIONAL EMPLOYEES acknowledge their responsibilities as specified under ¶ 2-201.11(E) and (F), and*

(c) *Documentation that the PERSON IN CHARGE acknowledges the responsibilities as specified under ¶¶ 2-201.11(B), (C) and (D), and §§ 2-201.12 and 2-201.13;*

(4) *Documentation that FOOD EMPLOYEES acknowledge that they have received training in:*

(a) *The RISKS of contacting the specific READY-TO-EAT FOODS with bare hands,*

(b) *Proper handwashing as specified under § 2-301.12,*

(c) *When to wash their hands as specified under § 2-301.14,*

(d) *Where to wash their hands as specified under § 2-301.15,*

(e) *Proper fingernail maintenance as specified under § 2-302.11,*

(f) *Prohibition of jewelry as specified under § 2-303.11, and*

(g) *Good hygienic practices as specified under §§2-401.11 and 2-401.12;*

(5) *Documentation that hands are washed before FOOD preparation and as necessary to prevent cross contamination by FOOD EMPLOYEES as specified under §§ 2-301.11, 2-301.12, 2-301.14, and 2-301.15 during all hours of operation when the specific READY-TO-EAT FOODS are prepared;*

(6) *Documentation that FOOD EMPLOYEES contacting READY-TO-EAT FOOD with bare hands use two or more of the following control measures to provide additional safeguards to HAZARDS associated with bare hand contact:*

(a) *Double handwashing,*

(b) *Nail brushes,*

(c) *A hand antiseptic after handwashing as specified under § 2-301.16,*

(d) *Incentive programs such as paid sick leave that assist or encourage FOOD EMPLOYEES not to work when they are ill, or*

(e) *Other control measures APPROVED by the REGULATORY AUTHORITY; and*

(7) *Documentation that corrective action is taken when Subparagraphs (D)(1) - (6) of this section are not followed.*

3-301.12   Preventing Contamination When Tasting.

A FOOD EMPLOYEE may not use a UTENSIL more than once to taste FOOD that is to be sold or served. [P]

**3-302.11   Packaged and Unpackaged Food - Separation,
Packaging, and Segregation.**

(A) FOOD shall be protected from cross contamination by:

(1) Except as specified in (1)(c) below, separating raw animal
FOODS during storage, preparation, holding, and display from:

(a) Raw READY-TO-EAT FOOD including other raw animal
FOOD such as FISH for sushi or MOLLUSCAN SHELLFISH, or
other raw READY-TO-EAT FOOD such as fruits and
vegetables, [P] and

(b) Cooked READY-TO-EAT FOOD; [P]

(c) *Frozen, commercially processed and packaged raw
animal FOOD may be stored or displayed with or above
frozen, commercially processed and packaged, ready-to-
eat food.*

(2) *Except when combined as ingredients*, separating types of
raw animal FOODS from each other such as beef, FISH, lamb,
pork, and POULTRY during storage, preparation, holding, and
display by:

(a) Using separate EQUIPMENT for each type, [P] or

(b) Arranging each type of FOOD in EQUIPMENT so that
cross contamination of one type with another is
prevented, [P] and

(c) Preparing each type of FOOD at different times or in
separate areas; [P]

(3) Cleaning EQUIPMENT and UTENSILS as specified under
¶ 4-602.11(A) and SANITIZING as specified under § 4-703.11;

(4) Except as specified under Subparagraph 3-501.15(B)(2)
and in ¶ (B) of this section, storing the FOOD in packages,
covered containers, or wrappings;

(5) Cleaning HERMETICALLY SEALED CONTAINERS of FOOD of
visible soil before opening;

(6) Protecting FOOD containers that are received packaged together in a case or overwrap from cuts when the case or overwrap is opened;

(7) Storing damaged, spoiled, or recalled FOOD being held in the FOOD ESTABLISHMENT as specified under § 6-404.11; and

(8) Separating fruits and vegetables, before they are washed as specified under § 3-302.15 from READY-TO-EAT FOOD.

(B) *Subparagraph (A)(4) of this section does not apply to:*

(1) Whole, uncut, raw fruits and vegetables and nuts in the shell, that require peeling or hulling before consumption;

(2) PRIMAL CUTS, quarters, or sides of raw MEAT or slab bacon that are hung on clean, SANITIZED hooks or placed on clean, SANITIZED racks;

(3) Whole, uncut, processed MEATS such as country hams, and smoked or cured sausages that are placed on clean, SANITIZED racks;

(4) FOOD being cooled as specified under Subparagraph 3-501.15(B)(2); or

(5) SHELLSTOCK.

3-302.12   Food Storage Containers, Identified with Common Name of Food.

Except for containers holding FOOD that can be readily and unmistakably recognized such as dry pasta, working containers holding FOOD or FOOD ingredients that are removed from their original packages for use in the FOOD ESTABLISHMENT, such as cooking oils, flour, herbs, potato flakes, salt, spices, and sugar shall be identified with the common name of the FOOD.

3-302.13   Pasteurized Eggs, Substitute for Raw Eggs for Certain Recipes.

Pasteurized EGGS or EGG PRODUCTS shall be substituted for raw EGGS in the preparation of FOODS such as Caesar salad, hollandaise or Béarnaise sauce, mayonnaise, meringue, eggnog, ice cream, and EGG-fortified BEVERAGES that are not: [P]

(A) Cooked as specified under Subparagraphs 3-401.11(A)(1) or (2); [P] or

(B) Included in ¶ 3-401.11(D). [P]

3-302.14   Protection from Unapproved Additives.

(A) FOOD shall be protected from contamination that may result from the addition of, as specified in § 3-202.12:

(1) Unsafe or unAPPROVED FOOD or COLOR ADDITIVES; [P] and

(2) Unsafe or unAPPROVED levels of APPROVED FOOD and COLOR ADDITIVES. [P]

(B) A FOOD EMPLOYEE may not:

(1) Apply sulfiting agents to fresh fruits and vegetables intended for raw consumption or to a FOOD considered to be a good source of vitamin B_1; [P] or

(2) *Except for grapes,* serve or sell FOOD specified under Subparagraph (B)(1) of this section that is treated with sulfiting agents before receipt by the FOOD ESTABLISHMENT. [P]

3-302.15   Washing Fruits and Vegetables.

(A) *Except as specified in ¶ (B) of this section and except for whole,* raw *fruits and vegetables that are intended for washing by the* CONSUMER *before consumption,* raw fruits and vegetables shall be thoroughly washed in water to remove soil and other contaminants before being cut, combined with other ingredients, cooked, served, or offered for human consumption in READY-TO-EAT form.

(B) *Fruits and vegetables may be washed by using chemicals as specified under § 7-204.12.*

66

Preventing
Contamination
from Ice Used
as a Coolant

3-303.11   Ice Used as Exterior Coolant, Prohlblted as Ingredient.

After use as a medium for cooling the exterior surfaces of FOOD such as melons or FISH, PACKAGED FOODS such as canned BEVERAGES, or cooling coils and tubes of EQUIPMENT, ice may not be used as FOOD. [P]

3-303.12   Storage or Display of Food in Contact with Water or Ice.

(A) PACKAGED FOOD may not be stored in direct contact with ice or water if the FOOD is subject to the entry of water because of the nature of its packaging, wrapping, or container or its positioning in the ice or water.

((B) Except as specified in ¶¶ (C) and (D) of this section, unPACKAGED FOOD may not be stored in direct contact with undrained ice.

(C) *Whole, raw fruits or vegetables; cut, raw vegetables such as celery or carrot sticks or cut potatoes; and tofu may be immersed in ice or water.*

(D) *Raw poultry and raw FISH that are received immersed in ice in shipping containers may remain in that condition while in storage awaiting preparation, display, service, or sale.*

Preventing
Contamination
from Equipment,
Utensils, and
Linens

3-304.11   Food Contact with Equipment and Utensils.

FOOD shall only contact surfaces of:

(A) EQUIPMENT and UTENSILS that are cleaned as specified under Part 4-6 of this Code and SANITIZED as specified under Part 4-7 of this Code; [P] or

(B) SINGLE-SERVICE and SINGLE-USE ARTICLES. [P]

3-304.12   In-Use Utensils, Between-Use Storage.

During pauses in FOOD preparation or dispensing, FOOD preparation and dispensing UTENSILS shall be stored:

(A) Except as specified under ¶ (B) of this section, in the FOOD with their handles above the top of the FOOD and the container;

(B) In FOOD that is not POTENTIALLY HAZARDOUS (TIME/TEMPERATURE CONTROL FOR SAFETY FOOD) with their handles above the top of the FOOD within containers or EQUIPMENT that can be closed, such as bins of sugar, flour, or cinnamon;

(C) On a clean portion of the FOOD preparation table or cooking EQUIPMENT only if the in-use UTENSIL and the FOOD-CONTACT surface of the FOOD preparation table or cooking EQUIPMENT are cleaned and SANITIZED at a frequency specified under §§ 4-602.11 and 4-702.11;

(D) In running water of sufficient velocity to flush particulates to the drain, if used with moist FOOD such as ice cream or mashed potatoes;

(E) In a clean, protected location if the UTENSILS, such as ice scoops, are used only with a FOOD that is not POTENTIALLY HAZARDOUS (TIME/TEMPERATURE CONTROL FOR SAFETY FOOD); or

(F) In a container of water if the water is maintained at a temperature of at least 57°C (135°F) and the container is cleaned at a frequency specified under Subparagraph 4-602.11(D)(7).

3-304.13   Linens and Napkins, Use Limitation.

LINENS and napkins may not be used in contact with FOOD *unless they are used to line a container for the service of FOODS and the LINENS and napkins are replaced each time the container is refilled for a new CONSUMER.*

3-304.14   Wiping Cloths, Use Limitation.

(A) Cloths in-use for wiping FOOD spills from TABLEWARE and carry-out containers that occur as FOOD is being served shall be:

(1) Maintained dry; and

(2) Used for no other purpose.

68

(B) Cloths in-use for wiping counters and other EQUIPMENT surfaces shall be:

(1) Held between uses in a chemical sanitizer solution at a concentration specified under § 4-501.114; and

(2) Laundered daily as specified under ¶ 4-802.11(D).

(C) Cloths in-use for wiping surfaces in contact with raw animal FOODS shall be kept separate from cloths used for other purposes.

(D) Dry wiping cloths and the chemical sanitizing solutions specified in Subparagraph (B)(1) of this section in which wet wiping cloths are held between uses shall be free of FOOD debris and visible soil.

(E) Containers of chemical sanitizing solutions specified in Subparagraph (B)(1) of this section in which wet wiping cloths are held between uses shall be stored off the floor and used in a manner that prevents contamination of FOOD, EQUIPMENT, UTENSILS, LINENS, SINGLE-SERVICE, or SINGLE-USE ARTICLES.

(F) SINGLE-USE disposable sanitizer wipes shall be used in accordance with EPA-approved manufacturer's label use instructions.

3-304.15   Gloves, Use Limitation.

(A) If used, SINGLE-USE gloves shall be used for only one task such as working with READY-TO-EAT FOOD or with raw animal FOOD, used for no other purpose, and discarded when damaged or soiled, or when interruptions occur in the operation. ^P

(B) Except as specified in ¶ (C) of this section, slash-resistant gloves that are used to protect the hands during operations requiring cutting shall be used in direct contact only with FOOD that is subsequently cooked as specified under Part 3-4 such as frozen FOOD or a PRIMAL CUT of MEAT.

(C) *Slash-resistant gloves may be used with READY-TO-EAT FOOD that will not be subsequently cooked if the slash-resistant gloves have a SMOOTH, durable, and nonabsorbent outer surface; or if* the slash-resistant gloves are covered with a SMOOTH, durable, nonabsorbent glove, or a SINGLE-USE glove.

(D) Cloth gloves may not be used in direct contact with FOOD unless the FOOD is subsequently cooked as required under Part 3-4 such as frozen FOOD or a PRIMAL CUT of MEAT.

3-304.16 Using Clean Tableware for Second Portions and Refills.

(A) Except for refilling a CONSUMER'S drinking cup or container without contact between the pouring UTENSIL and the lip-contact area of the drinking cup or container, FOOD EMPLOYEES may not use TABLEWARE, including SINGLE-SERVICE ARTICLES, soiled by the CONSUMER, to provide second portions or refills.

(B) Except as specified in ¶ (C) of this section, self-service CONSUMERS may not be allowed to use soiled TABLEWARE, including SINGLE-SERVICE ARTICLES, to obtain additional FOOD from the display and serving EQUIPMENT.

(C) Drinking cups and containers may be reused by self-service CONSUMERS if refilling is a contamination-free process as specified under ¶¶ 4-204.13(A), (B), and (D).

3-304.17 Refilling Returnables.

(A) A take-home FOOD container returned to a FOOD ESTABLISHMENT may not be refilled at a FOOD ESTABLISHMENT with a POTENTIALLY HAZARDOUS FOOD (TIME/TEMPERATURE CONTROL FOR SAFETY FOOD).

(B) Except as specified in ¶ (C), a take-home FOOD container refilled with FOOD that is not POTENTIALLY HAZARDOUS (TIME/TEMPERATURE CONTROL FOR SAFETY FOOD) shall be cleaned as specified under ¶ 4-603.17(B).

(C) Personal take-out BEVERAGE containers, such as thermally insulated bottles, nonspill coffee cups, and promotional BEVERAGE glasses, may be refilled by EMPLOYEES or the CONSUMER if refilling is a contamination-free process as specified under ¶¶ 4-204.13(A), (B), and (D).

3-305.11   Food Storage.

(A) Except as specified in ¶¶ (B) and (C) of this section, FOOD shall be protected from contamination by storing the FOOD:

(1) In a clean, dry location;

(2) Where it is not exposed to splash, dust, or other contamination; and

(3) At least 15 cm (6 inches) above the floor.

(B) *FOOD in packages and working containers may be stored less than 15 cm (6 inches) above the floor on case lot handling EQUIPMENT as specified under § 4-204.122.*

(C) *Pressurized BEVERAGE containers, cased FOOD in waterproof containers such as bottles or cans, and milk containers in plastic crates may be stored on a floor that is clean and not exposed to floor moisture.*

3-305.12   Food Storage, Prohibited Areas.

FOOD may not be stored:

(A) In locker rooms;

(B) In toilet rooms;

(C) In dressing rooms;

(D) In garbage rooms;

(E) In mechanical rooms;

(F) Under sewer lines that are not shielded to intercept potential drips;

(G) Under leaking water lines, including leaking automatic fire sprinkler heads, or under lines on which water has condensed;

(H) Under open stairwells; or

(I) Under other sources of contamination.

71

3-305.13 Vended Potentially Hazardous Food (Time/Temperature Control for Safety Food), Original Container.

POTENTIALLY HAZARDOUS FOOD (TIME/TEMPERATURE CONTROL FOR SAFETY FOOD) dispensed through a VENDING MACHINE shall be in the PACKAGE in which it was placed at the FOOD ESTABLISHMENT or FOOD PROCESSING PLANT at which it was prepared.

3-305.14 Food Preparation.

During preparation, unPACKAGED FOOD shall be protected from environmental sources of contamination.

Preventing Contamination by Consumers

3-306.11 Food Display.

Except for nuts in the shell and whole, raw fruits and vegetables that are intended for hulling, peeling, or washing by the CONSUMER before consumption, FOOD on display shall be protected from contamination by the use of PACKAGING; counter, service line, or salad bar FOOD guards; display cases; or other effective means. [P]

3-306.12 Condiments, Protection.

(A) Condiments shall be protected from contamination by being kept in dispensers that are designed to provide protection, protected FOOD displays provided with the proper UTENSILS, original containers designed for dispensing, or individual PACKAGES or portions.

(B) Condiments at a VENDING MACHINE LOCATION shall be in individual PACKAGES or provided in dispensers that are filled at an APPROVED location, such as the FOOD ESTABLISHMENT that provides FOOD to the VENDING MACHINE LOCATION, a FOOD PROCESSING PLANT that is regulated by the agency that has jurisdiction over the operation, or a properly equipped facility that is located on the site of the VENDING MACHINE LOCATION.

3-306.13 Consumer Self-Service Operations.

(A) Raw, unPACKAGED animal FOOD, such as beef, lamb, pork, POULTRY, and FISH may not be offered for CONSUMER self-service. [P] *This paragraph does not apply to:*

> (1) *CONSUMER self-service of READY-TO-EAT FOODS at buffets or salad bars that serve FOODS such as sushi or raw shellfish;*

> (2) *Ready-to-cook individual portions for immediate cooking and consumption on the PREMISES such as CONSUMER-cooked MEATS or CONSUMER-selected ingredients for Mongolian barbecue; or*

> (3) *Raw, frozen, shell-on shrimp, or lobster.*

(B) CONSUMER self-service operations for READY-TO-EAT FOODS shall be provided with suitable UTENSILS or effective dispensing methods that protect the FOOD from contamination. [Pf]

(C) CONSUMER self-service operations such as buffets and salad bars shall be monitored by FOOD EMPLOYEES trained in safe operating procedures. [Pf]

3-306.14 Returned Food and Re-Service of Food.

(A) Except as specified in ¶ (B) of this section, after being served or sold and in the possession of a CONSUMER, FOOD that is unused or returned by the CONSUMER may not be offered as FOOD for human consumption. [P]

(B) Except as specified under ¶ 3-801.11(G), *a container of FOOD that is not POTENTIALLY HAZARDOUS (TIME/TEMPERATURE CONTROL FOR SAFETY FOOD) may be RE-SERVED from one CONSUMER to another if:*

> (1) *The FOOD is dispensed so that it is protected from contamination and the container is closed between uses, such as a narrow-neck bottle containing catsup, steak sauce, or wine; or*

> (2) *The FOOD, such as crackers, salt, or pepper, is in an unopened original PACKAGE and is maintained in sound condition.*

3-307.11   Miscellaneous Sources of Contamination.

FOOD shall be protected from contamination that may result from a factor or source not specified under Subparts 3-301 - 3-306.

3-4	DESTRUCTION OF ORGANISMS OF PUBLIC HEALTH CONCERN
	Subparts
	3-401 Cooking
	3-402 Freezing
	3-403 Reheating
	3-404 Other Methods

Cooking

3-401.11   Raw Animal Foods.

(A) Except as specified under ¶ (B) and in ¶¶ (C) and (D) of this section, raw animal FOODS such as EGGS, FISH, MEAT, POULTRY, and FOODS containing these raw animal FOODS, shall be cooked to heat all parts of the FOOD to a temperature and for a time that complies with one of the following methods based on the FOOD that is being cooked:

(1) 63°C (145°F) or above for 15 seconds for: [P]

(a) Raw EGGS that are broken and prepared in response to a CONSUMER'S order and for immediate service, [P] and

(b) Except as specified under Subparagraphs (A)(2) and (A)(3) and ¶ (B), and in ¶ (C) of this section, FISH and MEAT including GAME ANIMALS commercially raised for FOOD as specified under Subparagraph 3-201.17(A)(1) and GAME ANIMALS under a voluntary inspection program as specified under Subparagraph 3-201.17(A)(2); [P]

(2) 68°C (155°F) for 15 seconds or the temperature specified in the following chart that corresponds to the holding time for RATITES, MECHANICALLY TENDERIZED, and INJECTED MEATS; the following if they are COMMINUTED: FISH, MEAT, GAME ANIMALS commercially raised for FOOD as specified under Subparagraph 3-201.17(A)(1), and GAME ANIMALS under a voluntary inspection program as specified under Subparagraph 3-201.17(A)(2); and raw EGGS that are not

prepared as specified under Subparagraph (A)(1)(a) of this section: [P]

Minimum	
Temperature °C (°F)	Time
63 (145)	3 minutes
66 (150)	1 minute
70 (158)	< 1 second (instantaneous)

;or

(3) 74°C (165°F) or above for 15 seconds for POULTRY, BALUTS, wild GAME ANIMALS as specified under Subparagraphs 3-201.17(A)(3) and (4), stuffed FISH, stuffed MEAT, stuffed pasta, stuffed POULTRY, stuffed RATITES, or stuffing containing FISH, MEAT, POULTRY, or RATITES. [P]

(B) Whole MEAT roasts including beef, corned beef, lamb, pork, and cured pork roasts such as ham shall be cooked:

(1) In an oven that is preheated to the temperature specified for the roast's weight in the following chart and that is held at that temperature: [Pf]

Oven Type	Oven Temperature Based on Roast Weight	
	Less than 4.5 kg (10 lbs)	4.5 kg (10 lbs) or More
Still Dry	177°C (350°F) or more	121°C (250°F) or more
Convection	163°C (325°F) or more	121°C (250°F) or more
High Humidity[1]	121°C (250°F) or less	121°C (250°F) or less

[1]Relative humidity greater than 90% for at least 1 hour as measured in the cooking chamber or exit of the oven; or in a moisture-impermeable bag that provides 100% humidity.

;and

(2) As specified in the following chart, to heat all parts of the FOOD to a temperature and for the holding time that corresponds to that temperature: [P]

Temperature °C (°F)	Time[1] in Minutes	Temperature °C (°F)	Time[1] in Seconds
54.4 (130)	112	63.9 (147)	134
55.0 (131)	89	65.0 (149)	85
56.1 (133)	56	66.1 (151)	54
57.2 (135)	36	67.2 (153)	34
57.8 (136)	28	68.3 (155)	22
58.9 (138)	18	69.4 (157)	14
60.0 (140)	12	70.0 (158)	0
61.1 (142)	8		
62.2 (144)	5		
62.8 (145)	4		

[1]Holding time may include postoven heat rise.

(C) *A raw or undercooked WHOLE-MUSCLE, INTACT BEEF steak may be served or offered for sale in a READY-TO-EAT form if:*

> (1) *The FOOD ESTABLISHMENT serves a population that is not a HIGHLY SUSCEPTIBLE POPULATION,*

> (2) *The steak is labeled to indicate that it meets the definition of "WHOLE-MUSCLE, INTACT BEEF" as specified under ¶ 3-201.11(E), and*

> (3) *The steak is cooked on both the top and bottom to a surface temperature of 63°C (145°F) or above and a cooked color change is achieved on all external surfaces.*

(D) *A raw animal FOOD such as raw EGG, raw FISH, raw-marinated FISH, raw MOLLUSCAN SHELLFISH, or steak tartare; or a partially cooked FOOD such as lightly cooked FISH, soft cooked EGGS, or rare MEAT other than WHOLE-MUSCLE, INTACT BEEF steaks as specified in ¶ (C) of this section, may be served or offered for sale upon CONSUMER request or selection in a READY-TO-EAT form if:*

> (1) *As specified under ¶¶ 3-801.11(C)(1) and (2), the FOOD ESTABLISHMENT serves a population that is not a HIGHLY SUSCEPTIBLE POPULATION;*

76

(2) *The FOOD, if served or offered for service by CONSUMER selection from a children's menu, does not contain COMMINUTED MEAT;* [Pf] *and*

(3) *The CONSUMER is informed as specified under § 3-603.11 that to ensure its safety, the FOOD should be cooked as specified under ¶ (A) or (B) of this section; or*

(4) *The REGULATORY AUTHORITY grants a VARIANCE from ¶ (A) or (B) of this section as specified in § 8-103.10 based on a HACCP PLAN that:*

> (a) *Is submitted by the PERMIT HOLDER and APPROVED as specified under § 8-103.11,*
>
> (b) *Documents scientific data or other information showing that a lesser time and temperature regimen results in a safe FOOD, and*
>
> (c) *Verifies that EQUIPMENT and procedures for FOOD preparation and training of FOOD EMPLOYEES at the FOOD ESTABLISHMENT meet the conditions of the VARIANCE.*

3-401.12   Microwave Cooking.

Raw animal FOODS cooked in a microwave oven shall be:

(A) Rotated or stirred throughout or midway during cooking to compensate for uneven distribution of heat;

(B) Covered to retain surface moisture;

(C) Heated to a temperature of at least 74°C (165°F) in all parts of the FOOD; and

(D) Allowed to stand covered for 2 minutes after cooking to obtain temperature equilibrium.

3-401.13   Plant Food Cooking for Hot Holding.

Fruits and vegetables that are cooked for hot holding shall be cooked to a temperature of 57°C (135°F). [Pf]

3-401.14   Non-Continuous Cooking of Raw Animal Foods.

Raw animal FOODS that are cooked using a NON-CONTINUOUS COOKING process shall be:

(A) Subject to an initial heating process that is no longer than sixty minutes in duration; [P]

(B) Immediately after initial heating, cooled according to the time and temperature parameters specified for cooked POTENTIALLY HAZARDOUS FOOD (TIME /TEMPERATURE CONTROL FOR SAFETY FOOD) under ¶ 3-501.14(A); [P]

(C) After cooling, held frozen or cold, as specified for POTENTIALLY HAZARDOUS FOOD (TIME/TEMPERATURE CONTROL FOR SAFETY FOOD) under ¶ 3-501.16(A)(2); [P]

(D) Prior to sale or service, cooked using a process that heats all parts of the FOOD to a temperature of at least 74°C (165°F) for 15 seconds; [P]

(E) Cooled according to the time and temperature parameters specified for cooked POTENTIALLY HAZARDOUS FOOD (TIME /TEMPERATURE CONTROL FOR SAFETY FOOD) under ¶ 3-501.14(A) if not either hot held as specified under ¶3-501.16(A), served immediately, or held using time as a public health control as specified under §3-501.19 after complete cooking; [P] and

(F) Prepared and stored according to written procedures that:

(1) Have obtained prior APPROVAL from the REGULATORY AUTHORITY; [Pf]

(2) Are maintained in the FOOD ESTABLISHMENT and are available to the REGULATORY AUTHORITY upon request; [Pf]

(3) Describe how the requirements specified under ¶ (A)-(E) of this Section are to be monitored and documented by the PERMIT HOLDER and the corrective actions to be taken if the requirements are not met; [Pf]

(4) Describe how the FOODS, after initial heating, but prior to complete cooking, are to be marked or otherwise identified as FOODS that must be cooked as specified under ¶ (D) of this section prior to being offered for sale or service; ^{Pf} and

(5) Describe how the FOODS, after initial heating but prior to cooking as specified under ¶(D) of this section, are to be separated from READY-TO-EAT FOODS as specified under ¶ 3-302.11 (D). ^{Pf}

Freezing   3-402.11   **Parasite Destruction.**

(A) Except as specified in ¶ (B) of this section, before service or sale in READY-TO-EAT form, raw, raw-marinated, partially cooked, or marinated-partially cooked FISH shall be:

(1) Frozen and stored at a temperature of -20°C (-4°F) or below for a minimum of 168 hours (7 days) in a freezer; ^P

(2) Frozen at -35°C (-31°F) or below until solid and stored at -35°C (-31°F) or below for a minimum of 15 hours; ^P or

(3) Frozen at -35°C (-31°F) or below until solid and stored at -20°C (-4°F) or below for a minimum of 24 hours. ^P

(B) *Paragraph (A) of this section does not apply to*:

(1) *MOLLUSCAN SHELLFISH*;

(2) *Tuna of the species Thunnus alalunga, Thunnus albacares (Yellowfin tuna), Thunnus atlanticus, Thunnus maccoyii (Bluefin tuna, Southern), Thunnus obesus (Bigeye tuna), or Thunnus thynnus (Bluefin tuna, Northern); or*

(3) *Aquacultured FISH, such as salmon, that*:

(a) *If raised in open water, are raised in net-pens, or*

(b) *Are raised in land-based operations such as ponds or tanks, and*

(c) *Are fed formulated feed, such as pellets, that contains no live parasites infective to the aquacultured FISH.*

(4) FISH eggs that have been removed from the skein and rinsed.

3-402.12   Records, Creation and Retention.

(A) Except as specified in ¶ 3-402.11(B) and ¶ (B) of this section, if raw, raw-marinated, partially cooked, or marinated-partially cooked FISH are served or sold in READY-TO-EAT form, the PERSON IN CHARGE shall record the freezing temperature and time to which the FISH are subjected and shall retain the records of the FOOD ESTABLISHMENT for 90 calendar days beyond the time of service or sale of the FISH. ^{Pf}

(B) *If the FISH are frozen by a supplier, a written agreement or statement from the supplier stipulating that the FISH supplied are frozen to a temperature and for a time specified under § 3-402.11 may substitute for the records specified under ¶ (A) of this section.*

(C) If raw, raw-marinated, partially cooked, or marinated-partially cooked FISH are served or sold in READY-TO-EAT form, and the FISH are raised and fed as specified in Subparagraph 3-402.11(B)(3), a written agreement or statement from the supplier or aquaculturist stipulating that the FISH were raised and fed as specified in Subparagraph 3-402.11(B)(3) shall be obtained by the PERSON IN CHARGE and retained in the records of the FOOD ESTABLISHMENT for 90 calendar days beyond the time of service or sale of the FISH. ^{Pf}

3-403.10   Preparation for Immediate Service.

Cooked and refrigerated FOOD that is prepared for immediate service in response to an individual CONSUMER order, such as a roast beef sandwich au jus, may be served at any temperature.

Reheating   ### 3-403.11   Reheating for Hot Holding.

(A) Except as specified under ¶¶ (B) and (C) and in ¶ (E) of this section, POTENTIALLY HAZARDOUS FOOD (TIME/TEMPERATURE CONTROL FOR SAFETY FOOD) that is cooked, cooled, and reheated for hot holding shall be reheated so that all parts of the FOOD reach a temperature of at least 74°C (165°F) for 15 seconds. ^P

80

(B) Except as specified under ¶ (C) of this section, POTENTIALLY HAZARDOUS FOOD (TIME/TEMPERATURE CONTROL FOR SAFETY FOOD) reheated in a microwave oven for hot holding shall be reheated so that all parts of the FOOD reach a temperature of at least 74°C (165°F) and the FOOD is rotated or stirred, covered, and allowed to stand covered for 2 minutes after reheating. [P]

(C) READY-TO-EAT FOOD taken from a commercially processed, HERMETICALLY SEALED CONTAINER, or from an intact PACKAGE from a FOOD PROCESSING PLANT that is inspected by the FOOD REGULATORY AUTHORITY that has jurisdiction over the plant, shall be heated to a temperature of at least 57°C (135°F) for hot holding. [P]

(D) Reheating for hot holding as specified under ¶¶ (A) - (C) of this section shall be done rapidly and the time the FOOD is between 5°C (41°F) and the temperatures specified under ¶¶ (A) - (C) of this section may not exceed 2 hours. [P]

(E) *Remaining unsliced portions of MEAT roasts that are cooked as specified under ¶ 3-401.11(B) may be reheated for hot holding using the oven parameters and minimum time and temperature conditions specified under ¶ 3-401.11(B).*

Other Methods   **3-404.11   Treating Juice.**

JUICE PACKAGED in a FOOD ESTABLISHMENT shall be:

(A) Treated under a HACCP PLAN as specified in ¶¶ 8-201.14(B) - (E) to attain a 5-log reduction, which is equal to a 99.999% reduction, of the most resistant microorganism of public health significance; [P] or

(B) Labeled, if not treated to yield a 5-log reduction of the most resistant microorganism of public health significance: [Pf]

(1) As specified under § 3-602.11, [Pf] and

(2) As specified in 21 CFR 101.17(g) Food labeling, warning, notice, and safe handling statements, JUICES that have not been specifically processed to prevent, reduce, or eliminate the presence of pathogens with the following, "WARNING: This product has not been pasteurized and,

81

therefore, may contain harmful bacteria that can cause serious illness in children, the elderly, and persons with weakened immune systems."[Pf]

3-5	**LIMITATION OF GROWTH OF ORGANISMS OF PUBLIC HEALTH CONCERN**
	Subparts
	3-501 **Temperature and Time Control**
	3-502 **Specialized Processing Methods**

Temperature and Time Control

3-501.11   Frozen Food.

Stored frozen FOODS shall be maintained frozen.

3-501.12   Potentially Hazardous Food (Time/Temperature Control for Safety Food), Slacking.

Frozen POTENTIALLY HAZARDOUS FOOD (TIME/TEMPERATURE CONTROL FOR SAFETY FOOD) that is slacked to moderate the temperature shall be held:

(A) Under refrigeration that maintains the FOOD temperature at 5°C (41°F) or less; or

(B) At any temperature if the FOOD remains frozen.

3-501.13   Thawing.

Except as specified in ¶ (D) of this section, POTENTIALLY HAZARDOUS FOOD (TIME/TEMPERATURE CONTROL FOR SAFETY FOOD) shall be thawed:

(A) Under refrigeration that maintains the FOOD temperature at 5°C (41°F) or less; or

(B) Completely submerged under running water:

(1) At a water temperature of 21°C (70°F) or below,

82

(2) With sufficient water velocity to agitate and float off loose particles in an overflow, and

(3) For a period of time that does not allow thawed portions of READY-TO-EAT FOOD to rise above 5°C (41°F), or

(4) For a period of time that does not allow thawed portions of a raw animal FOOD requiring cooking as specified under ¶ 3-401.11(A) or (B) to be above 5°C (41°F), for more than 4 hours including:

    (a) The time the FOOD is exposed to the running water and the time needed for preparation for cooking, or

    (b) The time it takes under refrigeration to lower the FOOD temperature to 5°C (41°F);

(C) As part of a cooking process if the FOOD that is frozen is:

    (1) Cooked as specified under ¶ 3-401.11(A) or (B) or § 3-401.12, or

    (2) Thawed in a microwave oven and immediately transferred to conventional cooking EQUIPMENT, with no interruption in the process; or

(D) *Using any procedure if a portion of frozen READY-TO-EAT FOOD is thawed and prepared for immediate service in response to an individual CONSUMER'S order.*

3-501.14   Cooling.

(A) Cooked POTENTIALLY HAZARDOUS FOOD (TIME/TEMPERATURE CONTROL FOR SAFETY FOOD) shall be cooled:

(1) Within 2 hours from 57°C (135°F) to 21°C (70°F); [P] and

(2) Within a total of 6 hours from 57°C (135°F) to 5°C (41°F) or less. [P]

(B) POTENTIALLY HAZARDOUS FOOD (TIME/TEMPERATURE CONTROL FOR SAFETY FOOD) shall be cooled within 4 hours to 5°C (41°F) or less if prepared from ingredients at ambient temperature, such as reconstituted FOODS and canned tuna. [P]

(C) Except as specified under ¶ (D) of this section, a POTENTIALLY
HAZARDOUS FOOD (TIME/TEMPERATURE CONTROL FOR SAFETY FOOD)
received in compliance with LAWS allowing a temperature above
5°C (41°F) during shipment from the supplier as specified in
¶ 3-202.11(B), shall be cooled within 4 hours to 5°C (41°F) or
less. [P]

(D) Raw EGGS shall be received as specified under
¶ 3-202.11(C) and immediately placed in refrigerated EQUIPMENT
that maintains an ambient air temperature of 7°C (45°F) or less. [P]

3-501.15   Cooling Methods.

(A) Cooling shall be accomplished in accordance with the time
and temperature criteria specified under § 3-501.14 by using one
or more of the following methods based on the type of FOOD being
cooled:

(1) Placing the FOOD in shallow pans; [Pf]

(2) Separating the FOOD into smaller or thinner portions; [Pf]

(3) Using rapid cooling EQUIPMENT; [Pf]

(4) Stirring the FOOD in a container placed in an ice water
bath; [Pf]

(5) Using containers that facilitate heat transfer; [Pf]

(6) Adding ice as an ingredient; [Pf] or

(7) Other effective methods. [Pf]

(B) When placed in cooling or cold holding EQUIPMENT, FOOD
containers in which FOOD is being cooled shall be:

(1) Arranged in the EQUIPMENT to provide maximum heat
transfer through the container walls; and

(2) Loosely covered, or uncovered if protected from overhead
contamination as specified under Subparagraph
3-305.11(A)(2), during the cooling period to facilitate heat
transfer from the surface of the FOOD.

3-501.16   Potentially Hazardous Food (Time/Temperature Control for Safety Food), Hot and Cold Holding.

(A) *Except during preparation, cooking, or cooling, or when time is used as the public health control as specified under §3-501.19,* and except as specified under ¶ (B) and in ¶ (C) of this section, POTENTIALLY HAZARDOUS FOOD (TIME/TEMPERATURE CONTROL FOR SAFETY FOOD) shall be maintained:

(1) At 57°C (135°F) or above, *except that roasts cooked to a temperature and for a time specified in ¶ 3-401.11(B) or reheated as specified in ¶ 3-403.11(E) may be held at a temperature of 54°C (130°F) or above;* [P] or

(2) At 5°C (41°F) or less. [P]

(B) EGGS that have not been treated to destroy all viable **Salmonellae** shall be stored in refrigerated EQUIPMENT that maintains an ambient air temperature of 7°C (45°F) or less. [P]

(C) POTENTIALLY HAZARDOUS FOOD (TIME/TEMPERATURE CONTROL FOR SAFETY FOOD) in a homogenous liquid form *may be maintained outside of the temperature control requirements, as specified under ¶ (A) of this section, while contained within specially designed* EQUIPMENT *that complies with the design and construction requirements as specified under ¶ 4-204.13(E).*

3-501.17   Ready-to-Eat, Potentially Hazardous Food (Time/Temperature Control for Safety Food), Date Marking.

*on-premises
preparation*
• *prepare and
hold cold*

(A) Except when PACKAGING FOOD using a REDUCED OXYGEN PACKAGING method as specified under § 3-502.12, and except as specified in ¶¶ (D) and (E) of this section, refrigerated, READY-TO -EAT, POTENTIALLY HAZARDOUS FOOD (TIME/TEMPERATURE CONTROL FOR SAFETY FOOD) prepared and held in a FOOD ESTABLISHMENT for more than 24 hours shall be clearly marked to indicate the date or day by which the FOOD shall be consumed on the PREMISES, sold, or discarded when held at a temperature of 5°C (41°F) or less for a maximum of 7 days. [Pf]

commercially
processed food
• *open and hold*
cold

(B) Except as specified in ¶¶ (D) - (F) of this section, refrigerated, READY-TO-EAT, POTENTIALLY HAZARDOUS FOOD (TIME/TEMPERATURE CONTROL FOR SAFETY FOOD) prepared and PACKAGED by a FOOD PROCESSING PLANT shall be clearly marked, at the time the original container is opened in a FOOD ESTABLISHMENT and if the FOOD is held for more than 24 hours, to indicate the date or day by which the FOOD shall be consumed on the PREMISES, sold, or discarded, based on the temperature and time combinations specified in ¶ (A) of this section and: ^{Pf}

(1) The day the original container is opened in the FOOD ESTABLISHMENT shall be counted as Day 1; ^{Pf} and

(2) The day or date marked by the FOOD ESTABLISHMENT may not exceed a manufacturer's use-by date if the manufacturer determined the use-by date based on FOOD safety. ^{Pf}

(C) A refrigerated, READY-TO-EAT, POTENTIALLY HAZARDOUS FOOD (TIME/TEMPERATURE CONTROL FOR SAFETY FOOD) ingredient or a portion of a refrigerated, READY-TO-EAT, POTENTIALLY HAZARDOUS FOOD (TIME/TEMPERATURE CONTROL FOR SAFETY FOOD) that is subsequently combined with additional ingredients or portions of FOOD shall retain the date marking of the earliest-prepared or first-prepared ingredient. ^{Pf}

(D) *A date marking system that meets the criteria stated in ¶¶ (A) and (B) of this section may include:*

(1) *Using a method APPROVED by the REGULATORY AUTHORITY for refrigerated, READY-TO-EAT POTENTIALLY HAZARDOUS FOOD (TIME/TEMPERATURE CONTROL FOR SAFETY FOOD) that is frequently rewrapped, such as lunchmeat or a roast, or for which date marking is impractical, such as soft serve mix or milk in a dispensing machine;*

(2) *Marking the date or day of preparation, with a procedure to discard the FOOD on or before the last date or day by which the FOOD must be consumed on the premises, sold, or discarded as specified under ¶ (A) of this section;*

(3) *Marking the date or day the original container is opened in a FOOD ESTABLISHMENT, with a procedure to discard the FOOD on or before the last date or day by which the FOOD must be consumed on the premises, sold, or discarded as specified under ¶ (B) of this section; or*

(4) *Using calendar dates, days of the week, color-coded marks, or other effective marking methods, provided that the marking system is disclosed to the REGULATORY AUTHORITY upon request.*

(E) *Paragraphs (A) and (B) of this section do not apply to individual meal portions served or rePACKAGED for sale from a bulk container upon a consumer's request.*

(F) *Paragraph (B) of this section does not apply to the following FOODS prepared and PACKAGED by a FOOD PROCESSING PLANT inspected by a REGULATORY AUTHORITY:*

(1) *Deli salads, such as ham salad, seafood salad, chicken salad, egg salad, pasta salad, potato salad, and macaroni salad, manufactured in accordance with 21 CFR 110 Current good manufacturing practice in manufacturing, packing, or holding human food;*

(2) *Hard cheeses containing not more than 39% moisture as defined in 21 CFR 133 Cheeses and related cheese products, such as cheddar, gruyere, parmesan and reggiano, and romano;*

(3) *Semi-soft cheeses containing more than 39% moisture, but not more than 50% moisture, as defined in 21 CFR 133 Cheeses and related cheese products, such as blue, edam, gorgonzola, gouda, and monterey jack;*

(4) *Cultured dairy products as defined in 21 CFR 131 Milk and cream, such as yogurt, sour cream, and buttermilk;*

(5) *Preserved FISH products, such as pickled herring and dried or salted cod, and other acidified FISH products defined in 21 CFR 114 Acidified foods;*

(6) *Shelf stable, dry fermented sausages, such as pepperoni and Genoa salami that are not labeled "Keep Refrigerated" as specified in 9 CFR 317 Labeling, marking devices, and containers, and which retain the original CASING on the product; and*

(7) *Shelf stable salt-cured products such as prosciutto and Parma (ham) that are not labeled "Keep Refrigerated" as specified in 9 CFR 317 Labeling, marking devices, and containers.*

3-501.18 Ready-to-Eat, Potentially Hazardous Food (Time/Temperature Control for Safety Food), Disposition.

(A) A FOOD specified in ¶ 3-501.17(A) or (B) shall be discarded if it:

(1) Exceeds the temperature and time combination specified in ¶ 3-501.17(A), except time that the product is frozen; [P]

(2) Is in a container or PACKAGE that does not bear a date or day; [P] or

(3) Is appropriately marked with a date or day that exceeds a temperature and time combination as specified in ¶ 3-501.17(A). [P]

(B) Refrigerated, READY-TO-EAT, POTENTIALLY HAZARDOUS FOOD (TIME/TEMPERATURE CONTROL FOR SAFETY FOOD) prepared in a FOOD ESTABLISHMENT and dispensed through a VENDING MACHINE with an automatic shutoff control shall be discarded if it exceeds a temperature and time combination as specified in ¶ 3-501.17(A). [P]

3-501.19 Time as a Public Health Control.

(A) Except as specified under ¶ (D) of this section, if time without temperature control is used as the public health control for a working supply of POTENTIALLY HAZARDOUS FOOD (TIME/TEMPERATURE CONTROL FOR SAFETY FOOD) before cooking, or for READY-TO-EAT POTENTIALLY HAZARDOUS FOOD (TIME/TEMPERATURE CONTROL FOR SAFETY FOOD) that is displayed or held for sale or service:

(1) Written procedures shall be prepared in advance, maintained in the FOOD ESTABLISHMENT and made available to the REGULATORY AUTHORITY upon request that specify: [Pf]

(a) Methods of compliance with Subparagraphs (B)(1)-(3) or C)(1)-(5) of this section; [Pf] and

(b) Methods of compliance with § 3-501.14 for FOOD that is prepared, cooked, and refrigerated before time is used as a public health control. [Pf]

Time –
maximum up to
4 hours

(B) If time temperature control is used as the public health control up to a maximum of 4 hours:

  (1) The FOOD shall have an initial temperature of 5°C (41°F) or less when removed from cold holding temperature control, or 57°C (135°F) or greater when removed from hot holding temperature control; [P]

  (2) The FOOD shall be marked or otherwise identified to indicate the time that is 4 hours past the point in time when the FOOD is removed from temperature control; [Pf]

  (3) The FOOD shall be cooked and served, served at any temperature if READY-TO-EAT, or discarded, within 4 hours from the point in time when the FOOD is removed from temperature control; [P] and

  (4) The FOOD in unmarked containers or PACKAGES, or marked to exceed a 4-hour limit shall be discarded. [P]

Time –
maximum up to
6 hours

(C) If time without temperature control is used as the public health control up to a maximum of 6 hours:

  (1) The FOOD shall have an initial temperature of 5°C (41°F) or less when removed from temperature control and the FOOD temperature may not exceed 21°C (70°F) within a maximum time period of 6 hours; [P]

  (2) The FOOD shall be monitored to ensure the warmest portion of the FOOD does not exceed 21°C (70°F) during the 6-hour period, *unless an ambient air temperature is maintained that ensures the FOOD does not exceed 21°C (70°F) during the 6-hour holding period*; [Pf]

  (3) The FOOD shall be marked or otherwise identified to indicate: [Pf]

    (a) The time when the FOOD is removed from 5°C (41°F) or less cold holding temperature control, [Pf] and

    (b) The time that is 6 hours past the point in time when the FOOD is removed from cold holding temperature control; [Pf]

  (4) The FOOD shall be:

(a) Discarded if the temperature of the FOOD exceeds 21°C (70°F), [P] or

(b) Cooked and served, served at any temperature if READY-TO-EAT, or discarded within a maximum of 6 hours from the point in time when the FOOD is removed from 5°C (41°F) or less cold holding temperature control; [P] and

(5) The FOOD in unmarked containers or PACKAGES, or marked with a time that exceeds the 6-hour limit shall be discarded. [P]

(D) A FOOD ESTABLISHMENT that serves a HIGHLY SUSCEPTIBLE POPULATION may not use time as specified under ¶¶ (A), (B) or (C) of this section as the public health control for raw EGGS.

*Specialized
Processing
Methods*

3-502.11   Variance Requirement.

A FOOD ESTABLISHMENT shall obtain a VARIANCE from the REGULATORY AUTHORITY as specified in § 8-103.10 and under § 8-103.11 before: [Pf]

(A) Smoking FOOD as a method of FOOD preservation rather than as a method of flavor enhancement; [Pf]

(B) Curing FOOD; [Pf]

(C) Using FOOD ADDITIVES or adding components such as vinegar: [Pf]

(1) As a method of FOOD preservation rather than as a method of flavor enhancement, [Pf] or

(2) To render a FOOD so that it is not POTENTIALLY HAZARDOUS (TIME/TEMPERATURE CONTROL OF SAFETY FOOD); [Pf]

(D) Packaging FOOD using a REDUCED OXYGEN PACKAGING method *except where the growth of and toxin formation by **Clostridium botulinum** and the growth of **Listeria monocytogenes** are controlled as specified under § 3-502.12;* [Pf]

90

(E) Operating a MOLLUSCAN SHELLFISH life-support system display tank used to store or display shellfish that are offered for human consumption;^{Pf}

(F) Custom processing animals that are for personal use as FOOD and not for sale or service in a FOOD ESTABLISHMENT;^{Pf}

(G) Preparing FOOD by another method that is determined by the REGULATORY AUTHORITY to require a VARIANCE;^{Pf} or

(H) Sprouting seeds or beans.^{Pf}

Clostridium botulinum and Listeria monocytogenes Controls

3-502.12   Reduced Oxygen Packaging Without a Variance, Criteria.

(A) Except for a FOOD ESTABLISHMENT that obtains a VARIANCE as specified under § 3-502.11, a FOOD ESTABLISHMENT that PACKAGES POTENTIALLY HAZARDOUS FOOD (TIME/TEMPERATURE CONTROL FOR SAFETY FOOD) using a REDUCED OXYGEN PACKAGING method shall control the growth and toxin formation of ***Clostridium botulinum*** and the growth of ***Listeria monocytogenes***.^P

(B) A FOOD ESTABLISHMENT that PACKAGES POTENTIALLY HAZARDOUS FOOD (TIME/TEMPERATURE CONTROL FOR SAFETY FOOD) using a REDUCED OXYGEN PACKAGING method shall have a HACCP PLAN that contains the information specified under ¶ 8-201.14(D) and that:^{Pf}

(1) Identifies the FOOD to be PACKAGED;^{Pf}

(2) Except as specified under ¶¶ (C) - (E) of this section, requires that the PACKAGED FOOD shall be maintained at 5°C (41°F) or less and meet at least one of the following criteria:^{Pf}

(a) Has an A_W of 0.91 or less,^{Pf}

(b) Has a PH of 4.6 or less,^{Pf}

(c) Is a MEAT or POULTRY product cured at a FOOD PROCESSING PLANT regulated by the USDA using substances specified in 9 CFR 424.21, Use of food ingredients and sources of radiation, and is received in an intact PACKAGE,^{Pf} or

(d) Is a FOOD with a high level of competing organisms such as raw MEAT, raw POULTRY, or raw vegetables; [Pf]

(3) Describes how the PACKAGE shall be prominently and conspicuously labeled on the principal display panel in bold type on a contrasting background, with instructions to: [Pf]

(a) Maintain the FOOD at 5°C (41°F) or below, [Pf] and

(b) Discard the FOOD if within 14 calendar days of its PACKAGING it is not served for on-PREMISES consumption, or consumed if served or sold for off-PREMISES consumption; [Pf]

(4) Limits the refrigerated shelf life to no more than 14 calendar days from PACKAGING to consumption, except the time the product is maintained frozen, or the original manufacturer's "sell by" or "use by" date, whichever occurs first; [P]

(5) Includes operational procedures that:

(a) Prohibit contacting READY-TO-EAT FOOD with bare hands as specified under ¶ 3-301.11(B), [Pf]

(b) Identify a designated work area and the method by which: [Pf]

(i) Physical barriers or methods of separation of raw FOODS and READY-TO-EAT FOODS minimize cross contamination, [Pf] and

(ii) Access to the processing EQUIPMENT is limited to responsible trained personnel familiar with the potential HAZARDS of the operation, [Pf] and

(c) Delineate cleaning and SANITIZATION procedures for FOOD-CONTACT SURFACES; [Pf] and

(6) Describes the training program that ensures that the individual responsible for the REDUCED OXYGEN PACKAGING operation understands the: [Pf]

(a) Concepts required for a safe operation, [Pf]

(b) EQUIPMENT and facilities, [Pf] and

92

(c) Procedures specified under Subparagraph (B)(5) of this section and ¶ 8-201.14(D). [Pf]

Fish

(C) *Except for* FISH *that is frozen before, during, and after* PACKAGING, a FOOD ESTABLISHMENT may not PACKAGE FISH using a REDUCED OXYGEN PACKAGING method. [P]

Cook-Chill or Sous Vide

(D) Except as specified under ¶ (C) of this section, a FOOD ESTABLISHMENT that PACKAGES FOOD using a cook-chill or sous vide process shall:

(1) Implement a HACCP PLAN that contains the information as specified under ¶ 8-201.14(D); [Pf]

(2) Ensure the FOOD is:

(a) Prepared and consumed on the PREMISES, or prepared and consumed off the PREMISES but within the same business entity with no distribution or sale of the PACKAGED product to another business entity or the CONSUMER, [Pf]

(b) Cooked to heat all parts of the FOOD to a temperature and for a time as specified under § 3-401.11, [P]

(c) Protected from contamination before and after cooking as specified under Parts 3-3 and 3-4, [P]

(d) Placed in a PACKAGE with an oxygen barrier and sealed before cooking, or placed in a PACKAGE and sealed immediately after cooking and before reaching a temperature below 57°C (135°F), [P]

(e) Cooled to 5°C (41°F) in the sealed PACKAGE or bag as specified under § 3-501.14 and subsequently: [P]

(i) *Cooled to 1°C (34°F) within 48 hours of reaching 5°C (41°F) and held at that temperature until consumed or discarded within 30 days after the date of* PACKAGING; [P]

(ii) *Cooled to 1°C (34°F) within 48 hours of reaching 5°C (41°F), removed from refrigeration equipment that maintains a 1°C (34°F) food temperature and then held at 5°C (41°F) or less for no more than 72 hours, at which time the* FOOD *must be consumed or discarded;* [P]

93

(iii) *Cooled to 3°C (38°F) or less within 24 hours of reaching 5°C (41°F) and held there for no more than 72 hours from* PACKAGING, *at which time the food must be consumed or discarded;* [P] or

(iv) Held frozen with no shelf life restriction while frozen until consumed or used. [P]

(f) Held in a refrigeration unit that is equipped with an electronic system that continuously monitors time and temperature and is visually examined for proper operation twice daily, [Pf]

(g) If transported off-site to a satellite location of the same business entity, equipped with verifiable electronic monitoring devices to ensure that times and temperatures are monitored during transportation, [Pf] and

(h) Labeled with the product name and the date PACKAGED; [Pf] and

(3) Maintain the records required to confirm that cooling and cold holding refrigeration time/temperature parameters are required as part of the HACCP PLAN and:

(a) Make such records available to the REGULATORY AUTHORITY upon request, [Pf] and

(b) Hold such records for at least 6 months; [Pf] and

(4) Implement written operational procedures as specified under Subparagraph (B)(5) of this section and a training program as specified under Subparagraph (B)(6) of this section. [Pf]

Cheese

(E) A FOOD ESTABLISHMENT that PACKAGES cheese using a REDUCED OXYGEN PACKAGING method shall:

(1) Limit the cheeses PACKAGED to those that are commercially manufactured in a FOOD PROCESSING PLANT with no ingredients added in the FOOD ESTABLISHMENT and that meet the Standards of Identity as specified in 21 CFR 133.150 Hard cheeses, 21 CFR 133.169 Pasteurized process cheese or 21 CFR 133.187 Semisoft cheeses; [P]

(2) Have a HACCP PLAN that contains the information specified under ¶ 8-201.14(D) and as specified under ¶¶ (B)(1), (B)(3)(a), (B)(5) and (B)(6) of this section; Pf

(3) Labels the PACKAGE on the principal display panel with a "use by" date that does not exceed 30 days from its packaging or the original manufacturer's "sell by" or "use by" date, whichever occurs first; Pf and

(4) Discards the REDUCED OXYGEN PACKAGED cheese if it is not sold for off-PREMISES consumption or consumed within 30 calendar days of its PACKAGING. Pf

---

3-6   FOOD IDENTITY, PRESENTATION, AND ON-PREMISES LABELING

Subparts

3-601	**Accurate Representation**
3-602	**Labeling**
3-603	**Consumer Advisory**

Accurate Representation

3-601.11   Standards of Identity.

PACKAGED FOOD shall comply with standard of identity requirements in 21 CFR 131-169 and 9 CFR 319 Definitions and standards of identity or composition, and the general requirements in 21 CFR 130 – Food Standards: General and 9 CFR 319 Subpart A – General.

3-601.12   Honestly Presented.

(A) FOOD shall be offered for human consumption in a way that does not mislead or misinform the CONSUMER.

(B) FOOD or COLOR ADDITIVES, colored overwraps, or lights may not be used to misrepresent the true appearance, color, or quality of a FOOD.

3-602.11   Food Labels.

(A) FOOD PACKAGED in a FOOD ESTABLISHMENT, shall be labeled as specified in LAW, including 21 CFR 101 - Food labeling, and 9 CFR 317 Labeling, marking devices, and containers.

(B) Label information shall include:

(1) The common name of the FOOD, or absent a common name, an adequately descriptive identity statement;

(2) If made from two or more ingredients, a list of ingredients in descending order of predominance by weight, including a declaration of artificial color or flavor and chemical preservatives, if contained in the FOOD;

(3) An accurate declaration of the quantity of contents;

(4) The name and place of business of the manufacturer, packer, or distributor; and

(5) The name of the FOOD source for each MAJOR FOOD ALLERGEN contained in the FOOD unless the FOOD source is already part of the common or usual name of the respective ingredient (Effective January 1, 2006). [Pf]

(6) Except as exempted in the Federal Food, Drug, and Cosmetic Act § 403(Q)(3) - (5), nutrition labeling as specified in 21 CFR 101 - Food Labeling and 9 CFR 317 Subpart B Nutrition Labeling.

(7) For any salmonid FISH containing canthaxanthin as a COLOR ADDITIVE, the labeling of the bulk FISH container, including a list of ingredients, displayed on the retail container or by other written means, such as a counter card, that discloses the use of canthaxanthin.

(C) Bulk FOOD that is available for CONSUMER self-dispensing shall be prominently labeled with the following information in plain view of the CONSUMER:

(1) The manufacturer's or processor's label that was provided with the FOOD; or

(2) A card, sign, or other method of notification that includes the information specified under Subparagraphs (B)(1), (2), and (5) of this section.

(D) *Bulk, unPACKAGED FOODS such as bakery products and unPACKAGED FOODS that are portioned to CONSUMER specification need not be labeled if:*

(1) *A health, nutrient content, or other claim is not made;*

(2) *There are no state or local LAWS requiring labeling; and*

(3) *The FOOD is manufactured or prepared on the PREMISES of the FOOD ESTABLISHMENT or at another FOOD ESTABLISHMENT or a FOOD PROCESSING PLANT that is owned by the same PERSON and is regulated by the FOOD regulatory agency that has jurisdiction.*

3-602.12   Other Forms of Information.

(A) If required by LAW, CONSUMER warnings shall be provided.

(B) FOOD ESTABLISHMENT or manufacturers' dating information on FOODS may not be concealed or altered.

Consumer Advisory

3-603.11   Consumption of Animal Foods that are Raw, Undercooked, or Not Otherwise Processed to Eliminate Pathogens.

(A) Except as specified in ¶ 3-401.11(C) and Subparagraph 3-401.11(D)(4) and under ¶ 3-801.11(C), if an animal FOOD such as beef, EGGS, FISH, lamb, milk, pork, POULTRY, or shellfish is served or sold raw, undercooked, or without otherwise being processed to eliminate pathogens, either in READY-TO-EAT form or as an ingredient in another READY-TO-EAT FOOD, the PERMIT HOLDER shall inform CONSUMERS of the significantly increased RISK of consuming such FOODS by way of a DISCLOSURE and REMINDER, as specified in ¶¶ (B) and (C) of this section using brochures, deli case or menu advisories, label statements, table tents, placards, or other effective written means. [Pf]

(B) DISCLOSURE shall include:

(1) A description of the animal-derived FOODS, such as "oysters on the half shell (raw oysters)," "raw-EGG Caesar salad," and "hamburgers (can be cooked to order)"; [Pf] or

(2) Identification of the animal-derived FOODS by asterisking them to a footnote that states that the items are served raw or undercooked, or contain (or may contain) raw or undercooked ingredients. [Pf]

(C) REMINDER shall include asterisking the animal-derived FOODS requiring DISCLOSURE to a footnote that states:

(1) Regarding the safety of these items, written information is available upon request; [Pf]

(2) Consuming raw or undercooked MEATS, POULTRY, seafood, shellfish, or EGGS may increase your RISK of foodborne illness; [Pf] or

(3) Consuming raw or undercooked MEATS, POULTRY, seafood, shellfish, or EGGS may increase your RISK of foodborne illness, especially if you have certain medical conditions. [Pf]

3-7	CONTAMINATED FOOD	
	Subpart	
	3-701	Disposition

Disposition   3-701.11   **Discarding or Reconditioning Unsafe, Adulterated, or Contaminated Food.**

(A) A FOOD that is unsafe, ADULTERATED, or not honestly presented as specified under § 3-101.11 shall be discarded or reconditioned according to an APPROVED procedure. [P]

(B) FOOD that is not from an APPROVED source as specified under §§ 3-201.11 - .17 shall be discarded. [P]

98

(C) READY-TO-EAT FOOD that may have been contaminated by an EMPLOYEE who has been RESTRICTED or EXCLUDED as specified under § 2-201.12 shall be discarded. [P]

(D) FOOD that is contaminated by FOOD EMPLOYEES, CONSUMERS, or other PERSONS through contact with their hands, bodily discharges, such as nasal or oral discharges, or other means shall be discarded. [P]

3-8	SPECIAL REQUIREMENTS FOR HIGHLY SUSCEPTIBLE POPULATIONS
	Subpart
	3-801 Additional Safeguards

Additional Safeguards

3-801.11   **Pasteurized Foods, Prohibited Re-Service, and Prohibited Food.**

In a FOOD ESTABLISHMENT that serves a HIGHLY SUSCEPTIBLE POPULATION:

(A) The following criteria apply to JUICE:

(1) For the purposes of this paragraph only, children who are age 9 or less and receive FOOD in a school, day care setting, or similar facility that provides custodial care are included as HIGHLY SUSCEPTIBLE POPULATIONS;

(2) PrePACKAGED JUICE or a prePACKAGED BEVERAGE containing JUICE, that bears a warning label as specified in 21 CFR, 101.17(g) Food labeling, warning, notice, and safe handling statements, Juices that have not been specifically processed to prevent, reduce, or eliminate the presence of pathogens, or a PACKAGED JUICE or BEVERAGE containing JUICE, that bears a warning label as specified under ¶ 3-404.11(B) may not be served or offered for sale; [P] and

(3) UNPACKAGED JUICE that is prepared on the premises for service or sale in a READY-TO-EAT form shall be processed under a HACCP PLAN that contains the information specified under ¶¶ 8-201.14(B) - (E) and as specified in

21 CFR Part 120 – Hazard Analysis and Critical Control Point (HACCP) Systems, Subpart B Pathogen Reduction, 120.24 Process controls. [P]

(B) Pasteurized EGGS or EGG PRODUCTS shall be substituted for raw EGGS in the preparation of: [P]

(1) FOODS such as Caesar salad, hollandaise or Béarnaise sauce, mayonnaise, meringue, EGGnog, ice cream, and EGG-fortified BEVERAGES, [P] and

(2) Except as specified in ¶ (F) of this section, recipes in which more than one EGG is broken and the EGGS are combined; [P]

(C) The following FOODS may not be served or offered for sale in a READY-TO-EAT form: [P]

(1) Raw animal FOODS such as raw FISH, raw-marinated FISH, raw MOLLUSCAN SHELLFISH, and steak tartare, [P]

(2) A partially cooked animal FOOD such as lightly cooked FISH, rare MEAT, soft-cooked EGGS that are made from raw EGGS, and meringue; [P] and

(3) Raw seed sprouts. [P]

(D) FOOD EMPLOYEES may not contact READY-TO-EAT FOOD as specified under ¶¶ 3-301.11(B) and (D). [P]

(E) Time only, as the public health control as specified under ¶ 3-501.19(D), may not be used for raw EGGS. [P]

(F) *Subparagraph (B)(2) of this section does not apply if:*

(1) *The raw EGGS are combined immediately before cooking for one CONSUMER'S serving at a single meal, cooked as specified under Subparagraph 3-401.11(A)(1), and served immediately, such as an omelet, soufflé, or scrambled EGGS;*

(2) *The raw EGGS are combined as an ingredient immediately before baking and the EGGS are thoroughly cooked to a READY-TO-EAT form, such as a cake, muffin, or bread; or*

100

(3) *The preparation of the food is conducted under a HACCP PLAN that:*

    (a) *Identifies the FOOD to be prepared,*

    (b) *Prohibits contacting READY-TO-EAT FOOD with bare hands,*

    (c) *Includes specifications and practices that ensure*:

        (i) ***Salmonella* Enteritidis** *growth is controlled before and after cooking, and*

        (ii) ***Salmonella* Enteritidis** *is destroyed by cooking the EGGS according to the temperature and time specified in Subparagraph 3-401.11(A)(2),*

    (d) *Contains the information specified under ¶ 8-201.14(D) including procedures that:*

        (i) *Control cross contamination of READY-TO-EAT FOOD with raw EGGS, and*

        (ii) *Delineate cleaning and SANITIZATION procedures for FOOD-CONTACT SURFACES,* and

    (e) *Describes the training program that ensures that the FOOD EMPLOYEE responsible for the preparation of the FOOD understands the procedures to be used.*

Re-service of Food

(G) Except as specified in paragraph (H) of this section, FOOD may be re-served as specified under Subparagraph 3-306.14(B)(1) and (2).

Prohibited Re-service of Food

(H) *FOOD may not be re-served under the following conditions:*

    (1) *Any FOOD served to patients or clients who are under contact precautions in medical isolation or quarantine, or protective environment isolation may not be re-served to others outside.*

(2) *Packages of FOOD from any patients, clients, or other CONSUMERS should not be re-served to PERSONS in protective environment isolation.*

Chapter

4 Equipment, Utensils, and Linens

Parts

4-1   MATERIALS FOR CONSTRUCTION AND REPAIR

Subparts

Multiuse   4-101.11   Characteristics.

Materials that are used in the construction of UTENSILS and FOOD-CONTACT SURFACES of EQUIPMENT may not allow the migration of deleterious substances or impart colors, odors, or tastes to FOOD and under normal use conditions shall be: [P]

(A) Safe; [P]

(B) Durable, CORROSION-RESISTANT, and nonabsorbent;

(C) Sufficient in weight and thickness to withstand repeated WAREWASHING;

103

(D) Finished to have a SMOOTH, EASILY CLEANABLE surface; and

(E) Resistant to pitting, chipping, crazing, scratching, scoring, distortion, and decomposition.

4-101.12   Cast Iron, Use Limitation.

(A) Except as specified in ¶¶ (B) and (C) of this section, cast iron may not be used for UTENSILS or FOOD-CONTACT SURFACES of EQUIPMENT.

(B) *Cast iron may be used as a surface for cooking.*

(C) *Cast iron may be used in UTENSILS for serving FOOD if the UTENSILS are used only as part of an uninterrupted process from cooking through service.*

4-101.13   Lead, Use Limitation.

(A) Ceramic, china, and crystal UTENSILS, and decorative UTENSILS such as hand painted ceramic or china that are used in contact with FOOD shall be lead-free or contain levels of lead not exceeding the limits of the following UTENSIL categories: [P]

UTENSIL Category	Ceramic Article Description	Maximum Lead MG/L
Beverage Mugs, Cups, Pitchers	Coffee Mugs	0.5
Large Hollowware (excluding pitchers)	Bowls ≥ 1.1 Liter (1.16 Quart)	1
Small Hollowware (excluding cups & mugs)	Bowls < 1.1 Liter (1.16 Quart)	2.0
Flat TABLEWARE	Plates, Saucers	3.0

(B) Pewter alloys containing lead in excess of 0.05% may not be used as a FOOD-CONTACT SURFACE. [P]

(C) Solder and flux containing lead in excess of 0.2% may not be used as a FOOD-CONTACT SURFACE.

104

4-101.14   Copper, Use Limitation.

(A) Except as specified in ¶ (B) of this section, copper and copper alloys such as brass may not be used in contact with a FOOD that has a pH below 6 such as vinegar, fruit JUICE, or wine or for a fitting or tubing installed between a backflow prevention device and a carbonator. [P]

(B) *Copper and copper alloys may be used in contact with beer brewing ingredients that have a pH below 6 in the preformation and fermentation steps of a beer brewing operation such as a brewpub or microbrewery.*

4-101.15   Galvanized Metal, Use Limitation.

Galvanized metal may not be used for UTENSILS or FOOD-CONTACT SURFACES of EQUIPMENT that are used in contact with acidic FOOD. [P]

4-101.16   Sponges, Use Limitation.

Sponges may not be used in contact with cleaned and SANITIZED or in-use FOOD-CONTACT SURFACES.

4-101.17   Wood, Use Limitation.

(A) Except as specified in ¶¶ (B), (C), and (D) of this section, wood and wood wicker may not be used as a FOOD-CONTACT SURFACE.

(B) *Hard maple or an equivalently hard, close-grained wood may be used for:*

(1) *Cutting boards; cutting blocks; bakers' tables; and UTENSILS such as rolling pins, doughnut dowels, salad bowls, and chopsticks; and*

(2) *Wooden paddles used in confectionery operations for pressure scraping kettles when manually preparing confections at a temperature of $110^{\circ}C$ ($230^{\circ}F$) or above.*

105

(C) *Whole, uncut, raw fruits and vegetables, and nuts in the shell may be kept in the wood shipping containers in which they were received, until the fruits, vegetables, or nuts are used.*

(D) *If the nature of the FOOD requires removal of rinds, peels, husks, or shells before consumption, the whole, uncut, raw FOOD may be kept in:*

  (1) *Untreated wood containers; or*

  (2) *Treated wood containers if the containers are treated with a preservative that meets the requirements specified in 21 CFR 178.3800 Preservatives for wood.*

4-101.18   Nonstick Coatings, Use Limitation.

Multiuse KITCHENWARE such as frying pans, griddles, sauce pans, cookie sheets, and waffle bakers that have a perfluorocarbon resin coating shall be used with nonscoring or nonscratching UTENSILS and cleaning aids.

4-101.19   Nonfood-Contact Surfaces.

NonFOOD-CONTACT SURFACES of EQUIPMENT that are exposed to splash, spillage, or other FOOD soiling or that require frequent cleaning shall be constructed of a CORROSION-RESISTANT, nonabsorbent, and SMOOTH material.

Single-Service and Single-Use

4-102.11   Characteristics.

Materials that are used to make SINGLE-SERVICE and SINGLE-USE ARTICLES:

  (A) May not:

  (1) Allow the migration of deleterious substances, [P] or

  (2) Impart colors, odors, or tastes to FOOD; and

(B) Shall be:

   (1) Safe, [P] and

   (2) Clean.

4-2   DESIGN AND CONSTRUCTION

   Subparts

4-201	Durability and Strength
4-202	Cleanability
4-203	Accuracy
4-204	Functionality
4-205	Acceptability

Durability and Strength

4-201.11   Equipment and Utensils.

EQUIPMENT and UTENSILS shall be designed and constructed to be durable and to retain their characteristic qualities under normal use conditions.

4-201.12   Food Temperature Measuring Devices.

FOOD TEMPERATURE MEASURING DEVICES may not have sensors or stems constructed of glass, *except that thermometers with glass sensors or stems that are encased in a shatterproof coating such as candy thermometers may be used.* [P]

Cleanability

4-202.11   Food-Contact Surfaces.

(A) Multiuse FOOD-CONTACT SURFACES shall be:

   (1) SMOOTH; [Pf]

   (2) Free of breaks, open seams, cracks, chips, inclusions, pits, and similar imperfections; [Pf]

   (3) Free of sharp internal angles, corners, and crevices; [Pf]

   (4) Finished to have SMOOTH welds and joints; [Pf] and

107

(5) Except as specified in ¶ (B) of this section, accessible for cleaning and inspection by one of the following methods:

(a) Without being disassembled, [Pf]

(b) By disassembling without the use of tools, [Pf] or

(c) By easy disassembling with the use of handheld tools commonly available to maintenance and cleaning personnel such as screwdrivers, pliers, open-end wrenches, and Allen wrenches. [Pf]

(B) *Subparagraph (A)(5) of this section does not apply to cooking oil storage tanks, distribution lines for cooking oils, or* BEVERAGE *syrup lines or tubes.*

4-202.12   CIP Equipment.

(A) CIP EQUIPMENT shall meet the characteristics specified under § 4-202.11 and shall be designed and constructed so that:

(1) Cleaning and SANITIZING solutions circulate throughout a fixed system and contact all interior FOOD-CONTACT SURFACES, [Pf] and

(2) The system is self-draining or capable of being completely drained of cleaning and SANITIZING solutions; and

(B) CIP EQUIPMENT that is not designed to be disassembled for cleaning shall be designed with inspection access points to ensure that all interior FOOD-CONTACT SURFACES throughout the fixed system are being effectively cleaned.

4-202.13   "V" Threads, Use Limitation.

Except for hot oil cooking or filtering EQUIPMENT, "V" type threads may not be used on FOOD-CONTACT SURFACES.

4-202.14   Hot Oil Filtering Equipment.

Hot oil filtering EQUIPMENT shall meet the characteristics specified under § 4-202.11 or § 4-202.12 and shall be readily accessible for filter replacement and cleaning of the filter.

4-202.15   Can Openers.

Cutting or piercing parts of can openers shall be readily removable for cleaning and for replacement.

4-202.16   Nonfood-Contact Surfaces.

NonFOOD-CONTACT SURFACES shall be free of unnecessary ledges, projections, and crevices, and designed and constructed to allow easy cleaning and to facilitate maintenance.

4-202.17   Kick Plates, Removable.

Kick plates shall be designed so that the areas behind them are accessible for inspection and cleaning by being:

(A) Removable by one of the methods specified under Subparagraph 4-202.11(A)(5) or capable of being rotated open; and

(B) Removable or capable of being rotated open without unlocking EQUIPMENT doors.

4-202.18   Ventilation Hood Systems, Filters.

Filters or other grease extracting EQUIPMENT shall be designed to be readily removable for cleaning and replacement if not designed to be cleaned in place.

Accuracy   ## 4-203.11   Temperature Measuring Devices, Food.

(A) FOOD TEMPERATURE MEASURING DEVICES that are scaled only in Celsius or dually scaled in Celsius and Fahrenheit shall be accurate to $\pm 1^{\circ}C$ in the intended range of use. [Pf]

(B) FOOD TEMPERATURE MEASURING DEVICES that are scaled only in Fahrenheit shall be accurate to ±2°F in the intended range of use. [Pf]

4-203.12 Temperature Measuring Devices, Ambient Air and Water.

(A) Ambient air and water TEMPERATURE MEASURING DEVICES that are scaled in Celsius or dually scaled in Celsius and Fahrenheit shall be designed to be easily readable and accurate to ±1.5°C in the intended range of use. [Pf]

(B) Ambient air and water TEMPERATURE MEASURING DEVICES that are scaled only in Fahrenheit shall be accurate to ±3°F in the intended range of use. [Pf]

4-203.13 Pressure Measuring Devices, Mechanical Warewashing Equipment.

Pressure measuring devices that display the pressures in the water supply line for the fresh hot water SANITIZING rinse shall have increments of 7 kilopascals (1 pound per square inch) or smaller and shall be accurate to ±14 kilopascals (±2 pounds per square inch) in the range indicated on the manufacturer's data plate.

Functionality

4-204.11 Ventilation Hood Systems, Drip Prevention.

Exhaust ventilation hood systems in FOOD preparation and WAREWASHING areas including components such as hoods, fans, guards, and ducting shall be designed to prevent grease or condensation from draining or dripping onto FOOD, EQUIPMENT, UTENSILS, LINENS, and SINGLE-SERVICE and SINGLE-USE ARTICLES.

4-204.12 Equipment Openings, Closures and Deflectors.

(A) A cover or lid for EQUIPMENT shall overlap the opening and be sloped to drain.

110

(B) An opening located within the top of a unit of EQUIPMENT that is designed for use with a cover or lid shall be flanged upward at least 5 millimeters (two-tenths of an inch).

(C) Except as specified under ¶ (D) of this section, fixed piping, TEMPERATURE MEASURING DEVICES, rotary shafts, and other parts extending into EQUIPMENT shall be provided with a watertight joint at the point where the item enters the EQUIPMENT.

(D) If a watertight joint is not provided:

(1) The piping, TEMPERATURE MEASURING DEVICES, rotary shafts, and other parts extending through the openings shall be equipped with an apron designed to deflect condensation, drips, and dust from openings into the FOOD; and

(2) The opening shall be flanged as specified under ¶ (B) of this section.

4-204.13 Dispensing Equipment, Protection of Equipment and Food.

In EQUIPMENT that dispenses or vends liquid FOOD or ice in unPACKAGED form:

(A) The delivery tube, chute, orifice, and splash surfaces directly above the container receiving the FOOD shall be designed in a manner, such as with barriers, baffles, or drip aprons, so that drips from condensation and splash are diverted from the opening of the container receiving the FOOD;

(B) The delivery tube, chute, and orifice shall be protected from manual contact such as by being recessed;

(C) The delivery tube or chute and orifice of EQUIPMENT used to vend liquid FOOD or ice in unPACKAGED form to self-service CONSUMERS shall be designed so that the delivery tube or chute and orifice are protected from dust, insects, rodents, and other contamination by a self-closing door if the EQUIPMENT is:

(1) Located in an outside area that does not otherwise afford the protection of an enclosure against the rain,

111

windblown debris, insects, rodents, and other contaminants that are present in the environment, or

(2) Available for self-service during hours when it is not under the full-time supervision of a FOOD EMPLOYEE; and

(D) The dispensing EQUIPMENT actuating lever or mechanism and filling device of CONSUMER self-service BEVERAGE dispensing EQUIPMENT shall be designed to prevent contact with the lip-contact surface of glasses or cups that are refilled.

(E) Dispensing EQUIPMENT in which POTENTIALLY HAZARDOUS FOOD (TIME/TEMPERATURE CONTROL FOR SAFETY FOOD) in a homogenous liquid form is maintained outside of the temperature control requirements as specified under §3-501.16(A) shall:

(1) be specifically designed and equipped to maintain the commercial sterility of aseptically PACKAGED FOOD in a homogenous liquid form for a specified duration from the time of opening the PACKAGING within the EQUIPMENT; [P] and

(2) conform to the requirements for this EQUIPMENT as specified in *NSF/ANSI 18-2006- Manual Food and Beverage Dispensing Equipment.* [P]

4-204.14   Vending Machine, Vending Stage Closure.

The dispensing compartment of a VENDING MACHINE including a machine that is designed to vend prePACKAGED snack FOOD that is not POTENTIALLY HAZARDOUS (TIME/TEMPERATURE CONTROL FOR SAFETY FOOD) such as chips, party mixes, and pretzels shall be equipped with a self-closing door or cover if the machine is:

(A) Located in an outside area that does not otherwise afford the protection of an enclosure against the rain, windblown debris, insects, rodents, and other contaminants that are present in the environment; or

(B) Available for self-service during hours when it is not under the full-time supervision of a FOOD EMPLOYEE.

4-204.15   Bearings and Gear Boxes, Leakproof.

EQUIPMENT containing bearings and gears that require lubricants shall be designed and constructed so that the lubricant cannot leak, drip, or be forced into FOOD or onto FOOD-CONTACT SURFACES.

4-204.16   Beverage Tubing, Separation.

Except for cold plates that are constructed integrally with an ice storage bin, BEVERAGE tubing and cold-plate BEVERAGE cooling devices may not be installed in contact with stored ice.

4-204.17   Ice Units, Separation of Drains.

Liquid waste drain lines may not pass through an ice machine or ice storage bin.

4-204.18   Condenser Unit, Separation.

If a condenser unit is an integral component of EQUIPMENT, the condenser unit shall be separated from the FOOD and FOOD storage space by a dustproof barrier.

4-204.19   Can Openers on Vending Machines.

Cutting or piercing parts of can openers on VENDING MACHINES shall be protected from manual contact, dust, insects, rodents, and other contamination.

4-204.110   Molluscan Shellfish Tanks.

(A) Except as specified under ¶ (B) of this section, MOLLUSCAN SHELLFISH life support system display tanks may not be used to store or display shellfish that are offered for human consumption and shall be conspicuously marked so that it is obvious to the CONSUMER that the shellfish are for display only.[P]

(B) MOLLUSCAN SHELLFISH life-support system display tanks that are used to store or display shellfish that are offered for human consumption shall be operated and maintained in accordance with a VARIANCE granted by the REGULATORY AUTHORITY as specified in § 8-103.10 and a HACCP PLAN that: [Pf]

(1) Is submitted by the PERMIT HOLDER and APPROVED as specified under § 8-103.11; [Pf] and

(2) Ensures that:

(a) Water used with FISH other than MOLLUSCAN SHELLFISH does not flow into the molluscan tank, [Pf]

(b) The safety and quality of the shellfish as they were received are not compromised by the use of the tank, [Pf] and

(c) The identity of the source of the SHELLSTOCK is retained as specified under § 3-203.12. [Pf]

4-204.111   Vending Machines, Automatic Shutoff.

(A) A machine vending POTENTIALLY HAZARDOUS FOOD (TIME/TEMPERATURE CONTROL FOR SAFETY FOOD) shall have an automatic control that prevents the machine from vending FOOD:

(1) If there is a power failure, mechanical failure, or other condition that results in an internal machine temperature that cannot maintain FOOD temperatures as specified under Chapter 3; [P] and

(2) If a condition specified under Subparagraph (A)(1) of this section occurs, until the machine is serviced and restocked with FOOD that has been maintained at temperatures specified under Chapter 3. [P]

(B) When the automatic shutoff within a machine vending POTENTIALLY HAZARDOUS FOOD (TIME/TEMPERATURE CONTROL FOR SAFETY FOOD) is activated:

(1) In a refrigerated vending machine, the ambient air temperature may not exceed 5°C (41°F) for more than 30 minutes immediately after the machine is filled, serviced, or restocked; [P] or

(2) In a hot holding vending machine, the ambient air temperature may not be less than 57 °C (135 °F) for more than 120 minutes immediately after the machine is filled, serviced, or restocked. [P]

4-204.112   Temperature Measuring Devices.

(A) In a mechanically refrigerated or hot FOOD storage unit, the sensor of a TEMPERATURE MEASURING DEVICE shall be located to measure the air temperature or a simulated product temperature in the warmest part of a mechanically refrigerated unit and in the coolest part of a hot FOOD storage unit.

(B) Except as specified in ¶ (C) of this section, cold or hot holding EQUIPMENT used for POTENTIALLY HAZARDOUS FOOD (TIME/TEMPERATURE CONTROL FOR SAFETY FOOD) shall be designed to include and shall be equipped with at least one integral or permanently affixed TEMPERATURE MEASURING DEVICE that is located to allow easy viewing of the device's temperature display.

(C) *Paragraph (B) of this section does not apply to EQUIPMENT for which the placement of a TEMPERATURE MEASURING DEVICE is not a practical means for measuring the ambient air surrounding the FOOD because of the design, type, and use of the EQUIPMENT, such as calrod units, heat lamps, cold plates, bainmaries, steam tables, insulated FOOD transport containers, and salad bars.*

(D) TEMPERATURE MEASURING DEVICES shall be designed to be easily readable.

(E) FOOD TEMPERATURE MEASURING DEVICES and water TEMPERATURE MEASURING DEVICES on WAREWASHING machines shall have a numerical scale, printed record, or digital readout in increments no greater than 1°C or 2°F in the intended range of use. [Pf]

4-204.113   Warewashing Machine, Data Plate Operating Specifications.

A WAREWASHING machine shall be provided with an easily accessible and readable data plate affixed to the machine by the manufacturer that indicates the machine's design and operation specifications including the:

(A) Temperatures required for washing, rinsing, and SANITIZING;

(B) Pressure required for the fresh water SANITIZING rinse *unless the machine is designed to use only a pumped SANITIZING rinse;* and

(C) Conveyor speed for conveyor machines or cycle time for stationary rack machines.

4-204.114   Warewashing Machines, Internal Baffles.

WAREWASHING machine wash and rinse tanks shall be equipped with baffles, curtains, or other means to minimize internal cross contamination of the solutions in wash and rinse tanks.

4-204.115   Warewashing Machines, Temperature Measuring Devices.

A WAREWASHING machine shall be equipped with a TEMPERATURE MEASURING DEVICE that indicates the temperature of the water:

(A) In each wash and rinse tank; [Pf] and

(B) As the water enters the hot water SANITIZING final rinse manifold or in the chemical SANITIZING solution tank. [Pf]

4-204.116   Manual Warewashing Equipment, Heaters and Baskets.

If hot water is used for SANITIZATION in manual WAREWASHING operations, the SANITIZING compartment of the sink shall be:

(A) Designed with an integral heating device that is capable of maintaining water at a temperature not less than 77°C (171°F); [Pf] and

(B) Provided with a rack or basket to allow complete immersion of equipment and utensils into the hot water. [Pf]

4-204.117   Warewashing Machines, Automatic Dispensing of Detergents and Sanitizers.

A WAREWASHING machine that is installed after adoption of this Code by the REGULATORY AUTHORITY, shall be equipped to:

(A) Automatically dispense detergents and SANITIZERS; [Pf] and

(B) Incorporate a visual means to verify that detergents and SANITIZERS are delivered or a visual or audible alarm to signal if the detergents and SANITIZERS are not delivered to the respective washing and SANITIZING cycles. [Pf]

4-204.118   Warewashing Machines, Flow Pressure Device.

(A) WAREWASHING machines that provide a fresh hot water SANITIZING rinse shall be equipped with a pressure gauge or similar device such as a transducer that measures and displays the water pressure in the supply line immediately before entering the WAREWASHING machine; and

(B) If the flow pressure measuring device is upstream of the fresh hot water SANITIZING rinse control valve, the device shall be mounted in a 6.4 millimeter or one-fourth inch Iron Pipe Size (IPS) valve.

(C) *Paragraphs (A) and (B) of this section do not apply to a machine that uses only a pumped or recirculated SANITIZING rinse.*

4-204.119 Warewashing Sinks and Drainboards, Self-Draining.

Sinks and drainboards of WAREWASHING sinks and machines shall be self-draining.

4-204.120 Equipment Compartments, Drainage.

EQUIPMENT compartments that are subject to accumulation of moisture due to conditions such as condensation, FOOD or BEVERAGE drip, or water from melting ice shall be sloped to an outlet that allows complete draining.

4-204.121 Vending Machines, Liquid Waste Products.

(A) VENDING MACHINES designed to store BEVERAGES that are PACKAGED in containers made from paper products shall be equipped with diversion devices and retention pans or drains for container leakage.

(B) VENDING MACHINES that dispense liquid FOOD in bulk shall be:

  (1) Provided with an internally mounted waste receptacle for the collection of drip, spillage, overflow, or other internal wastes; and

  (2) Equipped with an automatic shutoff device that will place the machine out of operation before the waste receptacle overflows.

(C) Shutoff devices specified under Subparagraph (B)(2) of this section shall prevent water or liquid FOOD from continuously running if there is a failure of a flow control device in the water or liquid FOOD system or waste accumulation that could lead to overflow of the waste receptacle.

4-204.122 Case Lot Handling Apparatuses, Moveability.

Apparatuses, such as dollies, pallets, racks, and skids used to store and transport large quantities of PACKAGED FOODS received from a supplier in a cased or overwrapped lot, shall be designed to be moved by hand or by conveniently available apparatuses such as hand trucks and forklifts.

4-204.123   Vending Machine Doors and Openings.

(A) VENDING MACHINE doors and access opening covers to FOOD and container storage spaces shall be tight-fitting so that the space along the entire interface between the doors or covers and the cabinet of the machine, if the doors or covers are in a closed position, is no greater than 1.5 millimeters or one-sixteenth inch by:

> (1) Being covered with louvers, screens, or materials that provide an equivalent opening of not greater than 1.5 millimeters or one-sixteenth inch. Screening of 12 or more mesh to 2.5 centimeters (12 mesh to 1 inch) meets this requirement;

> (2) Being effectively gasketed;

> (3) Having interface surfaces that are at least 13 millimeters or one-half inch wide; or

> (4) Jambs or surfaces used to form an L-shaped entry path to the interface.

(B) VENDING MACHINE service connection openings through an exterior wall of a machine shall be closed by sealants, clamps, or grommets so that the openings are no larger than 1.5 millimeters or one-sixteenth inch.

Acceptability   **4-205.10   Food Equipment, Certification and Classification.**

FOOD EQUIPMENT that is certified or classified for sanitation by an American National Standards Institute (ANSI)-accredited certification program is deemed to comply with Parts 4-1 and 4-2 of this chapter.

Subparts

Equipment   **4-301.11   Cooling, Heating, and Holding Capacities.**

EQUIPMENT for cooling and heating FOOD, and holding cold and hot FOOD, shall be sufficient in number and capacity to provide FOOD temperatures as specified under Chapter 3. [Pf]

4-301.12   Manual Warewashing, Sink Compartment Requirements.

(A) Except as specified in ¶ (C) of this section, a sink with at least 3 compartments shall be provided for manually washing, rinsing, and SANITIZING EQUIPMENT and UTENSILS. [Pf]

(B) Sink compartments shall be large enough to accommodate immersion of the largest EQUIPMENT and UTENSILS. If EQUIPMENT or UTENSILS are too large for the WAREWASHING sink, a WAREWASHING machine or alternative EQUIPMENT as specified in ¶ (C) of this section shall be used. [Pf]

(C) *Alternative manual WAREWASHING EQUIPMENT may be used when there are special cleaning needs or constraints and its use is APPROVED. Alternative manual WAREWASHING EQUIPMENT may include:*

(1) *High-pressure detergent sprayers;*

(2) *Low- or line-pressure spray detergent foamers;*

(3) *Other task-specific cleaning EQUIPMENT;*

(4) *Brushes or other implements;*

(5) *2-compartment sinks as specified under ¶¶ (D) and (E) of this section; or*

(6) *Receptacles that substitute for the compartments of a multicompartment sink.*

(D) Before a 2-compartment sink is used:

(1) The PERMIT HOLDER shall have its use APPROVED; and

(2) The PERMIT HOLDER shall limit the number of KITCHENWARE items cleaned and SANITIZED in the 2-compartment sink, and shall limit WAREWASHING to batch operations for cleaning KITCHENWARE such as between cutting one type of raw MEAT and another or cleanup at the end of a shift, and shall:

(a) Make up the cleaning and SANITIZING solutions immediately before use and drain them immediately after use, and

(b) Use a detergent-SANITIZER to SANITIZE and apply the detergent-SANITIZER in accordance with the manufacturer's label instructions and as specified under § 4-501.115, or

(c) Use a hot water SANITIZATION immersion step as specified under ¶ 4-603.16(C).

(E) A 2-compartment sink may not be used for WAREWASHING operations where cleaning and SANITIZING solutions are used for a continuous or intermittent flow of KITCHENWARE or TABLEWARE in an ongoing WAREWASHING process.

4-301.13   Drainboards.

Drainboards, UTENSIL racks, or tables large enough to accommodate all soiled and cleaned items that may accumulate during hours of operation shall be provided for necessary UTENSIL holding before cleaning and after SANITIZING.

4-301.14   Ventilation Hood Systems, Adequacy.

Ventilation hood systems and devices shall be sufficient in number and capacity to prevent grease or condensation from collecting on walls and ceilings.

4-301.15   Clothes Washers and Dryers.

(A) Except as specified in ¶ (B) of this section, if work clothes or LINENS are laundered on the PREMISES, a mechanical clothes washer and dryer shall be provided and used.

(B) *If on-PREMISES laundering is limited to wiping cloths intended to be used moist, or wiping cloths are air-dried as specified under § 4-901.12, a mechanical clothes washer and dryer need not be provided.*

Utensils, Temperature Measuring Devices, and Testing Devices

4-302.11   Utensils, Consumer Self-Service.

A FOOD dispensing UTENSIL shall be available for each container displayed at a CONSUMER self-service unit such as a buffet or salad bar. [Pf]

4-302.12   Food Temperature Measuring Devices.

(A) FOOD TEMPERATURE MEASURING DEVICES shall be provided and readily accessible for use in ensuring attainment and maintenance of FOOD temperatures as specified under Chapter 3. [Pf]

(B) A TEMPERATURE MEASURING DEVICE with a suitable small-diameter probe that is designed to measure the temperature of thin masses shall be provided and readily accessible to accurately measure the temperature in thin FOODS such as MEAT patties and FISH filets. [Pf]

4-302.13   Temperature Measuring Devices, Manual Warewashing.

In manual WAREWASHING operations, a TEMPERATURE MEASURING DEVICE shall be provided and readily accessible for frequently measuring the washing and SANITIZING temperatures.

4-302.14   Sanitizing Solutions, Testing Devices.

A test kit or other device that accurately measures the concentration in MG/L of SANITIZING solutions shall be provided.[Pf]

4-4	**LOCATION AND INSTALLATION**

Subparts

4-401	**Location**
4-402	**Installation**

Location   **4-401.11   Equipment, Clothes Washers and Dryers, and Storage Cabinets, Contamination Prevention.**

(A) Except as specified in ¶ (B) of this section, EQUIPMENT, a cabinet used for the storage of FOOD, or a cabinet that is used to store cleaned and SANITIZED EQUIPMENT, UTENSILS, laundered LINENS, and SINGLE-SERVICE and SINGLE-USE ARTICLES may not be located:

(1) In locker rooms;

(2) In toilet rooms;

(3) In garbage rooms;

(4) In mechanical rooms;

(5) Under sewer lines that are not shielded to intercept potential drips;

(6) Under leaking water lines including leaking automatic fire sprinkler heads or under lines on which water has condensed;

(7) Under open stairwells; or

(8) Under other sources of contamination.

(B) *A storage cabinet used for LINENS or SINGLE-SERVICE or SINGLE-USE ARTICLES may be stored in a locker room.*

123

(C) If a mechanical clothes washer or dryer is provided, it shall be located so that the washer or dryer is protected from contamination and only where there is no exposed FOOD; clean EQUIPMENT, UTENSILS, and LINENS; and unwrapped SINGLE-SERVICE and SINGLE-USE ARTICLES.

Installation

4-402.11   Fixed Equipment, Spacing or Sealing.

(A) EQUIPMENT that is fixed because it is not EASILY MOVABLE shall be installed so that it is:

(1) Spaced to allow access for cleaning along the sides, behind, and above the EQUIPMENT;

(2) Spaced from adjoining EQUIPMENT, walls, and ceilings a distance of not more than 1 millimeter or one thirty-second inch; or

(3) SEALED to adjoining EQUIPMENT or walls, if the EQUIPMENT is exposed to spillage or seepage.

(B) COUNTER-MOUNTED EQUIPMENT that is not EASILY MOVABLE shall be installed to allow cleaning of the EQUIPMENT and areas underneath and around the EQUIPMENT by being:

(1) SEALED; or

(2) Elevated on legs as specified under ¶ 4-402.12(D).

4-402.12   Fixed Equipment, Elevation or Sealing.

(A) Except as specified in ¶¶ (B) and (C) of this section, floor-mounted EQUIPMENT that is not EASILY MOVABLE shall be SEALED to the floor or elevated on legs that provide at least a 15 centimeter (6 inch) clearance between the floor and the EQUIPMENT.

(B) *If no part of the floor under the floor-mounted EQUIPMENT is more than 15 centimeters (6 inches) from the point of cleaning access, the clearance space may be only 10 centimeters (4 inches).*

(C) *This section does not apply to display shelving units, display refrigeration units, and display freezer units located in the CONSUMER shopping areas of a retail FOOD store, if the floor under the units is maintained clean.*

(D) Except as specified in ¶ (E) of this section, COUNTER-MOUNTED EQUIPMENT that is not EASILY MOVABLE shall be elevated on legs that provide at least a 10 centimeter (4 inch) clearance between the table and the EQUIPMENT.

(E) *The clearance space between the table and COUNTER-MOUNTED EQUIPMENT may be:*

   (1) *7.5 centimeters (3 inches) if the horizontal distance of the table top under the EQUIPMENT is no more than 50 centimeters (20 inches) from the point of access for cleaning; or*

   (2) *5 centimeters (2 inches) if the horizontal distance of the table top under the EQUIPMENT is no more than 7.5 centimeters (3 inches) from the point of access for cleaning*

4-5   MAINTENANCE AND OPERATION

Subparts

4-501	**Equipment**
4-502	**Utensils and Temperature and Pressure Measuring Devices**

Equipment

4-501.11   Good Repair and Proper Adjustment.

(A) EQUIPMENT shall be maintained in a state of repair and condition that meets the requirements specified under Parts 4-1 and 4-2.

(B) EQUIPMENT components such as doors, seals, hinges, fasteners, and kick plates shall be kept intact, tight, and adjusted in accordance with manufacturer's specifications.

(C) Cutting or piercing parts of can openers shall be kept sharp to minimize the creation of metal fragments that can contaminate FOOD when the container is opened.

125

4-501.12 Cutting Surfaces.

Surfaces such as cutting blocks and boards that are subject to scratching and scoring shall be resurfaced if they can no longer be effectively cleaned and SANITIZED, or discarded if they are not capable of being resurfaced.

4-501.13 Microwave Ovens.

Microwave ovens shall meet the safety standards specified in 21 CFR 1030.10 Microwave ovens.

4-501.14 Warewashing Equipment, Cleaning Frequency.

A WAREWASHING machine; the compartments of sinks, basins, or other receptacles used for washing and rinsing EQUIPMENT, UTENSILS, or raw FOODS, or laundering wiping cloths; and drainboards or other EQUIPMENT used to substitute for drainboards as specified under § 4-301.13 shall be cleaned:

  (A) Before use;

  (B) Throughout the day at a frequency necessary to prevent recontamination of EQUIPMENT and UTENSILS and to ensure that the EQUIPMENT performs its intended function; and

  (C) If used, at least every 24 hours.

4-501.15 Warewashing Machines, Manufacturers' Operating Instructions.

(A) A WAREWASHING machine and its auxiliary components shall be operated in accordance with the machine's data plate and other manufacturer's instructions.

(B) A WAREWASHING machine's conveyor speed or automatic cycle times shall be maintained accurately timed in accordance with manufacturer's specifications.

4-501.16   Warewashing Sinks, Use Limitation.

(A) A WAREWASHING sink may not be used for handwashing as specified under § 2-301.15.

(B) If a WAREWASHING sink is used to wash wiping cloths, wash produce, or thaw FOOD, the sink shall be cleaned as specified under § 4-501.14 before and after each time it is used to wash wiping cloths or wash produce or thaw FOOD. Sinks used to wash or thaw FOOD shall be SANITIZED as specified under Part 4-7 before and after using the sink to wash produce or thaw FOOD.

4-501.17   Warewashing Equipment, Cleaning Agents.

When used for WAREWASHING, the wash compartment of a sink, mechanical warewasher, or wash receptacle of alternative manual WAREWASHING EQUIPMENT as specified in ¶ 4-301.12(C), shall contain a wash solution of soap, detergent, acid cleaner, alkaline cleaner, degreaser, abrasive cleaner, or other cleaning agent according to the cleaning agent manufacturer's label instructions. [Pf]

4-501.18   Warewashing Equipment, Clean Solutions.

The wash, rinse, and SANITIZE solutions shall be maintained clean.

4-501.19   Manual Warewashing Equipment, Wash Solution Temperature.

The temperature of the wash solution in manual WAREWASHING EQUIPMENT shall be maintained at not less than 43°C (110°F) or the temperature specified on the cleaning agent manufacturer's label instructions. [Pf]

4-501.110   Mechanical Warewashing Equipment, Wash Solution Temperature.

(A) The temperature of the wash solution in spray type warewashers that use hot water to SANITIZE may not be less than:

(1) For a stationary rack, single temperature machine, 74°C (165°F); Pf

(2) For a stationary rack, dual temperature machine, 66°C (150°F); Pf

(3) For a single tank, conveyor, dual temperature machine, 71°C (160°F); Pf or

(4) For a multitank, conveyor, multitemperature machine, 66°C (150°F). Pf

(B) The temperature of the wash solution in spray-type warewashers that use chemicals to SANITIZE may not be less than 49°C (120°F). Pf

4-501.111   Manual Warewashing Equipment, Hot Water Sanitization Temperatures.

If immersion in hot water is used for SANITIZING in a manual operation, the temperature of the water shall be maintained at 77°C (171°F) or above. P

4-501.112   Mechanical Warewashing Equipment, Hot Water Sanitization Temperatures.

(A) Except as specified in ¶ (B) of this section, in a mechanical operation, the temperature of the fresh hot water SANITIZING rinse as it enters the manifold may not be more than 90°C (194°F), or less than: Pf

(1) For a stationary rack, single temperature machine, 74°C (165°F); Pf or

(2) For all other machines, 82°C (180°F). Pf

(B) *The maximum temperature specified under ¶ (A) of this section, does not apply to the high pressure and temperature systems with wand-type, hand-held, spraying devices used for the in-place cleaning and SANITIZING of EQUIPMENT such as meat saws.*

4-501.113   Mechanical Warewashing Equipment, Sanitization Pressure.

The flow pressure of the fresh hot water SANITIZING rinse in a WAREWASHING machine, as measured in the water line immediately downstream or upstream from the fresh hot water SANITIZING rinse control value, shall be within the range specified on the machine manufacturer's data plate and may not be less than 35 kilopascals (5 pounds per square inch) or more than 200 kilopascals (30 pounds per square inch).

4-501.114   Manual and Mechanical Warewashing Equipment, Chemical Sanitization - Temperature, pH, Concentration, and Hardness.

A chemical SANITIZER used in a SANITIZING solution for a manual or mechanical operation at contact times specified under ¶ 4-703.11(C) shall meet the criteria specified under § 7-204.11 Sanitizers, Criteria, shall be used in accordance with the EPA-registered label use instructions, and shall be used as follows [P]:

(A) A chlorine solution shall have a minimum temperature based on the concentration and pH of the solution as listed in the following chart; [P]

Concentration Range	Minimum Temperature	
MG/L	pH 10 or less °C (°F)	pH 8 or less °C (°F)
25 – 49	49 (120)	49 (120)
50 – 99	38 (100)	24 (75)
100	13 (55)	13 (55)

(B) An iodine solution shall have a:

(1) Minimum temperature of 20°C (68°F), [P]

(2) PH of 5.0 or less or a PH no higher than the level for which the manufacturer specifies the solution is effective, [P] and

(3) Concentration between 12.5 MG/L and 25 MG/L; [P]

(C) A quaternary ammonium compound solution shall:

(1) Have a minimum temperature of 24°C (75°F), [P]

(2) Have a concentration as specified under § 7-204.11 and as indicated by the manufacturer's use directions included in the labeling, [P] and

(3) Be used only in water with 500 MG/L hardness or less or in water having a hardness no greater than specified by the EPA-registered label use instructions; [P]

(D) If another solution of a chemical specified under ¶¶ (A) - (C) of this section is used, the PERMIT HOLDER shall demonstrate to the REGULATORY AUTHORITY that the solution achieves SANITIZATION and the use of the solution shall be APPROVED; [P] or

(E) If a chemical SANITIZER other than chlorine, iodine, or a quaternary ammonium compound is used, it shall be applied in accordance with the EPA-registered label use instructions. [P]

4-501.115   Manual Warewashing Equipment, Chemical Sanitization Using Detergent-Sanitizers.

If a detergent-SANITIZER is used to SANITIZE in a cleaning and SANITIZING procedure where there is no distinct water rinse between the washing and SANITIZING steps, the agent applied in the SANITIZING step shall be the same detergent-SANITIZER that is used in the washing step.

4-501.116   Warewashing Equipment, Determining Chemical Sanitizer Concentration.

Concentration of the SANITIZING solution shall be accurately determined by using a test kit or other device. [Pf]

130

Utensils and
Temperature
and Pressure
Measuring
Devices

4-502.11   Good Repair and Calibration.

(A) UTENSILS shall be maintained in a state of repair or condition that complies with the requirements specified under Parts 4-1 and 4-2 or shall be discarded.

(B) FOOD TEMPERATURE MEASURING DEVICES shall be calibrated in accordance with manufacturer's specifications as necessary to ensure their accuracy. [Pf]

(C) Ambient air temperature, water pressure, and water TEMPERATURE MEASURING DEVICES shall be maintained in good repair and be accurate within the intended range of use.

4-502.12   Single-Service and Single-Use Articles, Required Use.

A FOOD ESTABLISHMENT without facilities specified under Parts 4-6 and 4-7 for cleaning and SANITIZING KITCHENWARE and TABLEWARE shall provide only SINGLE-USE KITCHENWARE, SINGLE-SERVICE ARTICLES, and SINGLE-USE ARTICLES for use by FOOD EMPLOYEES AND SINGLE-SERVICE ARTICLES for use by CONSUMERS. [P]

4-502.13   Single-Service and Single-Use Articles, Use Limitation.

(A) SINGLE-SERVICE and SINGLE-USE ARTICLES may not be reused.

(B) The bulk milk container dispensing tube shall be cut on the diagonal leaving no more than one inch protruding from the chilled dispensing head.

4-502.14   Shells, Use Limitation.

Mollusk and crustacea shells may not be used more than once as serving containers.

Subparts

4-601	Objective
4-602	Frequency
4-603	Methods

Objective　　　　**4-601.11**　　**Equipment, Food-Contact Surfaces, Nonfood-Contact Surfaces, and Utensils.**

(A) EQUIPMENT FOOD-CONTACT SURFACES and UTENSILS shall be clean to sight and touch. [Pf]

(B) The FOOD-CONTACT SURFACES of cooking EQUIPMENT and pans shall be kept free of encrusted grease deposits and other soil accumulations.

(C) NonFOOD-CONTACT SURFACES of EQUIPMENT shall be kept free of an accumulation of dust, dirt, FOOD residue, and other debris.

Frequency　　　　**4-602.11**　　**Equipment Food-Contact Surfaces and Utensils.**

(A) EQUIPMENT FOOD-CONTACT SURFACES and UTENSILS shall be cleaned:

(1) Except as specified in ¶ (B) of this section, before each use with a different type of raw animal FOOD such as beef, FISH, lamb, pork, or POULTRY; [P]

(2) Each time there is a change from working with raw FOODS to working with READY-TO-EAT FOODS; [P]

(3) Between uses with raw fruits and vegetables and with POTENTIALLY HAZARDOUS FOOD (TIME/TEMPERATURE CONTROL FOR SAFETY FOOD); [P]

(4) Before using or storing a FOOD TEMPERATURE MEASURING DEVICE; [P] and

(5) At any time during the operation when contamination may have occurred. [P]

(B) *Subparagraph (A)(1) of this section does not apply if the* FOOD-CONTACT SURFACE *or* UTENSIL *is in contact with a succession of different raw animal* FOODS *each requiring a higher cooking temperature as specified under § 3-401.11 than the previous* FOOD, *such as preparing raw* FISH *followed by cutting raw poultry on the same cutting board.*

(C) Except as specified in ¶ (D) of this section, if used with POTENTIALLY HAZARDOUS FOOD (TIME/TEMPERATURE CONTROL FOR SAFETY FOOD), EQUIPMENT FOOD-CONTACT SURFACES and UTENSILS shall be cleaned throughout the day at least every 4 hours. [P]

(D) *Surfaces of* UTENSILS *and* EQUIPMENT *contacting* POTENTIALLY HAZARDOUS FOOD (TIME/TEMPERATURE CONTROL FOR SAFETY FOOD) *may be cleaned less frequently than every 4 hours if:*

(1) *In storage, containers of* POTENTIALLY HAZARDOUS FOOD (TIME/TEMPERATURE CONTROL FOR SAFETY FOOD) *and their contents are maintained at temperatures specified under Chapter 3 and the containers are cleaned when they are empty;*

(2) UTENSILS *and* EQUIPMENT *are used to prepare* FOOD *in a refrigerated room or area that is maintained at one of the temperatures in the following chart and:*

(a) *The* UTENSILS *and* EQUIPMENT *are cleaned at the frequency in the following chart that corresponds to the temperature; and*

133

Temperature	Cleaning Frequency
5.0°C (41°F) or less	24 hours
>5.0°C - 7.2°C (>41°F - 45°F)	20 hours
>7.2°C - 10.0°C (>45°F - 50°F)	16 hours
>10.0°C - 12.8°C (>50°F - 55°F)	10 hours

(b) *The cleaning frequency based on the ambient temperature of the refrigerated room or area is documented in the FOOD ESTABLISHMENT.*

(3) *Containers in serving situations such as salad bars, delis, and cafeteria lines hold READY-TO-EAT POTENTIALLY HAZARDOUS FOOD (TIME/TEMPERATURE CONTROL FOR SAFETY FOOD) that is maintained at the temperatures specified under Chapter 3, are intermittently combined with additional supplies of the same FOOD that is at the required temperature, and the containers are cleaned at least every 24 hours;*

(4) *TEMPERATURE MEASURING DEVICES are maintained in contact with FOOD, such as when left in a container of deli FOOD or in a roast, held at temperatures specified under Chapter 3;*

(5) *EQUIPMENT is used for storage of PACKAGED or unPACKAGED FOOD such as a reach-in refrigerator and the EQUIPMENT is cleaned at a frequency necessary to preclude accumulation of soil residues;*

(6) *The cleaning schedule is APPROVED based on consideration of:*

(a) *Characteristics of the EQUIPMENT and its use,*

(b) *The type of FOOD involved,*

134

(c) *The amount of* FOOD *residue accumulation, and*

(d) *The temperature at which the* FOOD *is maintained during the operation and the potential for the rapid and progressive multiplication of pathogenic or toxigenic microorganisms that are capable of causing foodborne disease; or*

(7) In-use UTENSILS *are intermittently stored in a container of water in which the water is maintained at 57ºC (135ºF) or more and the* UTENSILS *and container are cleaned at least every 24 hours or at a frequency necessary to preclude accumulation of soil residues.*

(E) *Except when dry cleaning methods are used as specified under § 4-603.11,* surfaces of UTENSILS and EQUIPMENT contacting FOOD that is not POTENTIALLY HAZARDOUS (TIME/TEMPERATURE CONTROL FOR SAFETY FOOD) shall be cleaned:

(1) At any time when contamination may have occurred;

(2) At least every 24 hours for iced tea dispensers and CONSUMER self-service UTENSILS such as tongs, scoops, or ladles;

(3) Before restocking CONSUMER self-service EQUIPMENT and UTENSILS such as condiment dispensers and display containers; and

(4) In EQUIPMENT such as ice bins and BEVERAGE dispensing nozzles and enclosed components of EQUIPMENT such as ice makers, cooking oil storage tanks and distribution lines, BEVERAGE and syrup dispensing lines or tubes, coffee bean grinders, and water vending EQUIPMENT:

(a) At a frequency specified by the manufacturer, or

(b) Absent manufacturer specifications, at a frequency necessary to preclude accumulation of soil or mold.

4-602.12   Cooking and Baking Equipment.

(A) The FOOD-CONTACT SURFACES of cooking and baking EQUIPMENT shall be cleaned at least every 24 hours. *This section does not apply to hot oil cooking and filtering EQUIPMENT if it is cleaned as specified in Subparagraph 4-602.11(D)(6).*

(B) The cavities and door seals of microwave ovens shall be cleaned at least every 24 hours by using the manufacturer's recommended cleaning procedure.

4-602.13   Nonfood-Contact Surfaces.

NonFOOD-CONTACT SURFACES of EQUIPMENT shall be cleaned at a frequency necessary to preclude accumulation of soil residues.

Methods

4-603.11   Dry Cleaning.

(A) If used, dry cleaning methods such as brushing, scraping, and vacuuming shall contact only SURFACES that are soiled with dry FOOD residues that are not POTENTIALLY HAZARDOUS (TIME/TEMPERATURE CONTROL FOR SAFETY FOOD).

(B) Cleaning EQUIPMENT used in dry cleaning FOOD-CONTACT SURFACES may not be used for any other purpose.

4-603.12   Precleaning.

(A) FOOD debris on EQUIPMENT and UTENSILS shall be scrapped over a waste disposal unit or garbage receptacle or shall be removed in a WAREWASHING machine with a prewash cycle.

(B) If necessary for effective cleaning, UTENSILS and EQUIPMENT shall be preflushed, presoaked, or scrubbed with abrasives.

4-603.13   Loading of Soiled Items, Warewashing Machines.

Soiled items to be cleaned in a WAREWASHING machine shall be loaded into racks, trays, or baskets or onto conveyors in a position that:

(A) Exposes the items to the unobstructed spray from all cycles; and

(B) Allows the items to drain.

4-603.14   Wet Cleaning.

(A) EQUIPMENT FOOD-CONTACT SURFACES and UTENSILS shall be effectively washed to remove or completely loosen soils by using the manual or mechanical means necessary such as the application of detergents containing wetting agents and emulsifiers; acid, alkaline, or abrasive cleaners; hot water; brushes; scouring pads; high-pressure sprays; or ultrasonic devices.

(B) The washing procedures selected shall be based on the type and purpose of the EQUIPMENT or UTENSIL, and on the type of soil to be removed.

4-603.15   Washing, Procedures for Alternative Manual Warewashing Equipment.

If washing in sink compartments or a WAREWASHING machine is impractical such as when the EQUIPMENT is fixed or the UTENSILS are too large, washing shall be done by using alternative manual WAREWASHING EQUIPMENT as specified in ¶ 4-301.12(C) in accordance with the following procedures:

(A) EQUIPMENT shall be disassembled as necessary to allow access of the detergent solution to all parts;

(B) EQUIPMENT components and UTENSILS shall be scrapped or rough cleaned to remove FOOD particle accumulation; and

(C) EQUIPMENT and UTENSILS shall be washed as specified under ¶ 4-603.14(A).

4-603.16   Rinsing Procedures.

Washed UTENSILS and EQUIPMENT shall be rinsed so that abrasives are removed and cleaning chemicals are removed or diluted through the use of water or a detergent-sanitizer solution by using one of the following procedures:

(A) Use of a distinct, separate water rinse after washing and before SANITIZING if using:

(1) A 3-compartment sink,

(2) Alternative manual WAREWASHING EQUIPMENT equivalent to a 3-compartment sink as specified in ¶ 4-301.12(C), or

(3) A 3-step washing, rinsing, and SANITIZING procedure in a WAREWASHING system for CIP EQUIPMENT;

(B) Use of a detergent-SANITIZER as specified under § 4-501.115 if using:

(1) Alternative WAREWASHING EQUIPMENT as specified in ¶ 4-301.12(C) that is APPROVED for use with a detergent-SANITIZER, or

(2) A WAREWASHING system for CIP EQUIPMENT;

(C) Use of a nondistinct water rinse that is integrated in the hot water SANITIZATION immersion step of a 2-compartment sink operation;

(D) If using a WAREWASHING machine that does not recycle the SANITIZING solution as specified under ¶ (E) of this section, or alternative manual WAREWASHING EQUIPMENT such as sprayers, use of a nondistinct water rinse that is:

(1) Integrated in the application of the SANITIZING solution, and

(2) Wasted immediately after each application; or

(E) If using a WAREWASHING machine that recycles the SANITIZING solution for use in the next wash cycle, use of a nondistinct water rinse that is integrated in the application of the SANITIZING solution.

138

4-603.17   Returnables, Cleaning for Refilling.

(A) Except as specified in ¶¶ (B) and (C) of this section, returned empty containers intended for cleaning and refilling with FOOD shall be cleaned and refilled in a regulated FOOD PROCESSING PLANT. ^P

(B) *A FOOD-specific container for BEVERAGES may be refilled at a FOOD ESTABLISHMENT if:*

> (1) *Only a BEVERAGE that is not a POTENTIALLY HAZARDOUS FOOD (TIME/TEMPERATURE CONTROL FOR SAFETY FOOD) is used as specified under ¶ 3-304.17(A);*

> (2) *The design of the container and of the rinsing EQUIPMENT and the nature of the BEVERAGE, when considered together, allow effective cleaning at home or in the FOOD ESTABLISHMENT;*

> (3) *Facilities for rinsing before refilling returned containers with fresh, hot water that is under pressure and not recirculated are provided as part of the dispensing system;*

> (4) *The CONSUMER-owned container returned to the FOOD ESTABLISHMENT for refilling is refilled for sale or service only to the same CONSUMER; and*

> (5) *The container is refilled by:*

>> (a) *An EMPLOYEE of the FOOD ESTABLISHMENT, or*

>> (b) *The owner of the container if the BEVERAGE system includes a contamination-free transfer process that cannot be bypassed by the container owner.*

(C) *CONSUMER-owned containers that are not FOOD-specific may be filled at a water VENDING MACHINE or system.*

4-7	SANITIZATION OF EQUIPMENT AND UTENSILS

Subparts

4-701	Objective
4-702	Frequency
4-703	Methods

Objective

4-701.10   Food-Contact Surfaces and Utensils.

EQUIPMENT FOOD-CONTACT SURFACES and UTENSILS shall be SANITIZED.

Frequency

4-702.11   Before Use After Cleaning.

UTENSILS and FOOD-CONTACT SURFACES of EQUIPMENT shall be SANITIZED before use after cleaning. [P]

Methods

4-703.11   Hot Water and Chemical.

After being cleaned, EQUIPMENT FOOD-CONTACT SURFACES and UTENSILS shall be SANITIZED in:

(A) Hot water manual operations by immersion for at least 30 seconds and as specified under § 4-501.111; [P]

(B) Hot water mechanical operations by being cycled through EQUIPMENT that is set up as specified under §§ 4-501.15, 4-501.112, and 4-501.113 and achieving a UTENSIL surface temperature of 71°C (160°F) as measured by an irreversible registering temperature indicator; [P] or

(C) Chemical manual or mechanical operations, including the application of SANITIZING chemicals by immersion, manual swabbing, brushing, or pressure spraying methods, using a solution as specified under § 4-501.114. Contact times shall be consistent with those on EPA-registered label use instructions by providing:

(1) Except as specified under Subparagraph (C)(2) of this section, a contact time of at least 10 seconds for a chlorine solution specified under ¶ 4-501.114(A), [P]

(2) A contact time of at least 7 seconds for a chlorine solution of 50 MG/L that has a PH of 10 or less and a temperature of at least 38°C (100°F) or a PH of 8 or less and a temperature of at least 24°C (75°F), [P]

(3) A contact time of at least 30 seconds for other chemical SANITIZING solutions, [P] or

(4) A contact time used in relationship with a combination of temperature, concentration, and PH that, when evaluated for efficacy, yields SANITIZATION as defined in ¶ 1-201.10(B). [P]

4-8   LAUNDERING

Subparts

4-801	Objective
4-802	Frequency
4-803	Methods

Objective   **4-801.11   Clean Linens.**

Clean LINENS shall be free from FOOD residues and other soiling matter.

Frequency   **4-802.11   Specifications.**

(A) LINENS that do not come in direct contact with FOOD shall be laundered between operations if they become wet, sticky, or visibly soiled.

(B) Cloth gloves used as specified in ¶ 3-304.15(D) shall be laundered before being used with a different type of raw animal FOOD such as beef, FISH, lamb, pork or POULTRY.

(C) LINENS and napkins that are used as specified under § 3-304.13 and cloth napkins shall be laundered between each use.

(D) Wet wiping cloths shall be laundered daily.

141

(E) Dry wiping cloths shall be laundered as necessary to prevent contamination of FOOD and clean serving UTENSILS.

4-803.11   Storage of Soiled Linens.

Soiled LINENS shall be kept in clean, nonabsorbent receptacles or clean, washable laundry bags and stored and transported to prevent contamination of FOOD, clean EQUIPMENT, clean UTENSILS, and SINGLE-SERVICE and SINGLE-USE ARTICLES.

4-803.12   Mechanical Washing.

(A) Except as specified in ¶ (B) of this section, LINENS shall be mechanically washed.

(B) *In FOOD ESTABLISHMENTS in which only wiping cloths are laundered as specified in ¶ 4-301.15(B), the wiping cloths may be laundered in a mechanical washer, sink designated only for laundering wiping cloths, or a WAREWASHING or FOOD preparation sink that is cleaned as specified under § 4-501.14.*

4-803.13   Use of Laundry Facilities.

(A) Except as specified in ¶ (B) of this section, laundry facilities on the PREMISES of a FOOD ESTABLISHMENT shall be used only for the washing and drying of items used in the operation of the establishment.

(B) *Separate laundry facilities located on the PREMISES for the purpose of general laundering such as for institutions providing boarding and lodging may also be used for laundering FOOD ESTABLISHMENT items.*

4-9   PROTECTION OF CLEAN ITEMS

Subparts

4-901	**Drying**
4-902	**Lubricating and Reassembling**
4-903	**Storing**
4-904	**Preventing Contamination**

Drying

4-901.11   Equipment and Utensils, Air-Drying Required.

After cleaning and SANITIZING, EQUIPMENT and UTENSILS:

(A) Shall be air-dried or used after adequate draining as specified in the first paragraph of 40 CFR 180.940 Tolerance exemptions for active and inert ingredients for use in antimicrobial formulations (food-contact surface SANITIZING solutions), before contact with FOOD; and

(B) May not be cloth dried *except that UTENSILS that have been air-dried may be polished with cloths that are maintained clean and dry.*

4-901.12   Wiping Cloths, Air-Drying Locations.

Wiping cloths laundered in a FOOD ESTABLISHMENT that does not have a mechanical clothes dryer as specified in ¶ 4-301.15(B) shall be air-dried in a location and in a manner that prevents contamination of FOOD, EQUIPMENT, UTENSILS, LINENS, and SINGLE-SERVICE and SINGLE-USE ARTICLES and the wiping cloths. *This section does not apply if wiping cloths are stored after laundering in a SANITIZING solution as specified under § 4-501.114.*

Lubricating and Reassembling

4-902.11   Food-Contact Surfaces.

Lubricants as specified under § 7-205.11 shall be applied to FOOD-CONTACT SURFACES that require lubrication in a manner that does not contaminate FOOD-CONTACT SURFACES.

4-902.12   Equipment.

EQUIPMENT shall be reassembled so that FOOD-CONTACT SURFACES are not contaminated.

Storing

4-903.11   Equipment, Utensils, Linens, and Single-Service and Single-Use Articles.

(A) Except as specified in ¶ (D) of this section, cleaned EQUIPMENT and UTENSILS, laundered LINENS, and SINGLE-SERVICE and SINGLE-USE ARTICLES shall be stored:

  (1) In a clean, dry location;

  (2) Where they are not exposed to splash, dust, or other contamination; and

  (3) At least 15 cm (6 inches) above the floor.

(B) Clean EQUIPMENT and UTENSILS shall be stored as specified under ¶ (A) of this section and shall be stored:

  (1) In a self-draining position that allows air drying; and

  (2) Covered or inverted.

(C) SINGLE-SERVICE and SINGLE-USE ARTICLES shall be stored as specified under ¶ (A) of this section and shall be kept in the original protective PACKAGE or stored by using other means that afford protection from contamination until used.

(D) *Items that are kept in closed PACKAGES may be stored less than 15 cm (6 inches) above the floor on dollies, pallets, racks, and skids that are designed as specified under § 4-204.122.*

4-903.12   Prohibitions.

(A) Except as specified in ¶ (B) of this section, cleaned and SANITIZED EQUIPMENT, UTENSILS, laundered LINENS, and SINGLE-SERVICE and SINGLE-USE ARTICLES may not be stored:

  (1) In locker rooms;

  (2) In toilet rooms;

144

(3) In garbage rooms;

(4) In mechanical rooms;

(5) Under sewer lines that are not shielded to intercept potential drips;

(6) Under leaking water lines including leaking automatic fire sprinkler heads or under lines on which water has condensed;

(7) Under open stairwells; or

(8) Under other sources of contamination.

(B) *Laundered* LINENS *and* SINGLE-SERVICE *and* SINGLE-USE ARTICLES *that are* PACKAGED *or in a facility such as a cabinet may be stored in a locker room.*

Preventing Contamination

4-904.11   Kitchenware and Tableware.

(A) SINGLE-SERVICE and SINGLE-USE ARTICLES and cleaned and SANITIZED UTENSILS shall be handled, displayed, and dispensed so that contamination of FOOD- and lip-contact surfaces is prevented.

(B) Knives, forks, and spoons that are not prewrapped shall be presented so that only the handles are touched by EMPLOYEES and by CONSUMERS if CONSUMER self-service is provided.

(C) Except as specified under ¶ (B) of this section, SINGLE-SERVICE ARTICLES that are intended for FOOD- or lip-contact shall be furnished for CONSUMER self-service with the original individual wrapper intact or from an APPROVED dispenser.

4-904.12   Soiled and Clean Tableware.

Soiled TABLEWARE shall be removed from CONSUMER eating and drinking areas and handled so that clean TABLEWARE is not contaminated.

4-904.13   Preset Tableware.

(A) Except as specified in ¶ (B) of this section, TABLEWARE that is preset shall be protected from contamination by being wrapped, covered, or inverted.

(B) *Preset TABLEWARE may be exposed if:*

> *(1) Unused settings are removed when a CONSUMER is seated; or*

> *(2) Settings not removed when a CONSUMER is seated are cleaned and SANITIZED before further use.*

4-904.14   Rinsing Equipment and Utensils after Cleaning and Sanitizing.

After being cleaned and SANITIZED, EQUIPMENT and UTENSILS shall not be rinsed before air drying or use unless:

(A) The rinse is applied directly from a potable water supply by a warewashing machine that is maintained and operated as specified under Subparts 4-204 and 4-501; and

(B) The rinse is applied only after the EQUIPMENT and UTENSILS have been SANITIZED by the application of hot water or by the application of a chemical SANITIZER solution whose EPA-registered label use instructions call for rinsing off the SANITIZER after it is applied in a commercial WAREWASHING machine.

5 Water, Plumbing, and Waste

Parts

5-1	WATER

Subparts

Source   5-101.11   Approved System.

DRINKING WATER shall be obtained from an APPROVED source that is:

(A) A PUBLIC WATER SYSTEM; [P] or

(B) A nonPUBLIC WATER SYSTEM that is constructed, maintained, and operated according to LAW. [P]

5-101.12   System Flushing and Disinfection.

A DRINKING WATER system shall be flushed and disinfected before being placed in service after construction, repair, or modification and after an emergency situation, such as a flood, that may introduce contaminants to the system. [P]

5-101.13   Bottled Drinking Water.

BOTTLED DRINKING WATER used or sold in a FOOD ESTABLISHMENT shall be obtained from APPROVED sources in accordance with 21 CFR 129 - Processing and Bottling of Bottled DRINKING WATER. [P]

Quality

5-102.11   Standards.

Except as specified under § 5-102.12:

(A) Water from a PUBLIC WATER SYSTEM shall meet 40 CFR 141 - National Primary Drinking Water Regulations and state DRINKING WATER quality standards; [P] and

(B) Water from a nonPUBLIC WATER SYSTEM shall meet state DRINKING WATER quality standards. [P]

5-102.12   Nondrinking Water.

(A) A nonDRINKING WATER supply shall be used only if its use is APPROVED. [P]

(B) NonDRINKING WATER shall be used only for nonculinary purposes such as air conditioning, nonFOOD EQUIPMENT cooling, and fire protection. [P]

5-102.13   Sampling.

Except when used as specified under § 5-102.12, water from a nonPUBLIC WATER SYSTEM shall be sampled and tested at least annually and as required by state water quality regulations. [Pf]

148

5-102.14   Sample Report.

The most recent sample report for the nonPUBLIC WATER SYSTEM shall be retained on file in the FOOD ESTABLISHMENT or the report shall be maintained as specified by state water quality regulations.

Quantity and Availability

5-103.11   Capacity.

(A) The water source and system shall be of sufficient capacity to meet the peak water demands of the FOOD ESTABLISHMENT. [Pf]

(B) Hot water generation and distribution systems shall be sufficient to meet the peak hot water demands throughout the FOOD ESTABLISHMENT. [Pf]

5-103.12   Pressure.

Water under pressure shall be provided to all fixtures, EQUIPMENT, and nonFOOD EQUIPMENT that are required to use water *except that water supplied as specified under ¶¶ 5-104.12(A) and (B) to a TEMPORARY FOOD ESTABLISHMENT or in response to a temporary interruption of a water supply need not be under pressure.* [Pf]

Distribution, Delivery, and Retention

5-104.11   System.

Water shall be received from the source through the use of:

(A) An APPROVED public water main; [Pf] or

(B) One or more of the following that shall be constructed, maintained, and operated according to LAW: [Pf]

(1) Nonpublic water main, water pumps, pipes, hoses, connections, and other appurtenances, [Pf]

(2) Water transport vehicles, [Pf] or

(3) Water containers. [Pf]

149

5-104.12   Alternative Water Supply.

Water meeting the requirements specified under Subparts 5-101, 5-102, and 5-103 shall be made available for a mobile facility, for a TEMPORARY FOOD ESTABLISHMENT without a permanent water supply, and for a FOOD ESTABLISHMENT with a temporary interruption of its water supply through:

(A) A supply of containers of commercially BOTTLED DRINKING WATER; [Pf]

(B) One or more closed portable water containers; [Pf]

(C) An enclosed vehicular water tank; [Pf]

(D) An on-PREMISES water storage tank; [Pf] or

(E) Piping, tubing, or hoses connected to an adjacent APPROVED source. [Pf]

5-2	PLUMBING SYSTEM
Subparts	
5-201	**Materials**
5-202	**Design, Construction, and Installation**
5-203	**Numbers and Capacities**
5-204	**Location and Placement**
5-205	**Operation and Maintenance**

Materials

5-201.11   Approved.

(A) A PLUMBING SYSTEM and hoses conveying water shall be constructed and repaired with APPROVED materials according to LAW. [P]

(B) A water filter shall be made of SAFE MATERIALS. [P]

*Design,
Construction,
and Installation*

5-202.11   Approved System and Cleanable Fixtures.

(A) A PLUMBING SYSTEM shall be designed, constructed, and installed according to LAW. [P]

(B) A PLUMBING FIXTURE such as a HANDWASHING SINK, toilet, or urinal shall be EASILY CLEANABLE.

5-202.12   Handwashing Sink, Installation.

(A) A HANDWASHING SINK shall be equipped to provide water at a temperature of at least 38°C (100°F) through a mixing valve or combination faucet. [Pf]

(B) A steam mixing valve may not be used at a HANDWASHING SINK.

(C) A self-closing, slow-closing, or metering faucet shall provide a flow of water for at least 15 seconds without the need to reactivate the faucet.

(D) An automatic handwashing facility shall be installed in accordance with manufacturer's instructions.

5-202.13   Backflow Prevention, Air Gap.

An air gap between the water supply inlet and the flood level rim of the PLUMBING FIXTURE, EQUIPMENT, or nonFOOD EQUIPMENT shall be at least twice the diameter of the water supply inlet and may not be less than 25 mm (1 inch). [P]

5-202.14   Backflow Prevention Device, Design Standard.

A backflow or backsiphonage prevention device installed on a water supply system shall meet American Society of Sanitary Engineering (A.S.S.E.) standards for construction, installation, maintenance, inspection, and testing for that specific application and type of device. [P]

5-202.15   Conditioning Device, Design.

A water filter, screen, and other water conditioning device installed on water lines shall be designed to facilitate disassembly for periodic servicing and cleaning. A water filter element shall be of the replaceable type.

5-203.11   Handwashing Sinks.

(A) Except as specified in ¶¶ (B) and (C) of this section, at least 1 HANDWASHING SINK, a number of HANDWASHING SINKS necessary for their convenient use by EMPLOYEES in areas specified under § 5-204.11, and not fewer than the number of HANDWASHING SINKS required by LAW shall be provided. [Pf]

(B) *If APPROVED and capable of removing the types of soils encountered in the FOOD operations involved, automatic handwashing facilities may be substituted for HANDWASHING SINKS in a FOOD ESTABLISHMENT that has at least 1 HANDWASHING SINK.*

(C) *If APPROVED, when FOOD exposure is limited and HANDWASHING SINKS are not conveniently available, such as in some mobile or TEMPORARY FOOD ESTABLISHMENTS or at some VENDING MACHINE LOCATIONS, EMPLOYEES may use chemically treated towelettes for handwashing.*

5-203.12   Toilets and Urinals.

At least 1 toilet and not fewer than the toilets required by LAW shall be provided. If authorized by LAW and urinals are substituted for toilets, the substitution shall be done as specified in LAW.

5-203.13   Service Sink.

(A) At least 1 service sink or 1 curbed cleaning facility equipped with a floor drain shall be provided and conveniently located for the cleaning of mops or similar wet floor cleaning tools and for the disposal of mop water and similar liquid waste.

(B) Toilets and urinals may not be used as a service sink for the disposal of mop water and similar liquid waste.

5-203.14   Backflow Prevention Device, When Required.

A PLUMBING SYSTEM shall be installed to preclude backflow of a solid, liquid, or gas contaminant into the water supply system at each point of use at the FOOD ESTABLISHMENT, including on a hose bibb if a hose is attached or on a hose bibb if a hose is not attached and backflow prevention is required by LAW, by:

(A) Providing an air gap as specified under § 5-202.13 [P]; or

(B) Installing an APPROVED backflow prevention device as specified under § 5-202.14. [P]

5-203.15   Backflow Prevention Device, Carbonator.

(A) If not provided with an air gap as specified under § 5-202.13, a dual check valve with an intermediate vent preceded by a screen of not less than 100 mesh to 25.4 mm (100 mesh to 1 inch) shall be installed upstream from a carbonating device and downstream from any copper in the water supply line.

(B) *A dual check valve attached to the carbonator need not be of the vented type if an air gap or vented backflow prevention device has been otherwise provided as specified under ¶ (A) of this section.*

Location and Placement

5-204.11   Handwashing Sinks.

A HANDWASHING SINK shall be located:

(A) To allow convenient use by EMPLOYEES in FOOD preparation, FOOD dispensing, and WAREWASHING areas; [Pf] and

(B) In, or immediately adjacent to, toilet rooms. [Pf]

5-204.12   Backflow Prevention Device, Location.

A backflow prevention device shall be located so that it may be serviced and maintained.

5-204.13   Conditioning Device, Location.

A water filter, screen, and other water conditioning device installed on water lines shall be located to facilitate disassembly for periodic servicing and cleaning.

Operation and Maintenance

5-205.11   Using a Handwashing Sink.

(A) A HANDWASHING SINK shall be maintained so that it is accessible at all times for EMPLOYEE use. [Pf]

153

(B) A HANDWASHING SINK may not be used for purposes other than handwashing. ^{Pf}

(C) An automatic handwashing facility shall be used in accordance with manufacturer's instructions. ^{Pf}

5-205.12   Prohibiting a Cross Connection.

(A) A PERSON may not create a cross connection by connecting a pipe or conduit between the DRINKING WATER system and a nonDRINKING WATER system or a water system of unknown quality.^P

(B) The piping of a nonDRINKING WATER system shall be durably identified so that it is readily distinguishable from piping that carries DRINKING WATER. ^{Pf}

5-205.13   Scheduling Inspection and Service for a Water System Device.

A device such as a water treatment device or backflow preventer shall be scheduled for inspection and service, in accordance with manufacturer's instructions and as necessary to prevent device failure based on local water conditions, and records demonstrating inspection and service shall be maintained by the PERSON IN CHARGE. ^{Pf}

5-205.14   Water Reservoir of Fogging Devices, Cleaning.

(A) A reservoir that is used to supply water to a device such as a produce fogger shall be:

(1) Maintained in accordance with manufacturer's specifications; ^P and

(2) Cleaned in accordance with manufacturer's specifications or according to the procedures specified under ¶ (B) of this section, whichever is more stringent. ^P

(B) Cleaning procedures shall include at least the following steps and shall be conducted at least once a week:

(1) Draining and complete disassembly of the water and aerosol contact parts; ^P

(2) Brush-cleaning the reservoir, aerosol tubing, and discharge nozzles with a suitable detergent solution; [P]

(3) Flushing the complete system with water to remove the detergent solution and particulate accumulation; [P] and

(4) Rinsing by immersing, spraying, or swabbing the reservoir, aerosol tubing, and discharge nozzles with at least 50 MG/L hypochlorite solution. [P]

5-205.15   System Maintained in Good Repair.

A PLUMBING SYSTEM shall be:

(A) Repaired according to LAW; [P] and

(B) Maintained in good repair.

5-3	**MOBILE WATER TANK AND MOBILE FOOD ESTABLISHMENT WATER TANK**
	Subparts
	5-301 **Materials**
	5-302 **Design and Construction**
	5-303 **Numbers and Capacities**
	5-304 **Operation and Maintenance**

Materials

5-301.11   Approved.

Materials that are used in the construction of a mobile water tank, mobile FOOD ESTABLISHMENT water tank, and appurtenances shall be:

(A) Safe; [P]

(B) Durable, CORROSION-RESISTANT, and nonabsorbent; and

(C) Finished to have a SMOOTH, EASILY CLEANABLE surface.

5-302.11   Enclosed System, Sloped to Drain.

A mobile water tank shall be:

(A) Enclosed from the filling inlet to the discharge outlet; and

(B) Sloped to an outlet that allows complete drainage of the tank.

5-302.12   Inspection and Cleaning Port, Protected and Secured.

If a water tank is designed with an access port for inspection and cleaning, the opening shall be in the top of the tank and:

(A) Flanged upward at least 13 mm (one-half inch); and

(B) Equipped with a port cover assembly that is:

(1) Provided with a gasket and a device for securing the cover in place, and

(2) Flanged to overlap the opening and sloped to drain.

5-302.13   "V" Type Threads, Use Limitation.

A fitting with "V" type threads on a water tank inlet or outlet shall be allowed only when a hose is permanently attached.

5-302.14   Tank Vent, Protected.

If provided, a water tank vent shall terminate in a downward direction and shall be covered with:

(A) 16 mesh to 25.4 mm (16 mesh to 1 inch) screen or equivalent when the vent is in a protected area; or

(B) A protective filter when the vent is in an area that is not protected from windblown dirt and debris.

5-302.15   Inlet and Outlet, Sloped to Drain.

(A) A water tank and its inlet and outlet shall be sloped to drain.

(B) A water tank inlet shall be positioned so that it is protected from contaminants such as waste discharge, road dust, oil, or grease.

5-302.16   Hose, Construction and Identification.

A hose used for conveying DRINKING WATER from a water tank shall be:

(A) Safe; [P]

(B) Durable, CORROSION-RESISTANT, and nonaborbent;

(C) Resistant to pitting, chipping, crazing, scratching, scoring, distortion, and decomposition;

(D) Finished with a SMOOTH interior surface; and

(E) Clearly and durably identified as to its use if not permanently attached.

Numbers and Capacities

5-303.11   Filter, Compressed Air.

A filter that does not pass oil or oil vapors shall be installed in the air supply line between the compressor and DRINKING WATER system when compressed air is used to pressurize the water tank system. [P]

5-303.12   Protective Cover or Device.

A cap and keeper chain, closed cabinet, closed storage tube, or other APPROVED protective cover or device shall be provided for a water inlet, outlet, and hose.

5-303.13   Mobile Food Establishment Tank Inlet.

A mobile FOOD ESTABLISHMENT'S water tank inlet shall be:

(A) 19.1 mm (three-fourths inch) in inner diameter or less; and

(B) Provided with a hose connection of a size or type that will prevent its use for any other service.

5-304.11   System Flushing and Sanitization.

A water tank, pump, and hoses shall be flushed and SANITIZED before being placed in service after construction, repair, modification, and periods of nonuse. [P]

5-304.12   Using a Pump and Hoses, Backflow Prevention.

A PERSON shall operate a water tank, pump, and hoses so that backflow and other contamination of the water supply are prevented.

5-304.13   Protecting Inlet, Outlet, and Hose Fitting.

If not in use, a water tank and hose inlet and outlet fitting shall be protected using a cover or device as specified under § 5-303.12.

5-304.14   Tank, Pump, and Hoses, Dedication.

(A) Except as specified in ¶ (B) of this section, a water tank, pump, and hoses used for conveying DRINKING WATER shall be used for no other purpose. [P]

(B) *Water tanks, pumps, and hoses APPROVED for liquid FOODS may be used for conveying DRINKING WATER if they are cleaned and SANITIZED before they are used to convey water.*

5-4	SEWAGE, OTHER LIQUID WASTE, AND RAINWATER

Subparts

5-401	**Mobile Holding Tank**
5-402	**Retention, Drainage, and Delivery**
5-403	**Disposal Facility**

Mobile Holding Tank

5-401.11   Capacity and Drainage.

A SEWAGE holding tank in a mobile FOOD ESTABLISHMENT shall be:

(A) Sized 15 percent larger in capacity than the water supply tank; and

(B) Sloped to a drain that is 25 mm (1 inch) in inner diameter or greater, equipped with a shut-off valve.

Retention, Drainage, and Delivery

design, construction, and installation

5-402.10   Establishment Drainage System.

FOOD ESTABLISHMENT drainage systems, including grease traps, that convey SEWAGE shall be designed and installed as specified under ¶ 5-202.11(A).

5-402.11   Backflow Prevention.

(A) Except as specified in ¶¶ (B), (C), and (D) of this section, a direct connection may not exist between the SEWAGE system and a drain originating from EQUIPMENT in which FOOD, portable EQUIPMENT, or UTENSILS are placed. [P]

(B) *Paragraph (A) of this section does not apply to floor drains that originate in refrigerated spaces that are constructed as an integral part of the building.*

(C) *If allowed by LAW, a WAREWASHING machine may have a direct connection between its waste outlet and a floor drain when the machine is located within 1.5 m (5 feet) of a trapped floor drain and the machine outlet is connected to the inlet side of a properly vented floor drain trap.*

(D) *If allowed by* LAW, *a* WAREWASHING *or culinary sink may have a direct connection.*

location and placement

5-402.12   Grease Trap.

If used, a grease trap shall be located to be easily accessible for cleaning.

operation and maintenance

5-402.13   Conveying Sewage.

SEWAGE shall be conveyed to the point of disposal through an APPROVED sanitary SEWAGE system or other system, including use of SEWAGE transport vehicles, waste retention tanks, pumps, pipes, hoses, and connections that are constructed, maintained, and operated according to LAW.[P]

5-402.14   Removing Mobile Food Establishment Wastes.

SEWAGE and other liquid wastes shall be removed from a mobile FOOD ESTABLISHMENT at an APPROVED waste SERVICING AREA or by a SEWAGE transport vehicle in such a way that a public health HAZARD or nuisance is not created. [Pf]

5-402.15   Flushing a Waste Retention Tank.

A tank for liquid waste retention shall be thoroughly flushed and drained in a sanitary manner during the servicing operation.

Disposal Facility

5-403.11   Approved Sewage Disposal System.

design and construction

SEWAGE shall be disposed through an APPROVED facility that is:

(A) A public SEWAGE treatment plant; [P] or

(B) An individual SEWAGE disposal system that is sized, constructed, maintained, and operated according to LAW. [P]

5-403.12   Other Liquid Wastes and Rainwater.

Condensate drainage and other nonSEWAGE liquids and rainwater shall be drained from point of discharge to disposal according to LAW.

5-5	REFUSE, RECYCLABLES, AND RETURNABLES

Subparts

5-501	Facilities on the Premises
5-502	Removal
5-503	Facilities for Disposal and Recycling

Facilities on the Premises
materials, design, construction, and installation

5-501.10   Indoor Storage Area.

If located within the FOOD ESTABLISHMENT, a storage area for REFUSE, recyclables, and returnables shall meet the requirements specified under §§ 6-101.11, 6-201.11 - 6-201.18, 6-202.15, and 6-202.16.

5-501.11   Outdoor Storage Surface.

An outdoor storage surface for REFUSE, recyclables, and returnables shall be constructed of nonabsorbent material such as concrete or asphalt and shall be SMOOTH, durable, and sloped to drain.

5-501.12   Outdoor Enclosure.

If used, an outdoor enclosure for REFUSE, recyclables, and returnables shall be constructed of durable and cleanable materials.

5-501.13   Receptacles.

(A) Except as specified in ¶ (B) of this section, receptacles and waste handling units for REFUSE, recyclables, and returnables and for use with materials containing FOOD residue shall be durable, cleanable, insect- and rodent-resistant, leakproof, and nonabsorbent.

161

(B) *Plastic bags and wet strength paper bags may be used to line receptacles for storage inside the* FOOD ESTABLISHMENT, *or within closed outside receptacles.*

5-501.14   Receptacles in Vending Machines.

Except for a receptacle for BEVERAGE *bottle crown closures,* a REFUSE receptacle may not be located within a VENDING MACHINE.

5-501.15   Outside Receptacles.

(A) Receptacles and waste handling units for REFUSE, recyclables, and returnables used with materials containing FOOD residue and used outside the FOOD ESTABLISHMENT shall be designed and constructed to have tight-fitting lids, doors, or covers.

(B) Receptacles and waste handling units for REFUSE and recyclables such as an on-site compactor shall be installed so that accumulation of debris and insect and rodent attraction and harborage are minimized and effective cleaning is facilitated around and, if the unit is not installed flush with the base pad, under the unit.

numbers and capacities

5-501.16   Storage Areas, Rooms, and Receptacles, Capacity and Availability.

(A) An inside storage room and area and outside storage area and enclosure, and receptacles shall be of sufficient capacity to hold REFUSE, recyclables, and returnables that accumulate.

(B) A receptacle shall be provided in each area of the FOOD ESTABLISHMENT or PREMISES where REFUSE is generated or commonly discarded, or where recyclables or returnables are placed.

(C) If disposable towels are used at handwashing lavatories, a waste receptacle shall be located at each lavatory or group of adjacent lavatories.

162

5-501.17 Toilet Room Receptacle, Covered.

A toilet room used by females shall be provided with a covered receptacle for sanitary napkins.

5-501.18 Cleaning Implements and Supplies.

(A) Except as specified in ¶ (B) of this section, suitable cleaning implements and supplies such as high pressure pumps, hot water, steam, and detergent shall be provided as necessary for effective cleaning of receptacles and waste handling units for REFUSE, recyclables, and returnables.

(B) *If APPROVED, off-PREMISES-based cleaning services may be used if on-PREMISES cleaning implements and supplies are not provided.*

location and placement

5-501.19 Storage Areas, Redeeming Machines, Receptacles and Waste Handling Units, Location.

(A) An area designated for REFUSE, recyclables, returnables, and, except as specified in ¶ (B) of this section, a redeeming machine for recyclables or returnables shall be located so that it is separate from FOOD, EQUIPMENT, UTENSILS, LINENS, and SINGLE-SERVICE and SINGLE-USE ARTICLES and a public health HAZARD or nuisance is not created.

(B) *A redeeming machine may be located in the PACKAGED FOOD storage area or CONSUMER area of a FOOD ESTABLISHMENT if FOOD, EQUIPMENT, UTENSILS, LINENS, and SINGLE-SERVICE and SINGLE-USE ARTICLES are not subject to contamination from the machines and a public health HAZARD or nuisance is not created.*

(C) The location of receptacles and waste handling units for REFUSE, recyclables, and returnables may not create a public health HAZARD or nuisance or interfere with the cleaning of adjacent space.

163

5-501.110   Storing Refuse, Recyclables, and Returnables.

REFUSE, recyclables, and returnables shall be stored in receptacles or waste handling units so that they are inaccessible to insects and rodents.

5-501.111   Areas, Enclosures, and Receptacles, Good Repair.

Storage areas, enclosures, and receptacles for REFUSE, recyclables, and returnables shall be maintained in good repair.

5-501.112   Outside Storage Prohibitions.

(A) Except as specified in ¶ (B) of this section, REFUSE receptacles not meeting the requirements specified under ¶ 5-501.13(A) such as receptacles that are not rodent-resistant, unprotected plastic bags and paper bags, or baled units that contain materials with FOOD residue may not be stored outside.

(B) *Cardboard or other packaging material that does not contain FOOD residues and that is awaiting regularly scheduled delivery to a recycling or disposal site may be stored outside without being in a covered receptacle if it is stored so that it does not create a rodent harborage problem.*

5-501.113   Covering Receptacles.

Receptacles and waste handling units for REFUSE, recyclables, and returnables shall be kept covered:

   (A) Inside the FOOD ESTABLISHMENT if the receptacles and units:

      (1) Contain FOOD residue and are not in continuous use; or

      (2) After they are filled; and

   (B) With tight-fitting lids or doors if kept outside the FOOD ESTABLISHMENT.

5-501.114   Using Drain Plugs.

Drains in receptacles and waste handling units for REFUSE, recyclables, and returnables shall have drain plugs in place.

5-501.115   Maintaining Refuse Areas and Enclosures.

A storage area and enclosure for REFUSE, recyclables, or returnables shall be maintained free of unnecessary items, as specified under § 6-501.114, and clean.

5-501.116   Cleaning Receptacles.

(A) Receptacles and waste handling units for REFUSE, recyclables, and returnables shall be thoroughly cleaned in a way that does not contaminate FOOD, EQUIPMENT, UTENSILS, LINENS, or SINGLE-SERVICE and SINGLE-USE ARTICLES, and waste water shall be disposed of as specified under § 5-402.13.

(B) Soiled receptacles and waste handling units for REFUSE, recyclables, and returnables shall be cleaned at a frequency necessary to prevent them from developing a buildup of soil or becoming attractants for insects and rodents.

Removal

5-502.11   Frequency.

REFUSE, recyclables, and returnables shall be removed from the PREMISES at a frequency that will minimize the development of objectionable odors and other conditions that attract or harbor insects and rodents.

5-502.12   Receptacles or Vehicles.

REFUSE, recyclables, and returnables shall be removed from the PREMISES by way of:

(A) Portable receptacles that are constructed and maintained according to LAW; or

(B) A transport vehicle that is constructed, maintained, and operated according to LAW.

**Facilities for
Disposal and
Recycling**

5-503.11   Community or Individual Facility.

Solid waste not disposed of through the SEWAGE system such
as through grinders and pulpers shall be recycled or disposed
of in an APPROVED public or private community recycling or
REFUSE facility; or solid waste shall be disposed of in an
individual REFUSE facility such as a landfill or incinerator which
is sized, constructed, maintained, and operated according to
LAW.

Chapter

6 Physical Facilities

Parts

6-1   **MATERIALS FOR CONSTRUCTION AND REPAIR**

Subparts

Indoor Areas   **6-101.11**   **Surface Characteristics.**

(A) Except as specified in ¶ (B) of this section, materials for indoor floor, wall, and ceiling surfaces under conditions of normal use shall be:

(1) SMOOTH, durable, and EASILY CLEANABLE for areas where FOOD ESTABLISHMENT operations are conducted;

(2) Closely woven and EASILY CLEANABLE carpet for carpeted areas; and

(3) Nonabsorbent for areas subject to moisture such as FOOD preparation areas, walk-in refrigerators, WAREWASHING areas, toilet rooms, mobile FOOD ESTABLISHMENT SERVICING AREAS, and areas subject to flushing or spray cleaning methods.

(B) *In a TEMPORARY FOOD ESTABLISHMENT:*

(1) *If graded to drain, a floor may be concrete, machine-laid asphalt, or dirt or gravel if it is covered with mats, removable platforms, duckboards, or other APPROVED materials that are effectively treated to control dust and mud; and*

167

(2) *Walls and ceilings may be constructed of a material that protects the interior from the weather and windblown dust and debris.*

Outdoor Areas   **6-102.11   Surface Characteristics.**

(A) The outdoor walking and driving areas shall be surfaced with concrete, asphalt, or gravel or other materials that have been effectively treated to minimize dust, facilitate maintenance, and prevent muddy conditions.

(B) Exterior surfaces of buildings and mobile FOOD ESTABLISHMENTS shall be of weather-resistant materials and shall comply with LAW.

(C) Outdoor storage areas for REFUSE, recyclables, or returnables shall be of materials specified under §§ 5-501.11 and 5-501.12.

6-2	**DESIGN, CONSTRUCTION, AND INSTALLATION**
	Subparts
	6-201 Cleanability
	6-202 Functionality

Cleanability   **6-201.11   Floors, Walls, and Ceilings.**

Except as specified under § 6-201.14 and *except for antislip floor coverings or applications that may be used for safety reasons,* floors, floor coverings, walls, wall coverings, and ceilings shall be designed, constructed, and installed so they are SMOOTH and EASILY CLEANABLE.

6-201.12   Floors, Walls, and Ceilings, Utility Lines.

(A) Utility service lines and pipes may not be unnecessarily exposed.

(B) Exposed utility service lines and pipes shall be installed so they do not obstruct or prevent cleaning of the floors, walls, or ceilings.

(C) Exposed horizontal utility service lines and pipes may not be installed on the floor.

6-201.13   Floor and Wall Junctures, Coved, and Enclosed or Sealed.

(A) In FOOD ESTABLISHMENTS in which cleaning methods other than water flushing are used for cleaning floors, the floor and wall junctures shall be coved and closed to no larger than 1 mm (one thirty-second inch).

(B) The floors in FOOD ESTABLISHMENTS in which water flush cleaning methods are used shall be provided with drains and be graded to drain, and the floor and wall junctures shall be coved and SEALED.

6-201.14   Floor Carpeting, Restrictions and Installation.

(A) A floor covering such as carpeting or similar material may not be installed as a floor covering in FOOD preparation areas, walk-in refrigerators, WAREWASHING areas, toilet room areas where handwashing lavatories, toilets, and urinals are located, REFUSE storage rooms, or other areas where the floor is subject to moisture, flushing, or spray cleaning methods.

(B) If carpeting is installed as a floor covering in areas other than those specified under ¶ (A) of this section, it shall be:

    (1) Securely attached to the floor with a durable mastic, by using a stretch and tack method, or by another method; and

    (2) Installed tightly against the wall under the coving or installed away from the wall with a space between the carpet and the wall and with the edges of the carpet secured by metal stripping or some other means.

6-201.15   Floor Covering, Mats and Duckboards.

Mats and duckboards shall be designed to be removable and EASILY CLEANABLE.

6-201.16   Wall and Ceiling Coverings and Coatings.

(A) Wall and ceiling covering materials shall be attached so that they are EASILY CLEANABLE.

(B) *Except in areas used only for dry storage*, concrete, porous blocks, or bricks used for indoor wall construction shall be finished and SEALED to provide a SMOOTH, nonabsorbent, EASILY CLEANABLE surface.

6-201.17   Walls and Ceilings, Attachments.

(A) Except as specified in ¶ (B) of this section, attachments to walls and ceilings such as light fixtures, mechanical room ventilation system components, vent covers, wall mounted fans, decorative items, and other attachments shall be EASILY CLEANABLE.

(B) *In a CONSUMER area, wall and ceiling surfaces and decorative items and attachments that are provided for ambiance need not meet this requirement if they are kept clean.*

6-201.18   Walls and Ceilings, Studs, Joists, and Rafters.

Except for TEMPORARY FOOD ESTABLISHMENTS, studs, joists, and rafters may not be exposed in areas subject to moisture.

Functionality

6-202.11   Light Bulbs, Protective Shielding.

(A) Except as specified in ¶ (B) of this section, light bulbs shall be shielded, coated, or otherwise shatter-resistant in areas where there is exposed FOOD; clean EQUIPMENT, UTENSILS, and LINENS; or unwrapped SINGLE-SERVICE and SINGLE-USE ARTICLES.

(B) *Shielded, coated, or otherwise shatter-resistant bulbs need not be used in areas used only for storing FOOD in unopened packages, if:*

  (1) *The integrity of the packages cannot be affected by broken glass falling onto them; and*

  (2) *The packages are capable of being cleaned of debris from broken bulbs before the packages are opened.*

(C) An infrared or other heat lamp shall be protected against breakage by a shield surrounding and extending beyond the bulb so that only the face of the bulb is exposed.

6-202.12   Heating, Ventilating, Air Conditioning System Vents.

Heating, ventilating, and air conditioning systems shall be designed and installed so that make-up air intake and exhaust vents do not cause contamination of FOOD, FOOD-CONTACT SURFACES, EQUIPMENT, or UTENSILS.

6-202.13   Insect Control Devices, Design and Installation.

(A) Insect control devices that are used to electrocute or stun flying insects shall be designed to retain the insect within the device.

(B) Insect control devices shall be installed so that:

(1) The devices are not located over a FOOD preparation area; and

(2) Dead insects and insect fragments are prevented from being impelled onto or falling on exposed FOOD; clean EQUIPMENT, UTENSILS, and LINENS; and unwrapped SINGLE-SERVICE and SINGLE-USE ARTICLES.

6-202.14   Toilet Rooms, Enclosed.

Except where a toilet room is located outside a FOOD ESTABLISHMENT and does not open directly into the FOOD ESTABLISHMENT such as a toilet room that is provided by the management of a shopping mall, a toilet room located on the PREMISES shall be completely enclosed and provided with a tight-fitting and self-closing door.

6-202.15   Outer Openings, Protected.

(A) Except as specified in ¶¶ (B), (C), and (E) and under ¶ (D) of this section, outer openings of a FOOD ESTABLISHMENT shall be protected against the entry of insects and rodents by:

(1) Filling or closing holes and other gaps along floors, walls, and ceilings;

(2) Closed, tight-fitting windows; and

(3) Solid, self-closing, tight-fitting doors.

(B) *Paragraph (A) of this section does not apply if a* FOOD ESTABLISHMENT *opens into a larger structure, such as a mall, airport, or office building, or into an attached structure, such as a porch, and the outer openings from the larger or attached structure are protected against the entry of insects and rodents.*

(C) *Exterior doors used as exits need not be self-closing if they are:*

(1) *Solid and tight-fitting;*

(2) *Designated for use only when an emergency exists, by the fire protection authority that has jurisdiction over the* FOOD ESTABLISHMENT; *and*

(3) *Limited-use so they are not used for entrance or exit from the building for purposes other than the designated emergency exit use.*

(D) Except as specified in ¶¶ (B) and (E) of this section, if the windows or doors of a FOOD ESTABLISHMENT, or of a larger structure within which a FOOD ESTABLISHMENT is located, are kept open for ventilation or other purposes or a TEMPORARY FOOD ESTABLISHMENT is not provided with windows and doors as specified under ¶ (A) of this section, the openings shall be protected against the entry of insects and rodents by:

(1) 16 mesh to 25.4 mm (16 mesh to 1 inch) screens;

(2) Properly designed and installed air curtains to control flying insects; or

(3) Other effective means.

172

(E) *Paragraph (D) of this section does not apply if flying insects and other pests are absent due to the location of the* ESTABLISHMENT, *the weather, or other limiting condition.*

6-202.16   Exterior Walls and Roofs, Protective Barrier.

Perimeter walls and roofs of a FOOD ESTABLISHMENT shall effectively protect the establishment from the weather and the entry of insects, rodents, and other animals.

6-202.17   Outdoor Food Vending Areas, Overhead Protection.

Except for machines that vend canned BEVERAGES, if located outside, a machine used to vend FOOD shall be provided with overhead protection.

6-202.18   Outdoor Servicing Areas, Overhead Protection.

Except for areas used only for the loading of water or the discharge of SEWAGE *and other liquid waste, through the use of a closed system of hoses,* SERVICING AREAS shall be provided with overhead protection.

6-202.19   Outdoor Walking and Driving Surfaces, Graded to Drain.

Exterior walking and driving surfaces shall be graded to drain.

6-202.110   Outdoor Refuse Areas, Curbed and Graded to Drain.

Outdoor REFUSE areas shall be constructed in accordance with LAW and shall be curbed and graded to drain to collect and dispose of liquid waste that results from the REFUSE and from cleaning the area and waste receptacles.

6-202.111   **Private Homes and Living or Sleeping Quarters, Use Prohibition.**

A private home, a room used as living or sleeping quarters, or an area directly opening into a room used as living or sleeping quarters may not be used for conducting FOOD ESTABLISHMENT operations. [P]

6-202.112   **Living or Sleeping Quarters, Separation.**

Living or sleeping quarters located on the PREMISES of a FOOD ESTABLISHMENT such as those provided for lodging registration clerks or resident managers shall be separated from rooms and areas used for FOOD ESTABLISHMENT operations by complete partitioning and solid self-closing doors.

6-3	NUMBERS AND CAPACITIES
	Subparts
	6-301 Handwashing Sinks
	6-302 Toilets and Urinals
	6-303 Lighting
	6-304 Ventilation
	6-305 Dressing Areas and Lockers
	6-306 Service Sinks

Handwashing Sinks

6-301.10   **Minimum Number.**

HANDWASHING SINKS shall be provided as specified under § 5-203.11.

6-301.11   **Handwashing Cleanser, Availability.**

Each HANDWASHING SINK or group of 2 adjacent HANDWASHING SINKS shall be provided with a supply of hand cleaning liquid, powder, or bar soap. [Pf]

6-301.12   Hand Drying Provision.

Each HANDWASHING SINK or group of adjacent HANDWASHING SINKS shall be provided with:

(A) Individual, disposable towels; [Pf]

(B) A continuous towel system that supplies the user with a clean towel; [Pf] or

(C) A heated-air hand drying device; [Pf] or

(D) A hand drying device that employs an air-knife system that delivers high velocity, pressurized air at ambient temperatures. [Pf]

6-301.13   Handwashing Aids and Devices, Use Restrictions.

A sink used for FOOD preparation or UTENSIL washing, or a service sink or curbed cleaning facility used for the disposal of mop water or similar wastes, may not be provided with the handwashing aids and devices required for a HANDWASHING SINK as specified under §§ 6-301.11 and 6-301.12 and ¶ 5-501.16(C).

6-301.14   Handwashing Signage.

A sign or poster that notifies FOOD EMPLOYEES to wash their hands shall be provided at all HANDWASHING SINKS used by FOOD EMPLOYEES and shall be clearly visible to FOOD EMPLOYEES.

6-301.20   Disposable Towels, Waste Receptacle.

A HANDWASHING SINK or group of adjacent HANDWASHING SINKS that is provided with disposable towels shall be provided with a waste receptacle as specified under ¶ 5-501.16(C).

Toilets and Urinals   ### 6-302.10   Minimum Number.

Toilets and urinals shall be provided as specified under § 5-203.12.

6-302.11   Toilet Tissue, Availability.

A supply of toilet tissue shall be available at each toilet. [Pf]

Lighting

6-303.11   Intensity.

The light intensity shall be:

(A) At least 108 lux (10 foot candles) at a distance of 75 cm (30 inches) above the floor, in walk-in refrigeration units and dry FOOD storage areas and in other areas and rooms during periods of cleaning;

(B) At least 215 lux (20 foot candles):

(1) At a surface where FOOD is provided for CONSUMER self-service such as buffets and salad bars or where fresh produce or PACKAGED FOODS are sold or offered for consumption,

(2) Inside EQUIPMENT such as reach-in and under-counter refrigerators; and

(3) At a distance of 75 cm (30 inches) above the floor in areas used for handwashing, WAREWASHING, and EQUIPMENT and UTENSIL storage, and in toilet rooms; and

(C) At least 540 lux (50 foot candles) at a surface where a FOOD EMPLOYEE is working with FOOD or working with UTENSILS or EQUIPMENT such as knives, slicers, grinders, or saws where EMPLOYEE safety is a factor.

Ventilation

6-304.11   Mechanical.

If necessary to keep rooms free of excessive heat, steam, condensation, vapors, obnoxious odors, smoke, and fumes, mechanical ventilation of sufficient capacity shall be provided.

Dressing Areas and Lockers

6-305.11   Designation.

(A) Dressing rooms or dressing areas shall be designated if EMPLOYEES routinely change their clothes in the establishment.

176

(B) Lockers or other suitable facilities shall be provided for the orderly storage of EMPLOYEES' clothing and other possessions.

Service Sinks   **6-306.10   Availability.**

A service sink or curbed cleaning facility shall be provided as specified under ¶ 5-203.13(A).

6-4	**LOCATION AND PLACEMENT**

Subparts

6-401	**Handwashing Sinks**
6-402	**Toilet Rooms**
6-403	**Employee Accommodations**
6-404	**Distressed Merchandise**
6-405	**Refuse, Recyclables, and Returnables**

Handwashing   **6-401.10   Conveniently Located.**
Sinks

HANDWASHING SINKS shall be conveniently located as specified under § 5-204.11.

Toilet Rooms   **6-402.11   Convenience and Accessibility.**

Toilet rooms shall be conveniently located and accessible to EMPLOYEES during all hours of operation.

Employee   **6-403.11   Designated Areas.**
Accommodations

(A) Areas designated for EMPLOYEES to eat, drink, and use tobacco shall be located so that FOOD, EQUIPMENT, LINENS, and SINGLE-SERVICE and SINGLE-USE ARTICLES are protected from contamination.

(B) Lockers or other suitable facilities shall be located in a designated room or area where contamination of FOOD, EQUIPMENT, UTENSILS, LINENS, and SINGLE-SERVICE and SINGLE-USE ARTICLES can not occur.

177

Distressed
Merchandise

6-404.11   Segregation and Location.

Products that are held by the PERMIT HOLDER for credit, redemption, or return to the distributor, such as damaged, spoiled, or recalled products, shall be segregated and held in designated areas that are separated from FOOD, EQUIPMENT, UTENSILS, LINENS, and SINGLE-SERVICE and SINGLE-USE ARTICLES.^{Pf}

Refuse,
Recyclables, and
Returnables

6-405.10   Receptacles, Waste Handling Units, and Designated Storage Areas.

Units, receptacles, and areas designated for storage of REFUSE and recyclable and returnable containers shall be located as specified under § 5-501.19.

6-5   MAINTENANCE AND OPERATION

Subpart

6-501   Premises, Structures, Attachments, and Fixtures - Methods

---

Premises,
Structures,
Attachments,
and Fixtures
- Methods

6-501.11   Repairing.

PHYSICAL FACILITIES shall be maintained in good repair.

6-501.12   Cleaning, Frequency and Restrictions.

(A) PHYSICAL FACILITIES shall be cleaned as often as necessary to keep them clean.

(B) *Except for cleaning that is necessary due to a spill or other accident,* cleaning shall be done during periods when the least amount of FOOD is exposed such as after closing.

6-501.13   Cleaning Floors, Dustless Methods.

(A) Except as specified in ¶ (B) of this section, only dustless methods of cleaning shall be used, such as wet cleaning, vacuum cleaning, mopping with treated dust mops, or sweeping using a broom and dust-arresting compounds.

(B) *Spills or drippage on floors that occur between normal floor cleaning times may be cleaned:*

   (1) *Without the use of dust-arresting compounds; and*

   (2) *In the case of liquid spills or drippage, with the use of a small amount of absorbent compound such as sawdust or diatomaceous earth applied immediately before spot cleaning.*

6-501.14   Cleaning Ventilation Systems, Nuisance and Discharge Prohibition.

(A) Intake and exhaust air ducts shall be cleaned and filters changed so they are not a source of contamination by dust, dirt, and other materials.

(B) If vented to the outside, ventilation systems may not create a public health HAZARD or nuisance or unLAWful discharge.

6-501.15   Cleaning Maintenance Tools, Preventing Contamination.

FOOD preparation sinks, HANDWASHING SINKS, and WAREWASHING EQUIPMENT may not be used for the cleaning of maintenance tools, the preparation or holding of maintenance materials, or the disposal of mop water and similar liquid wastes. [Pf]

6-501.16   Drying Mops.

After use, mops shall be placed in a position that allows them to air-dry without soiling walls, EQUIPMENT, or supplies.

6-501.17   Absorbent Materials on Floors, Use Limitation.

Except as specified in ¶ 6-501.13(B), sawdust, wood shavings, granular salt, baked clay, diatomaceous earth, or similar materials may not be used on floors.

6-501.18   Cleaning of Plumbing Fixtures.

PLUMBING FIXTURES such as HANDWASHING SINKS, toilets, and urinals shall be cleaned as often as necessary to keep them clean.

6-501.19   Closing Toilet Room Doors.

Except during cleaning and maintenance operations, toilet room doors as specified under § 6-202.14 shall be kept closed.

6-501.110   Using Dressing Rooms and Lockers.

(A) Dressing rooms shall be used by EMPLOYEES if the EMPLOYEES regularly change their clothes in the establishment.

(B) Lockers or other suitable facilities shall be used for the orderly storage of EMPLOYEE clothing and other possessions.

6-501.111   Controlling Pests.

The PREMISES shall be maintained free of insects, rodents, and other pests. The presence of insects, rodents, and other pests shall be controlled to eliminate their presence on the PREMISES by:

   (A) Routinely inspecting incoming shipments of FOOD and supplies;

   (B) Routinely inspecting the PREMISES for evidence of pests;

   (C) Using methods, if pests are found, such as trapping devices or other means of pest control as specified under §§ 7-202.12, 7-206.12, and 7-206.13; [Pf] and

   (D) Eliminating harborage conditions.

180

6-501.112   Removing Dead or Trapped Birds, Insects, Rodents, and Other Pests.

Dead or trapped birds, insects, rodents, and other pests shall be removed from control devices and the PREMISES at a frequency that prevents their accumulation, decomposition, or the attraction of pests.

6-501.113   Storing Maintenance Tools.

Maintenance tools such as brooms, mops, vacuum cleaners, and similar items shall be:

(A) Stored so they do not contaminate FOOD, EQUIPMENT, UTENSILS, LINENS, and SINGLE-SERVICE and SINGLE-USE ARTICLES; and

(B) Stored in an orderly manner that facilitates cleaning the area used for storing the maintenance tools.

6-501.114   Maintaining Premises, Unnecessary Items and Litter.

The PREMISES shall be free of:

(A) Items that are unnecessary to the operation or maintenance of the establishment such as EQUIPMENT that is nonfunctional or no longer used; and

(B) Litter.

6-501.115   Prohibiting Animals.

(A) Except as specified in ¶¶ (B) and (C) of this section, live animals may not be allowed on the PREMISES of a FOOD ESTABLISHMENT. Pf

(B) *Live animals may be allowed in the following situations if the contamination of FOOD; clean EQUIPMENT, UTENSILS, and LINENS; and unwrapped SINGLE-SERVICE and SINGLE-USE ARTICLES can not result:*

181

(1) Edible FISH or decorative FISH in aquariums, shellfish or crustacea on ice or under refrigeration, and shellfish and crustacea in display tank systems;

(2) Patrol dogs accompanying police or security officers in offices and dining, sales, and storage areas, and sentry dogs running loose in outside fenced areas;

(3) In areas that are not used for FOOD preparation and that are usually open for customers, such as dining and sales areas, SERVICE ANIMALS that are controlled by the disabled EMPLOYEE or PERSON, if a health or safety HAZARD will not result from the presence or activities of the SERVICE ANIMAL;

(4) Pets in the common dining areas of institutional care facilities such as nursing homes, assisted living facilities, group homes, or residential care facilities at times other than during meals if:

  (a) Effective partitioning and self-closing doors separate the common dining areas from FOOD storage or FOOD preparation areas,

  (b) Condiments, EQUIPMENT, and UTENSILS are stored in enclosed cabinets or removed from the common dining areas when pets are present, and

  (c) Dining areas including tables, countertops, and similar surfaces are effectively cleaned before the next meal service; and

(5) In areas that are not used for FOOD preparation, storage, sales, display, or dining, in which there are caged animals or animals that are similarly confined, such as in a variety store that sells pets or a tourist park that displays animals.

(C) Live or dead FISH bait may be stored if contamination of FOOD; clean EQUIPMENT, UTENSILS, and LINENS; and unwrapped SINGLE-SERVICE and SINGLE-USE ARTICLES can not result.

7 Poisonous or Toxic Materials

Parts

7-1   **LABELING AND IDENTIFICATION**

Subparts

*Original
Containers*

7-101.11   **Identifying Information, Prominence.**

Containers of POISONOUS OR TOXIC MATERIALS and PERSONAL CARE ITEMS shall bear a legible manufacturer's label. [Pf]

*Working
Containers*

7-102.11   **Common Name.**

Working containers used for storing POISONOUS OR TOXIC MATERIALS such as cleaners and SANITIZERS taken from bulk supplies shall be clearly and individually identified with the common name of the material. [Pf]

7-2	OPERATIONAL SUPPLIES AND APPLICATIONS

Subparts

7-201	Storage
7-202	Presence and Use
7-203	Container Prohibitions
7-204	Chemicals
7-205	Lubricants
7-206	Pesticides
7-207	Medicines
7-208	First Aid Supplies
7-209	Other Personal Care Items

Storage

7-201.11   Separation.

POISONOUS OR TOXIC MATERIALS shall be stored so they can not contaminate FOOD, EQUIPMENT, UTENSILS, LINENS, and SINGLE-SERVICE and SINGLE-USE ARTICLES by:

(A) Separating the POISONOUS OR TOXIC MATERIALS by spacing or partitioning; [P] and

(B) Locating the POISONOUS OR TOXIC MATERIALS in an area that is not above FOOD, EQUIPMENT, UTENSILS, LINENS, and SINGLE-SERVICE or SINGLE-USE ARTICLES. *This paragraph does not apply to EQUIPMENT and UTENSIL cleaners and SANITIZERS that are stored in WAREWASHING areas for availability and convenience if the materials are stored to prevent contamination of FOOD, EQUIPMENT, UTENSILS, LINENS, and SINGLE-SERVICE and SINGLE-USE ARTICLES.* [P]

Presence and Use

7-202.11   Restriction.

(A) Only those POISONOUS OR TOXIC MATERIALS that are required for the operation and maintenance of a FOOD ESTABLISHMENT, such as for the cleaning and SANITIZING of EQUIPMENT and UTENSILS and the control of insects and rodents, shall be allowed in a FOOD ESTABLISHMENT. [Pf]

(B) *Paragraph (A) of this section does not apply to PACKAGED POISONOUS OR TOXIC MATERIALS that are for retail sale.*

7-202.12   Conditions of Use.

POISONOUS OR TOXIC MATERIALS shall be:

(A) Used according to:

(1) LAW and this Code,

(2) Manufacturer's use directions included in labeling, and, for a pesticide, manufacturer's label instructions that state that use is allowed in a FOOD ESTABLISHMENT, [P]

(3) The conditions of certification, if certification is required, for use of the pest control materials, [P] and

(4) Additional conditions that may be established by the REGULATORY AUTHORITY; and

(B) Applied so that:

(1) A HAZARD to EMPLOYEES or other PERSONS is not constituted, [P] and

(2) Contamination including toxic residues due to drip, drain, fog, splash or spray on FOOD, EQUIPMENT, UTENSILS, LINENS, and SINGLE-SERVICE and SINGLE-USE ARTICLES is prevented, and for a RESTRICTED USE PESTICIDE, this is achieved by: [P]

(a) Removing the items, [P]

(b) Covering the items with impermeable covers, [P] or

(c) Taking other appropriate preventive actions, [P] and

(d) Cleaning and SANITIZING EQUIPMENT and UTENSILS after the application. [P]

(C) A RESTRICTED USE PESTICIDE shall be applied only by an applicator certified as defined in 7 USC 136 Definitions, (e) Certified Applicator, of the Federal Insecticide, Fungicide, and Rodenticide Act, or a PERSON under the direct supervision of a certified applicator. [Pf]

185

7-203.11   Poisonous or Toxic Material Containers.

A container previously used to store POISONOUS OR TOXIC
MATERIALS may not be used to store, transport, or dispense
FOOD. [P]

7-204.11   Sanitizers, Criteria.

Chemical SANITIZERS and other chemical antimicrobials applied to
FOOD-CONTACT SURFACES shall meet the requirements specified in
40 CFR 180.940 Tolerance exemptions for active and inert
ingredients for use in antimicrobial formulations (food-contact
surface sanitizing solutions). [P]

**7-204.12   Chemicals for Washing, Treatment, Storage
and Processing Fruits and Vegetables, Criteria.**

(A) Chemicals used to wash or peel raw, whole fruits and
vegetables shall meet the requirements specified in 21 CFR
173.315 Chemicals used in washing or to assist in the peeling of
fruits and vegetables. [P]

(B) Ozone as an antimicrobial agent used in the treatment,
storage, and processing of fruits and vegetables in a food
establishment shall meet the requirements specified in 21 CFR
173.368 Ozone.

7-204.13   Boiler Water Additives, Criteria.

Chemicals used as boiler water ADDITIVES shall meet the
requirements specified in 21 CFR 173.310 Boiler water
additives. [P]

7-204.14   Drying Agents, Criteria.

Drying agents used in conjunction with SANITIZATION shall:

   (A) Contain only components that are listed as one of the
   following:

(1) Generally recognized as safe for use in FOOD as specified in 21 CFR 182 - Substances Generally Recognized as Safe, or 21 CFR 184 - Direct Food Substances Affirmed as Generally Recognized as Safe, [P]

(2) Generally recognized as safe for the intended use as specified in 21 CFR 186 - Indirect Food Substances Affirmed as Generally Recognized as Safe, [P]

(3) APPROVED for use as a drying agent under a prior sanction specified in 21 CFR 181 - Prior-Sanctioned Food Ingredients, [P]

(4) Specifically regulated as an indirect FOOD ADDITIVE for use as a drying agent as specified in 21 CFR Parts 175-178, [P] or

(5) APPROVED for use as a drying agent under the threshold of regulation process established by 21 CFR 170.39 Threshold of regulation for substances used in food-contact articles; [P] and

(B) When SANITIZATION is with chemicals, the approval required under Subparagraph (A)(3) or (A)(5) of this section or the regulation as an indirect FOOD ADDITIVE required under Subparagraph (A)(4) of this section, shall be specifically for use with chemical SANITIZING solutions. [P]

Lubricants

7-205.11   Incidental Food Contact, Criteria.

Lubricants shall meet the requirements specified in 21 CFR 178.3570 Lubricants with incidental food contact, if they are used on FOOD-CONTACT SURFACES, on bearings and gears located on or within FOOD-CONTACT SURFACES, or on bearings and gears that are located so that lubricants may leak, drip, or be forced into FOOD or onto FOOD-CONTACT SURFACES. [P]

Pesticides

7-206.11   Restricted Use Pesticides, Criteria.

RESTRICTED USE PESTICIDES specified under ¶ 7-202.12(C) shall meet the requirements specified in 40 CFR 152 Subpart I - Classification of Pesticides. [P]

187

7-206.12   Rodent Bait Stations.

Rodent bait shall be contained in a covered, tamper-resistant bait station. ^P

7-206.13   Tracking Powders, Pest Control and Monitoring.

(A) Except as specified in ¶ (B) of this section, a tracking powder pesticide may not be used in a FOOD ESTABLISHMENT. ^P

(B) If used, a nontoxic tracking powder such as talcum or flour may not contaminate FOOD, EQUIPMENT, UTENSILS, LINENS, and SINGLE-SERVICE and SINGLE-USE ARTICLES.

Medicines   **7-207.11   Restriction and Storage.**

(A) *Except for medicines that are stored or displayed for retail sale,* only those medicines that are necessary for the health of EMPLOYEES shall be allowed in a FOOD ESTABLISHMENT. ^{Pf}

(B) Medicines that are in a FOOD ESTABLISHMENT for the EMPLOYEES' use shall be labeled as specified under § 7-101.11 and located to prevent the contamination of FOOD, EQUIPMENT, UTENSILS, LINENS, and SINGLE-SERVICE and SINGLE-USE ARTICLES. ^P

7-207.12   Refrigerated Medicines, Storage.

Medicines belonging to EMPLOYEES or to children in a day care center that require refrigeration and are stored in a FOOD refrigerator shall be:

   (A) Stored in a package or container and kept inside a covered, leakproof container that is identified as a container for the storage of medicines; ^P and

   (B) Located so they are inaccessible to children. ^P

First Aid Supplies   **7-208.11   Storage.**

First aid supplies that are in a FOOD ESTABLISHMENT for the EMPLOYEES' use shall be:

(A) Labeled as specified under § 7-101.11; ^{Pf} and

(B) Stored in a kit or a container that is located to prevent the contamination of FOOD, EQUIPMENT, UTENSILS, and LINENS, and SINGLE-SERVICE and SINGLE-USE ARTICLES. ^P

Other Personal Care Items

7-209.11   Storage.

Except as specified under §§ 7-207.12 and 7-208.11, EMPLOYEES shall store their PERSONAL CARE ITEMS in facilities as specified under ¶ 6-305.11(B).

7-3   STOCK AND RETAIL SALE

Subpart

7-301   Storage and Display

Storage and Display

7-301.11   Separation.

POISONOUS or TOXIC MATERIALS shall be stored and displayed for retail sale so they can not contaminate FOOD, EQUIPMENT, UTENSILS, LINENS, and SINGLE-SERVICE and SINGLE-USE ARTICLES by:

(A) Separating the POISONOUS or TOXIC MATERIALS by spacing or partitioning; ^P and

(B) Locating the POISONOUS OR TOXIC MATERIALS in an area that is not above FOOD, EQUIPMENT, UTENSILS, LINENS, and SINGLE-SERVICE or SINGLE-USE ARTICLES. ^P

This page is intended to be blank.

Chapter 8 Compliance and Enforcement

8-1 CODE APPLICABILITY

Subparts

Use for Intended Purpose

8-101.10 Public Health Protection.

(A) The REGULATORY AUTHORITY shall apply this Code to promote its underlying purpose, as specified in § 1-102.10, of safeguarding public health and ensuring that FOOD is safe, unADULTERATED, and honestly presented when offered to the CONSUMER.

(B) In enforcing the provisions of this Code, the REGULATORY AUTHORITY shall assess existing facilities or EQUIPMENT that were in use before the effective date of this Code based on the following considerations:

(1) Whether the facilities or EQUIPMENT are in good repair and capable of being maintained in a sanitary condition;

191

(2) Whether FOOD-CONTACT SURFACES comply with Subpart 4-101;

(3) Whether the capacities of cooling, heating, and holding EQUIPMENT are sufficient to comply with § 4-301.11; and

(4) The existence of a documented agreement with the PERMIT HOLDER that the facilities or EQUIPMENT will be replaced as specified under ¶ 8-304.11(G).

Additional Requirements	**8-102.10** **Preventing Health Hazards, Provision for Conditions Not Addressed.**

(A) If necessary to protect against public health HAZARDS or nuisances, the REGULATORY AUTHORITY may impose specific requirements in addition to the requirements contained in this Code that are authorized by LAW.

(B) The REGULATORY AUTHORITY shall document the conditions that necessitate the imposition of additional requirements and the underlying public health rationale. The documentation shall be provided to the PERMIT applicant or PERMIT HOLDER and a copy shall be maintained in the REGULATORY AUTHORITY'S file for the FOOD ESTABLISHMENT.

Variances	**8-103.10** **Modifications and Waivers.**

The REGULATORY AUTHORITY may grant a VARIANCE by modifying or waiving the requirements of this Code if in the opinion of the REGULATORY AUTHORITY a health HAZARD or nuisance will not result from the VARIANCE. If a VARIANCE is granted, the REGULATORY AUTHORITY shall retain the information specified under § 8-103.11 in its records for the FOOD ESTABLISHMENT.

8-103.11   **Documentation of Proposed Variance and Justification.**

Before a VARIANCE from a requirement of this Code is APPROVED, the information that shall be provided by the PERSON requesting the VARIANCE and retained in the REGULATORY AUTHORITY's file on the FOOD ESTABLISHMENT includes:

(A) A statement of the proposed VARIANCE of the Code requirement citing relevant Code section numbers;[Pf]

(B) An analysis of the rationale for how the potential public health HAZARDS and nuisances addressed by the relevant Code sections will be alternatively addressed by the proposal; [Pf] and

(C) A HACCP PLAN if required as specified under ¶ 8-201.13(A) that includes the information specified under § 8-201.14 as it is relevant to the VARIANCE requested. [Pf]

8-103.12   Conformance with Approved Procedures.

If the REGULATORY AUTHORITY grants a VARIANCE as specified in § 8-103.10, or a HACCP PLAN is otherwise required as specified under § 8-201.13, the PERMIT HOLDER shall:

(A) Comply with the HACCP PLANs and procedures that are submitted as specified under § 8-201.14 and APPROVED as a basis for the modification or waiver; [P] and

(B) Maintain and provide to the REGULATORY AUTHORITY, upon request, records specified under ¶¶ 8-201.14(D) and (E) that demonstrate that the following are routinely employed;

(1) Procedures for monitoring the CRITICAL CONTROL POINTS, [Pf]

(2) Monitoring of the CRITICAL CONTROL POINTS, [Pf]

(3) Verification of the effectiveness of the operation or process, [Pf] and

(4) Necessary corrective actions if there is failure at a CRITICAL CONTROL POINT. [Pf]

193

Subparts

8-201	Facility and Operating Plans
8-202	Confidentiality
8-203	Construction Inspection and Approval

Facility and Operating Plans

8-201.11   When Plans Are Required.

A PERMIT applicant or PERMIT HOLDER shall submit to the REGULATORY AUTHORITY properly prepared plans and specifications for review and approval before:

(A) The construction of a FOOD ESTABLISHMENT; [Pf]

(B) The conversion of an existing structure for use as a FOOD ESTABLISHMENT; [Pf] or

(C) The remodeling of a FOOD ESTABLISHMENT or a change of type of FOOD ESTABLISHMENT or FOOD operation as specified under ¶ 8-302.14(C) if the REGULATORY AUTHORITY determines that plans and specifications are necessary to ensure compliance with this Code. [Pf]

8-201.12   Contents of the Plans and Specifications.

The plans and specifications for a FOOD ESTABLISHMENT, including a FOOD ESTABLISHMENT specified under § 8-201.13, shall include, as required by the REGULATORY AUTHORITY based on the type of operation, type of FOOD preparation, and FOODS prepared, the following information to demonstrate conformance with Code provisions:

(A) Intended menu;

(B) Anticipated volume of FOOD to be stored, prepared, and sold or served;

(C) Proposed layout, mechanical schematics, construction materials, and finish schedules;

(D) Proposed EQUIPMENT types, manufacturers, model numbers, locations, dimensions, performance capacities, and installation specifications;

(E) Evidence that standard procedures that ensure compliance with the requirements of this Code are developed or are being developed; and

(F) Other information that may be required by the REGULATORY AUTHORITY for the proper review of the proposed construction, conversion or modification, and procedures for operating a FOOD ESTABLISHMENT.

8-201.13   When a HACCP Plan is Required.

(A) Before engaging in an activity that requires a HACCP PLAN, a PERMIT applicant or PERMIT HOLDER shall submit to the REGULATORY AUTHORITY for approval a properly prepared HACCP PLAN as specified under § 8-201.14 and the relevant provisions of this Code if:

(1) Submission of a HACCP PLAN is required according to LAW;

(2) A VARIANCE is required as specified under Subparagraph 3-401.11(D)(4), § 3-502.11, or ¶ 4-204.110(B);

(3) The REGULATORY AUTHORITY determines that a FOOD preparation or processing method requires a VARIANCE based on a plan submittal specified under § 8-201.12, an inspectional finding, or a VARIANCE request.

(B) A PERMIT applicant or PERMIT HOLDER shall have a properly prepared HACCP PLAN as specified under § 3-502.12.

8-201.14   Contents of a HACCP Plan.

For a FOOD ESTABLISHMENT that is required under § 8-201.13 to have a HACCP PLAN, the plan and specifications shall indicate:

(A) A categorization of the types of POTENTIALLY HAZARDOUS FOODS (TIME/TEMPERATURE CONTROL FOR SAFETY FOODS) that are specified in the menu such as soups and sauces, salads, and bulk, solid FOODS such as MEAT roasts, or of other FOODS that are specified by the REGULATORY AUTHORITY; [Pf]

(B) A flow diagram by specific FOOD or category type identifying CRITICAL CONTROL POINTS and providing information on the following:

(1) Ingredients, materials, and EQUIPMENT used in the preparation of that FOOD, [Pf] and

(2) Formulations or recipes that delineate methods and procedural control measures that address the FOOD safety concerns involved; [Pf]

(C) FOOD EMPLOYEE and supervisory training plan that addresses the FOOD safety issues of concern; [Pf]

(D) A statement of standard operating procedures for the plan under consideration including clearly identifying:

(1) Each CRITICAL CONTROL POINT, [Pf]

(2) The CRITICAL LIMITS for each CRITICAL CONTROL POINT, [Pf]

(3) The method and frequency for monitoring and controlling each CRITICAL CONTROL POINT by the FOOD EMPLOYEE designated by the PERSON IN CHARGE, [Pf]

(4) The method and frequency for the PERSON IN CHARGE to routinely verify that the FOOD EMPLOYEE is following standard operating procedures and monitoring CRITICAL CONTROL POINTS, [Pf]

(5) Action to be taken by the PERSON IN CHARGE if the CRITICAL LIMITS for each CRITICAL CONTROL POINT are not met, [Pf] and

(6) Records to be maintained by the PERSON IN CHARGE to demonstrate that the HACCP PLAN is properly operated and managed; [Pf] and

(E) Additional scientific data or other information, as required by the REGULATORY AUTHORITY, supporting the determination that FOOD safety is not compromised by the proposal. [Pf]

Confidentiality	**8-202.10** **Trade Secrets.**

The REGULATORY AUTHORITY shall treat as confidential in accordance with LAW, information that meets the criteria specified in LAW for a trade secret and is contained on inspection report forms and in the plans and specifications submitted as specified under §§ 8-201.12 and 8-201.14.

Construction Inspection and Approval	**8-203.10** **Preoperational Inspections.**

The REGULATORY AUTHORITY shall conduct one or more preoperational inspections to verify that the FOOD ESTABLISHMENT is constructed and equipped in accordance with the APPROVED plans and APPROVED modifications of those plans, has established standard operating procedures as specified under ¶ 8-201.12(E), and is in compliance with LAW and this Code.

8-3   **PERMIT TO OPERATE**

Subparts

8-301   **Requirement**
8-302   **Application Procedure**
8-303   **Issuance**
8-304   **Conditions of Retention**

Requirement   **8-301.11** **Prerequisite for Operation.**

A PERSON may not operate a FOOD ESTABLISHMENT without a valid PERMIT to operate issued by the REGULATORY AUTHORITY. [Pf]

**8-302.11   Submission 30 Calendar Days Before
                    Proposed Opening.**

An applicant shall submit an application for a PERMIT at least
30 calendar days before the date planned for opening a FOOD
ESTABLISHMENT or the expiration date of the current PERMIT for
an existing facility.

8-302.12   Form of Submission.

A PERSON desiring to operate a FOOD ESTABLISHMENT shall
submit to the REGULATORY AUTHORITY a written application for
a PERMIT on a form provided by the REGULATORY AUTHORITY.

**8-302.13   Qualifications and Responsibilities of
                    Applicants.**

To qualify for a PERMIT, an applicant shall:

(A) Be an owner of the FOOD ESTABLISHMENT or an officer of
the legal ownership;

(B) Comply with the requirements of this Code;

(C) As specified under § 8-402.11, agree to allow access
to the FOOD ESTABLISHMENT and to provide required
information; and

(D) Pay the applicable PERMIT fees at the time the
application is submitted.

8-302.14   Contents of the Application.

The application shall include:

(A) The name, birth date, mailing address, telephone
number, and signature of the PERSON applying for the
PERMIT and the name, mailing address, and location of the
FOOD ESTABLISHMENT;

(B) Information specifying whether the FOOD
ESTABLISHMENT is owned by an association, corporation,
individual, partnership, or other legal entity;

198

(C) A statement specifying whether the FOOD ESTABLISHMENT:

  (1) Is mobile or stationary and temporary or permanent, and

  (2) Is an operation that includes one or more of the following:

    (a) Prepares, offers for sale, or serves POTENTIALLY HAZARDOUS FOOD (TIME/TEMPERATURE CONTROL FOR SAFETY FOOD):

      (i) Only to order upon a CONSUMER'S request,

      (ii) In advance in quantities based on projected CONSUMER demand and discards FOOD that is not sold or served at an APPROVED frequency, or

      (iii) Using time as the public health control as specified under § 3-501.19,

    (b) Prepares POTENTIALLY HAZARDOUS FOOD (TIME/TEMPERATURE CONTROL FOR SAFETY FOOD) in advance using a FOOD preparation method that involves two or more steps which may include combining POTENTIALLY HAZARDOUS (TIME/TEMPERATURE CONTROL FOR SAFETY FOOD) ingredients; cooking; cooling; reheating; hot or cold holding; freezing; or thawing,

    (c) Prepares FOOD as specified under Subparagraph (C)(2)(b) of this section for delivery to and consumption at a location off the PREMISES of the FOOD ESTABLISHMENT where it is prepared,

    (d) Prepares FOOD as specified under Subparagraph (C)(2)(b) of this section for service to a HIGHLY SUSCEPTIBLE POPULATION,

    (e) Prepares only FOOD that is not POTENTIALLY HAZARDOUS (TIME/TEMPERATURE CONTROL OF SAFETY FOOD), or

    (f) Does not prepare, but offers for sale only prePACKAGED FOOD that is not POTENTIALLY HAZARDOUS (TIME/TEMPERATURE CONTROL FOR SAFETY FOOD);

199

(D) The name, title, address, and telephone number of the PERSON directly responsible for the FOOD ESTABLISHMENT;

(E) The name, title, address, and telephone number of the PERSON who functions as the immediate supervisor of the PERSON specified under ¶ (D) of this section such as the zone, district, or regional supervisor;

(F) The names, titles, and addresses of:

(1) The PERSONS comprising the legal ownership as specified under ¶ (B) of this section including the owners and officers, and

(2) The local resident agent if one is required based on the type of legal ownership;

(G) A statement signed by the applicant that:

(1) Attests to the accuracy of the information provided in the application, and

(2) Affirms that the applicant will:

(a) Comply with this Code, and

(b) Allow the REGULATORY AUTHORITY access to the establishment as specified under § 8-402.11 and to the records specified under §§ 3-203.12 and 5-205.13 and Subparagraph 8-201.14(D)(6); and

(H) Other information required by the REGULATORY AUTHORITY.

Issuance   8-303.10   **New, Converted, or Remodeled Establishments.**

For FOOD ESTABLISHMENTS that are required to submit plans as specified under § 8-201.11 the REGULATORY AUTHORITY shall issue a PERMIT to the applicant after:

(A) A properly completed application is submitted;

(B) The required fee is submitted;

(C) The required plans, specifications, and information are reviewed and APPROVED; and

(D) A preoperational inspection as specified in § 8-203.10 shows that the establishment is built or remodeled in accordance with the APPROVED plans and specifications and that the establishment is in compliance with this Code.

8-303.20 Existing Establishments, Permit Renewal, and Change of Ownership.

The REGULATORY AUTHORITY may renew a PERMIT for an existing FOOD ESTABLISHMENT or may issue a PERMIT to a new owner of an existing FOOD ESTABLISHMENT after a properly completed application is submitted, reviewed, and APPROVED, the fees are paid, and an inspection shows that the establishment is in compliance with this Code.

8-303.30 Denial of Application for Permit, Notice.

If an application for a PERMIT to operate is denied, the REGULATORY AUTHORITY shall provide the applicant with a notice that includes:

(A) The specific reasons and Code citations for the PERMIT denial;

(B) The actions, if any, that the applicant must take to qualify for a PERMIT; and

(C) Advisement of the applicant's right of appeal and the process and time frames for appeal that are provided in LAW.

Conditions of Retention

8-304.10 Responsibilities of the Regulatory Authority.

(A) At the time a PERMIT is first issued, the REGULATORY AUTHORITY shall provide to the PERMIT HOLDER a copy of this Code so that the PERMIT HOLDER is notified of the compliance requirements and the conditions of retention, as specified under § 8-304.11, that are applicable to the PERMIT.

(B) *Failure to provide the information specified in ¶ (A) of this section does not prevent the* REGULATORY AUTHORITY *from taking authorized action or seeking remedies if the* PERMIT HOLDER *fails to comply with this Code or an order, warning, or directive of the* REGULATORY AUTHORITY.

8-304.11   Responsibilities of the Permit Holder.

Upon acceptance of the PERMIT issued by the REGULATORY AUTHORITY, the PERMIT HOLDER in order to retain the PERMIT shall:

(A) Post the PERMIT in a location in the FOOD ESTABLISHMENT that is conspicuous to CONSUMERS;

(B) Comply with the provisions of this Code including the conditions of a granted VARIANCE as specified under § 8-103.12, and APPROVED plans as specified under § 8-201.12;

(C) If a FOOD ESTABLISHMENT is required under § 8-201.13 to operate under a HACCP PLAN, comply with the plan as specified under § 8-103.12;

(D) Immediately contact the REGULATORY AUTHORITY to report an illness of a FOOD EMPLOYEE or CONDITIONAL EMPLOYEE as specified under ¶ 2-201.11(B);

(E) Immediately discontinue operations and notify the REGULATORY AUTHORITY if an IMMINENT HEALTH HAZARD may exist as specified under § 8-404.11;

(F) Allow representatives of the REGULATORY AUTHORITY access to the FOOD ESTABLISHMENT as specified under § 8-402.11;

(G) Replace existing facilities and EQUIPMENT specified in § 8-101.10 with facilities and EQUIPMENT that comply with this Code if:

(1) The REGULATORY AUTHORITY directs the replacement because the facilities and EQUIPMENT constitute a public health HAZARD or nuisance or no longer comply with the criteria upon which the facilities and EQUIPMENT were accepted,

(2) The REGULATORY AUTHORITY directs the replacement of the facilities and EQUIPMENT because of a change of ownership, or

(3) The facilities and EQUIPMENT are replaced in the normal course of operation;

(H) Comply with directives of the REGULATORY AUTHORITY including time frames for corrective actions specified in inspection reports, notices, orders, warnings, and other directives issued by the REGULATORY AUTHORITY in regard to the PERMIT HOLDER'S FOOD ESTABLISHMENT or in response to community emergencies;

(I) Accept notices issued and served by the REGULATORY AUTHORITY according to LAW; and

(J) Be subject to the administrative, civil, injunctive, and criminal remedies authorized in LAW for failure to comply with this Code or a directive of the REGULATORY AUTHORITY, including time frames for corrective actions specified in inspection reports, notices, orders, warnings, and other directives.

8-304.20   Permits Not Transferable.

A PERMIT may not be transferred from one PERSON to another PERSON, from one FOOD ESTABLISHMENT to another, or from one type of operation to another if the FOOD operation changes from the type of operation specified in the application as specified under ¶ 8-302.14(C) and the change in operation is not APPROVED.

8-4	INSPECTION AND CORRECTION OF VIOLATIONS

Subparts

Frequency

8-401.10   Establishing Inspection Interval.

(A) Except as specified in ¶¶ (B) and (C) of this section, the REGULATORY AUTHORITY shall inspect a FOOD ESTABLISHMENT at least once every 6 months.

(B) *The REGULATORY AUTHORITY may increase the interval between inspections beyond 6 months if:*

   (1) *The FOOD ESTABLISHMENT is fully operating under an APPROVED and validated HACCP PLAN as specified under § 8-201.14 and ¶¶ 8-103.12(A) and (B);*

   (2) *The FOOD ESTABLISHMENT is assigned a less frequent inspection frequency based on a written RISK-based inspection schedule that is being uniformly applied throughout the jurisdiction and at least once every 6 months the establishment is contacted by telephone or other means by the REGULATORY AUTHORITY to ensure that the establishment manager and the nature of FOOD operation are not changed; or*

   (3) *The establishment's operation involves only coffee service and other unPACKAGED or prePACKAGED FOOD that is not POTENTIALLY HAZARDOUS (TIME/TEMPERATURE CONTROL FOR SAFETY FOOD) such as carbonated BEVERAGES and snack FOOD such as chips, nuts, popcorn, and pretzels.*

(C) The REGULATORY AUTHORITY shall periodically inspect throughout its PERMIT period a TEMPORARY FOOD ESTABLISHMENT that prepares, sells, or serves unPACKAGED POTENTIALLY HAZARDOUS FOOD (TIME/TEMPERATURE CONTROL FOR SAFETY FOOD) and that:

   (1) Has improvised rather than permanent facilities or EQUIPMENT for accomplishing functions such as handwashing, FOOD preparation and protection, FOOD temperature control, WAREWASHING, providing DRINKING WATER, waste retention and disposal, and insect and rodent control; or

   (2) Has inexperienced FOOD EMPLOYEES.

8-401.20   Performance- and Risk-Based.

204

Within the parameters specified in § 8-401.10, the REGULATORY AUTHORITY shall prioritize, and conduct more frequent inspections based upon its assessment of a FOOD ESTABLISHMENT'S history of compliance with this Code and the establishment's potential as a vector of foodborne illness by evaluating:

(A) Past performance, for nonconformance with Code or HACCP PLAN requirements that are PRIORITY ITEMS or PRIORITY FOUNDATION ITEMS;

(B) Past performance, for numerous or repeat violations of Code or HACCP PLAN requirements that are CORE ITEMS;

(C) Past performance, for complaints investigated and found to be valid;

(D) The HAZARDS associated with the particular FOODS that are prepared, stored, or served;

(E) The type of operation including the methods and extent of FOOD storage, preparation, and service;

(F) The number of people served; and

(G) Whether the population served is a HIGHLY SUSCEPTIBLE POPULATION.

8-402.10   Competency of Inspectors.

An authorized representative of the REGULATORY AUTHORITY who inspects a FOOD ESTABLISHMENT or conducts plan review for compliance with this Code shall have the knowledge, skills, and ability to adequately perform the required duties.

Access   8-402.11   **Allowed at Reasonable Times after Due
                                          Notice.**

After the REGULATORY AUTHORITY presents official credentials
and provides notice of the purpose of, and an intent to
conduct, an inspection, the PERSON IN CHARGE shall allow the
REGULATORY AUTHORITY to determine if the FOOD
ESTABLISHMENT is in compliance with this Code by allowing
access to the establishment, allowing inspection, and
providing information and records specified in this Code and
to which the REGULATORY AUTHORITY is entitled according to
LAW, during the FOOD ESTABLISHMENT'S hours of operation and
other reasonable times.

8-402.20   **Refusal, Notification of Right to Access,
              and Final Request for Access.**

If a PERSON denies access to the REGULATORY AUTHORITY, the
REGULATORY AUTHORITY shall:

(A) Inform the PERSON that:

(1) The PERMIT HOLDER is required to allow access to
the REGULATORY AUTHORITY as specified under
§ 8-402.11 of this Code,

(2) Access is a condition of the acceptance and
retention of a FOOD ESTABLISHMENT PERMIT to operate
as specified under ¶ 8-304.11(F), and

(3) If access is denied, an order issued by the
appropriate authority allowing access, hereinafter
referred to as an inspection order, may be obtained
according to LAW; and

(B) Make a final request for access.

8-402.30   Refusal, Reporting.

If after the REGULATORY AUTHORITY presents credentials and provides notice as specified under § 8-402.11, explains the authority upon which access is requested, and makes a final request for access as specified in § 8-402.20, the PERSON IN CHARGE continues to REFUSE access, the REGULATORY AUTHORITY shall provide details of the denial of access on an inspection report form.

8-402.40   Inspection Order to Gain Access.

If denied access to a FOOD ESTABLISHMENT for an authorized purpose and after complying with § 8-402.20, the REGULATORY AUTHORITY may issue, or apply for the issuance of, an inspection order to gain access as provided in LAW.

Report of
Findings

8-403.10   Documenting Information and Observations.

The REGULATORY AUTHORITY shall document on an inspection report form:

(A) Administrative information about the FOOD ESTABLISHMENT'S legal identity, street and mailing addresses, type of establishment and operation as specified under ¶ 8-302.14(C), inspection date, and other information such as type of water supply and SEWAGE disposal, status of the PERMIT, and personnel certificates that may be required; and

(B) Specific factual observations of violative conditions or other deviations from this Code that require correction by the PERMIT HOLDER including:

(1) Failure of the PERSON IN CHARGE to demonstrate the knowledge of foodborne illness prevention, application of HACCP principles, and the requirements of this Code as specified under § 2-102.11,

(2) Failure of FOOD EMPLOYEES, CONDITIONAL EMPLOYEES, and the PERSON IN CHARGE to report a disease or medical condition as specified under ¶¶ 2-201.11(B) and (D),

207

(3) Nonconformance with PRIORITY ITEMS OR PRIORITY FOUNDATION ITEMS of this Code,

(4) Failure of the appropriate FOOD EMPLOYEES to demonstrate their knowledge of, and ability to perform in accordance with, the procedural, monitoring, verification, and corrective action practices required by the REGULATORY AUTHORITY as specified under § 8-103.12,

(5) Failure of the PERSON IN CHARGE to provide records required by the REGULATORY AUTHORITY for determining conformance with a HACCP PLAN as specified under Subparagraph 8-201.14(D)(6), and

(6) Nonconformance with CRITICAL LIMITS of a HACCP PLAN.

8-403.20   Specifying Time Frame for Corrections.

The REGULATORY AUTHORITY shall specify on the inspection report form the time frame for correction of the violations as specified under §§ 8-404.11, 8-405.11, and 8-406.11.

8-403.30   Issuing Report and Obtaining Acknowledgment of Receipt.

At the conclusion of the inspection and according to LAW, the REGULATORY AUTHORITY shall provide a copy of the completed inspection report and the notice to correct violations to the PERMIT HOLDER or to the PERSON IN CHARGE, and request a signed acknowledgment of receipt.

8-403.40   Refusal to Sign Acknowledgment.

The REGULATORY AUTHORITY shall:

(A) Inform a PERSON who declines to sign an acknowledgment of receipt of inspectional findings as specified in § 8-403.30 that:

(1) An acknowledgment of receipt is not an agreement with findings,

(2) Refusal to sign an acknowledgment of receipt will not affect the PERMIT HOLDER'S obligation to correct the violations noted in the inspection report within the time frames specified, and

(3) A refusal to sign an acknowledgment of receipt is noted in the inspection report and conveyed to the REGULATORY AUTHORITY'S historical record for the FOOD ESTABLISHMENT; and

(B) Make a final request that the PERSON IN CHARGE sign an acknowledgment receipt of inspectional findings.

8-403.50   Public Information.

Except as specified in § 8-202.10, the REGULATORY AUTHORITY shall treat the inspection report as a public document and shall make it available for disclosure to a PERSON who requests it as provided in LAW.

Imminent Health Hazard

8-404.11   Ceasing Operations and Reporting.

(A) Except as specified in ¶ (B) of this section, a PERMIT HOLDER shall immediately discontinue operations and notify the REGULATORY AUTHORITY if an IMMINENT HEALTH HAZARD may exist because of an emergency such as a fire, flood, extended interruption of electrical or water service, SEWAGE backup, misuse of POISONOUS OR TOXIC MATERIALS, onset of an apparent foodborne illness outbreak, gross insanitary occurrence or condition, or other circumstance that may endanger public health. ^P

(B) *A PERMIT HOLDER need not discontinue operations in an area of an establishment that is unaffected by the IMMINENT HEALTH HAZARD.*

8-404.12   Resumption of Operations.

If operations are discontinued as specified under § 8-404.11 or otherwise according to LAW, the PERMIT HOLDER shall obtain approval from the REGULATORY AUTHORITY before resuming operations.

209

Violation of Priority Item or Priority Foundation Item

8-405.11 Timely Correction.

(A) Except as specified in ¶ (B) of this section, a PERMIT HOLDER shall at the time of inspection correct a violation of a PRIORITY ITEM OR PRIORITY FOUNDATION ITEM of this Code and implement corrective actions for a HACCP PLAN provision that is not in compliance with its CRITICAL LIMIT. Pf

(B) *Considering the nature of the potential HAZARD involved and the complexity of the corrective action needed, the REGULATORY AUTHORITY may agree to or specify a longer time frame, not to exceed 10 calendar days after the inspection, for the PERMIT HOLDER to correct violations of a PRIORITY ITEM OR PRIORITY FOUNDATION ITEM or HACCP PLAN deviations.*

8-405.20 Verification and Documentation of Correction.

(A) After observing at the time of inspection a correction of a violation of a PRIORITY ITEM or PRIORITY FOUNDATION ITEM or a HACCP PLAN deviation, the REGULATORY AUTHORITY shall enter the violation and information about the corrective action on the inspection report.

(B) As specified under ¶ 8-405.11(B), after receiving notification that the PERMIT HOLDER has corrected a violation of a PRIORITY ITEM OR PRIORITY FOUNDATION ITEM or HACCP PLAN deviation, or at the end of the specified period of time, the REGULATORY AUTHORITY shall verify correction of the violation, document the information on an inspection report, and enter the report in the REGULATORY AUTHORITY'S records.

Core Item Violation

8-406.11 Time Frame for Correction.

(A) Except as specified in ¶ (B) of this section, the PERMIT HOLDER shall correct CORE ITEMS by a date and time agreed to or specified by the REGULATORY AUTHORITY but no later than 90 calendar days after the inspection.

(B) *The REGULATORY AUTHORITY may approve a compliance schedule that extends beyond the time limits specified under ¶ (A) of this section if a written schedule of compliance is submitted by the PERMIT HOLDER and no health HAZARD exists or will result from allowing an extended schedule for compliance.*

8-5 PREVENTION OF FOODBORNE DISEASE TRANSMISSION BY EMPLOYEES

Subpart

8-501 Investigation and Control

Investigation and Control

8-501.10 Obtaining Information: Personal History of Illness, Medical Examination, and Specimen Analysis.

The REGULATORY AUTHORITY shall act when it has reasonable cause to believe that a FOOD EMPLOYEE or CONDITIONAL EMPLOYEE has possibly transmitted disease; may be infected with a disease in a communicable form that is transmissible through FOOD; may be a carrier of infectious agents that cause a disease that is transmissible through FOOD; or is affected with a boil, an infected wound, or acute respiratory infection, by:

(A) Securing a confidential medical history of the FOOD EMPLOYEE or CONDITIONAL EMPLOYEE suspected of transmitting disease or making other investigations as deemed appropriate; and

(B) Requiring appropriate medical examinations, including collection of specimens for laboratory analysis, of a suspected FOOD EMPLOYEE or CONDITIONAL EMPLOYEE.

8-501.20 Restriction or Exclusion of Food Employee, or Summary Suspension of Permit.

Based on the findings of an investigation related to a FOOD EMPLOYEE or CONDITIONAL EMPLOYEE who is suspected of being infected or diseased, the REGULATORY AUTHORITY may issue an order to the suspected FOOD EMPLOYEE, CONDITIONAL EMPLOYEE or PERMIT HOLDER instituting one or more of the following control measures:

(A) RESTRICTING the FOOD EMPLOYEE or CONDITIONAL EMPLOYEE;

(B) EXCLUDING the FOOD EMPLOYEE or CONDITIONAL EMPLOYEE; or

(C) Closing the FOOD ESTABLISHMENT by summarily suspending a PERMIT to operate in accordance with LAW.

8-501.30   Restriction or Exclusion Order: Warning or Hearing Not Required, Information Required in Order.

Based on the findings of the investigation as specified in § 8-501.10 and to control disease transmission, the REGULATORY AUTHORITY may issue an order of RESTRICTION or EXCLUSION to a suspected FOOD EMPLOYEE or the PERMIT HOLDER without prior warning, notice of a hearing, or a hearing if the order:

(A) States the reasons for the RESTRICTION or EXCLUSION that is ordered;

(B) States the evidence that the FOOD EMPLOYEE or PERMIT HOLDER shall provide in order to demonstrate that the reasons for the RESTRICTION or EXCLUSION are eliminated;

(C) States that the suspected FOOD EMPLOYEE or the PERMIT HOLDER may request an appeal hearing by submitting a timely request as provided in LAW; and

(D) Provides the name and address of the REGULATORY AUTHORITY representative to whom a request for an appeal hearing may be made.

8-501.40   Removal of Exclusions and Restrictions.

The REGULATORY AUTHORITY shall release a FOOD EMPLOYEE, OR CONDITIONAL EMPLOYEE from RESTRICTION or EXCLUSION according to LAW and the conditions specified under § 2-201.13.

INDEX

Equipment, utensils, and linens
cleaning, 132-139
design and construction, 107-119
laundering lines, 141-142
location and installation, 123-125
maintenance and operation, 125-131
materials for construction and repair,
103-107
numbers and capacities, 120-123
protection of clean items, 143-146
sanitization of equipment and utensils,
140-141
See also Physical facilities
Escargot. *See Fish*
Evidence at hearing
documentary, 220
excluded, 233
regulatory authority presentation, 233
written, 233
Exclude, definition, 7
Exclusion of employee
illness, 34-36
infection or disease, 34-36
release, 36-42, 212
removal, 36-42, 212
Exclusion order
for infected or diseased employee, 212
service, 217-218
Expiration time for potentially hazardous food, 85-90
See also Public Health Reasons Annex,
414-419; Model Forms, Guides, and
Other Aids Annex, Chart 4-C
Exposure, 31-33
Facilities
assessment for Code enforcement, 191-192
disposal, recycling, and refilling of waste,
166
necessary replacement, 203
on-premises for refuse, recyclables, and
returnables, 161-163
Facility plans and specifications, submission
and approval, 194-195
Faucet, handwashing sink, 151
Fee for operating permit, issuance criteria, 198
Fees, civil proceeding
enforcement and collection, 237
hearing officer's powers, 230-231
Fever with sore throat, employee symptom, 31
Filter, compressed air, for drinking water system, 157
Filtering equipment, hot oil, design and construction,
109
Final order, rendering by hearing officer, 231-232
Fines, criminal proceeding, 236-237
civil proceeding, 237
Fingernails
artificial, prohibition, 46
of employees, maintenance, 46
First aid supplies in food establishments, storage;
See also Personal care items
Fish
consumer self-service, 73
cooking requirements, 74-77

definition, 8
frozen by supplier, freezing records, 80
other than molluscan shellfish, 50, 79
raw, storage, 64-65
recreationally caught, 51-52; *See also Public*
Health Reasons, 374
use of clean equipment, 132; *See also*
Public Health Reasons Annex, 465-
466
use of laundered gloves, 142
Fish, lightly cooked or raw
aquacultured
consumer advisory, 97-98
freezing to control parasites, 79
immersion in ice or water, 67
restriction on reduced oxygen packaging, 93
Fitting or tubing, copper and copper alloys, use
limitation, 105
Fixtures. *See Physical facilities*
Flatware. *See Tableware*
Floor drains, cleanability, 169
Floor-mounted equipment, clearance, 124
Floors
absorbent materials, use limitation, 180
and floor coverings, cleanability, 168-170
dustless cleaning methods, 179
Flow pressure valve, warewashing machine, 117
Flushing
drinking water system, 148
mobile water tank and mobile food
establishment water tank, 157-158
waste retention tanks, 160
Flux, use limitation for food-contact surfaces, 104
Fogging devices, cleaning the water reservoir,
154-155
Food
additives, 55, 66, 90, 186-187
characteristics, 49
contact with equipment and utensils, 67
contaminated, 98-99
cooked, potentially hazardous, cooling,
83-84
damaged, spoiled, or recalled, storage, 64
definition, 8
destroying or denaturing, 223
destruction of organisms of public health
concern, 74-77
examining, sampling, and testing, 223
frozen, potentially hazardous, 55, 82
hermetically sealed, source, 51
honest presentation, 1, 95, 191
identity, presentation, and on-premises
labeling, 50-51, 95
in contact with water or ice, storage or
display, 67
limitation of growth of organisms of public
health concern, 82-90
official tagging, 222
packaged and unpackaged, separation,
packaging and segregation, 64-65
packaged, labeling, 50-51, 93-94
protection for contamination, 61-73

plans, standard operating procedures, *See Public Health Reasons Annex,* 498-499
water system service schedule, 154
Recyclables. *See Refuse*
Recycling facilities, 166
Redeeming machines, location, 163
Reduced oxygen packaging
conditions not requiring a variance, 91-95
conditions requiring variance, 90-91
definition, 19-20
HACCP plan and variance criteria, 90-91
References. *See References Annex*
Refilling
clean tableware, 70
consumer self-service, using facilities, 139
returnables, 70, 139
Refrigeration, cooling and cold holding, 83-85
Refusal of access
application for inspection order, 207
reporting, 207
Refusal to sign acknowledgment of inspection report receipt, 208-209
Refuse areas and enclosures, maintenance, 165
Refuse, definition, 20
Refuse, recyclables, and returnables
cleaning implements and supplies, 163
design and construction, 161-162
facilities, on the premises, 161-162
facilities for disposal and recycling, 166
indoor storage area, design, 161
location, 163
outdoor enclosure, construction, 161
outdoor storage areas, construction materials, 161
outdoor storage surface, design and construction, 161, 173
removal, 165
storage, operation, and maintenance, 162-165
storage areas
equipment, and receptacles, location, 163
rooms, and receptacles, capacity and availability, 162
storage prohibitions, 164
toilet room receptacle, covered, 163
Regulatory authority
definition, 20
responsibilities for permit issuance, 201
Reheating
food from a hermetically sealed container, 81
hot holding, temperature requirements, 80-81
ready-to-eat food, requirements, 81
Record of hearing procedure, 229
Reinspection after permit suspension, time frame, 224
Reinspection order, hearing officer's powers, 231-232
Reinstatement
excluded or restricted employee, 36-42
permit, 225
Releasing food from hold order, 223

Remedies, 219-237
administrative, 220-234
conditions warranting, 219-220
criteria for seeking, 219-220
judicial, 234-237
Remodeling of food establishment, plans and specifications 194-195
Removal, refuse, recyclables, and returnables, 165
Reporting, disease; medical condition
By conditional employee, 31
by food employee, 31
by permit holder, 202
by person in charge, 33
Reporting, imminent health hazard
by permit holder, 202, 209
Request for hearing, 225-229
Re-service of unopened packaged food and unused
definition, 21
food, prohibition, 73
HSP, 101-102
Response to hearing notice
basis and time frame, 225-226
required contents, 226
Responsibilities
food employee reporting illness, 31
person in charge duties and authorities, 28-30
person in charge reporting ill employee, 33
permit holder for ceasing operations, 209
permit holder for permit retention, 202-203
regulatory authority for permit issuance, 201
Restaurant. *See Food establishment*
Restrict, definition, 21
Restricted use pesticide, definition, 21
Restriction
employee, release, 36-42, 212
infected or diseased employee, 36-42, 211-212
Restriction order
for infected or diseased employee, 212
service, 211-212
Restrictions
employees, removal, 34-36, 212
ill employees, 34-36
Resumption of operations, 209
Retail food store. *See Food establishment*
Retention tank. *See Sewage, holding tank*
Retirement home. *See Group residence*
Returnables
on-site cleaning and refilling, 139
refilling, 70
See also Refuse
Reuse of shells, 131. *See also Public Health Reasons Annex,* 465
Review of plans. *See Facility plans and specifications; Public Health Reasons Annex,* 498-499
Revocation of permit. *See Summary permit suspension*
Rhea. *See Ratites*
Right of appeal, denial of application for operating permit, 201

Right to hearing, waiver, 225-234
Rights
    parties to hearing, 233
    preservation, 215
    recipients of orders or decisions, 215
    respondent to hearing notice, 228-229,
        232-233
Rinsing procedures, equipment and utensils, 137-138
Risk-based frequency of inspection, 205. *See
    also Annex 5*
Roasts, beef and pork
    Formed/chunked, *see Public Health
        Reasons Annex*, 396-397
    minimum holding times for cooking, 73-74
    oven parameters for cooking, 75-76
    reheating, 81
Rodent control, 180
    in food establishments, poisonous or toxic
        materials, 184-189
    outer openings protected, 172-173. *See
        also Pest control*
Rodents, dead or trapped, removal, 181
Roe. *See Fish*
Roofs, protective barrier, 173
Rooms. *See Physical facilities*

Safe material, definition, 21
Safeguards, procedural, 215
Salad bars, monitoring by food employees, 73
***Salmonella* Typhi**
    cause of disease outbreak and employee
        illness, 26-28, 30
    employee illness, reporting, 26, 28, 30-34,
        207
    infection, conditions for employee restriction
        or exclusion, 33-36
    reporting responsibility of person in charge,
        33
***Salmonella* Typhi**-free employee, removal of
    restriction or exclusion, 28-30, 192-193, *See
    Public Health Reasons Annex,* Tables 1
    and 2
Sample report, private water system, 149
Sampling, water, nonpublic system, 148
Sanctions or penalties, statement in hearing
    notice, 228-229
Sanitization
    chemical, manual, 129-130
    chemical, warewashing equipment, 129-130
    definition, 21
    equipment and utensils, 140-141
    hot water temperatures
        manual, 128
        warewashing equipment, 128
    pressure, mechanical warewashing
        equipment, 129. *See also
            Poisonous or toxic
            materials*
Sanitizing solutions
    chemical, determining concentration,
        129-130

    detergent-sanitizer, rinsing procedures,
        137-138
    testing devices, availability, 123
    wiping cloth storage, 68-69
Scallops. *See Molluscan shellfish*
Screening
    backflow prevention device, 151, 153
    outer openings protected, 172-173
    tank vent, 156
    vending machines, 119
    water conditioning device, 151
Seafood. *See Fish*
Sealed, definition, 21
Seeing Eye dog. *See Service animal*
Self-draining warewashing sinks and drainboards,
    118
Self-service
    clean tableware for refills, 70
    consumer, protection from contamination,
        73
    handling of single-service and single-use
        articles, 145
    utensil availability, 122
Sentences for violations, 236-237
Sentry dogs. *See Patrol dogs*
Service animal
    care and handling, 48
    definition, 21
    handwashing after handling, 44
    handling of single-service and single-use,
        181-182
    presence in dining and sales area, 181-182
Service of notice
    proper methods, 217
    proof of proper service, 218
    time of effectiveness, 218
Service sinks
    availability, 177
    plumbing system, numbers and capacity,
        152
    use limitation, 45
Servicing area
    definition, 21
    outdoor, overhead protection, 173
Serving dishes. *See Hollowware*
Settlement
    authorization, 234
    consent agreement, approval and final
        decision by hearing officer, 231
    request for, 226
    respondent acceptance as waiver of
        right to appeal, 234
Sewage
    definition, 22
    disposal, conveying, 160
    disposal system, approved, design and
        construction, 160
    holding tank, mobile, 158
Sewage, other liquid wastes, and rainwater
    backflow prevention, 159-160
    conveying, 160
    disposal facility, 160